Is God real?

DATE			

IS GOD REAL?

Is God Real?

Edited by

Joseph Runzo

Professor of Philosophy and of Religion
Chapman University, Orange, California

St. Martin's Press   New York

All rights reserved. For information, write:
Scholarly and Reference Division,
St. Martin's Press, Inc., 175 Fifth Avenue,
New York, N.Y. 10010

First published in the United States of America in 1993

Printed in Hong Kong

ISBN 0–312–08439–0

Library of Congress Cataloging-in-Publication Data
Is God real? / edited by Joseph Runzo.
p.   cm.
Includes bibliographical references and index.
ISBN 0–312–08439–0
1. God.   I. Runzo, Joseph, 1948–   .
BT102.I855   1993
211—dc20   92–20273
                                               CIP

In gratitude to
Bill Alston and John Hick
friends and teachers

nisi Dominus frustra

Contents

Contents

PART THREE: A FALSE DICHOTOMY?

PART FOUR: RELIGIOUS REALISM

PART FIVE: A FINAL OVERVIEW

Notes on the Contributors

Paul Badham is Professor and Head of the Department of Theology and Religious Studies at St David's University College, Lampeter, University of Wales. His books include *Christian Beliefs About Life After Death, Immortality or Extinctions?, Death and Immortality in the Religions of the World, Ethics on the Frontiers of Human Existence, Religion State and Society in Modern Britain* and *A John Hick Reader*.

Francis Cook is Associate Professor of Religious Studies Emeritus at the University of California, Riverside. He is the author of *Hua-yen Buddhism: The Jewel Net of Indra, How to Raise an Ox* and *Sounds of Valley Streams*.

Don Cupitt is Dean of Emmanuel College and University Lecturer in the Philosophy of Religion at Cambridge University. The most recent of his twenty books are *Taking Leave of God, The World to Come, The Sea of Faith, Only Human, Life Lines, The Long-Legged Fly, The New Christian Ethics, Radicals and the Future of the Church, Creation Out of Nothing, What is a Story?* and *The Time Being*.

Stephen T. Davis is Professor of Philosophy and Religion at Claremont McKenna College. His books include *The Debate About the Bible: Inerrancy Versus Infallibility; Faith, Scepticism and Evidence: An Essay in Religious Epistemology; Encountering Evil: Live Options in Theodicy, Logic and the Nature of God; Encountering Jesus: A Debate on Christology* and *Death and Afterlife*.

Brian L. Hebblethwaite is Fellow and Dean of Chapel at Queens' College, Cambridge and University Lecturer in Divinity at Cambridge University. He is the author of *Evil, Suffering and Religion; The Adequacy of Christian Ethics; The Problems of Theology; The Christian Hope; The Incarnation* and *The Ocean of Truth;* and editor of *Divine Action: Studies Inspired by the Philosophical Theology of Austin Farrer; The Philosophical Frontiers of Christian Theology* and *Christianity and Other Religions*.

John Hick is Danforth Professor of Philosophy of Religion at The Claremont Graduate School. His twenty books include *An Interpretation of Religion, Problems of Religious Pluralism, God Has Many Names,*

Death and Eternal Life, Evil and the God of Love, God and the Universe of Faiths, Arguments for the Existence of God and *Philosophy of Religion.*

Alfred Louch is Professor of Philosophy and Education at The Claremont Graduate School and the author of *Explanation and Human Action.*

Myra E. Moss is Professor of Philosophy at Claremont McKenna College, the author of *Benedetto Croce Reconsidered: Truth and Error in Theories of Art and History and Literature,* and the translator of *Benedetto Croce's Essays on Literature and Literary Criticism.*

June O'Connor is Professor of Religious Studies and Chair of the Program in Religious Studies at the University of California, Riverside. She is the author of *The Quest for Political and Spiritual Liberation: A Study in the Thought of Sri Aurobindo Ghose* and *The Moral Vision of Dorothy Day: A Feminist Perspective.*

D.Z. Phillips is Professor of Philosophy at the University College of Swansea, University of Wales. His fourteen books include *From Fantasy to Faith; Faith After Foundationalism; Belief, Change and Forms of Life; Religion Without Explanation; Death and Immortality; Faith and Philosophical Enquiry* and *The Concept of Prayer.*

Joseph Runzo is Professor of Philosophy and of Religion at Chapman University and President of the Philosophy of Religion Society. He is the author of *Reason, Relativism and God,* editor of *Ethics, Religion and the Good Society: New Directions in a Pluralistic World* and co-editor of *Religious Experience and Religious Belief: Essays in the Epistemology of Religion.*

Jack C. Verheyden is Professor of Theology at the School of Theology at Claremont and Professor of Religion at the Claremont Graduate School. He is the editor of *Schleiermacher's Life of Jesus.*

John H. Whittaker is Professor of Philosophy and Director of the Religious Studies Program at Louisiana State University. He is the author of *Matters of Faith and Matters of Principle: Religious Truth Claims and Their Logic* and *The Logic of Religious Persuasion.*

Introduction

JOSEPH RUNZO

This is an unusual collection of essays on an unusually important topic in the philosophy of religion. There are a number of salient issues in contemporary philosophy of religion: the epistemic status of religious beliefs, the problem of religious pluralism, whether and to what extent women and other members of the underclass bring a different voice to religion and offer different, viable models for God, the place of religious ethics in public morality. But no issue is more trenchant than that of religious realism vs. religious non-realism. Indeed, of the questions just mentioned, realism vs. non-realism has the longest history as a prominent issue in modern religious thought. And not only is the realist/non-realist question fundamental, the present collection of essays is unusual. Not only are the authors among the most prominent contemporary participants in the debate – Don Cupitt, D.Z. Phillips, John Hick, Brian Hebblethwaite and Paul Badham, among others – these essays constitute a *genuine* dialogue, with point and counterpoint, developed position and articulated response. Not merely presenting a set of collected essays, here religious realists and non-realists alike respond explicitly and directly to each other.

Religious realism, in brief, is the view that there is a transcendent divine reality independent of human thought. However, many realists allow for the post-Kantian notion of the mind's structuring of all perception. So it is better to say that realists hold that there exists a transcendent divine reality, independent *at least in part* of human thought, action or attitudes. Religious non-realists deny this.

Religious realism, in the form of theological realism, has been the dominant, orthodox position in the West: God possesses aseity. (In contrast, as Francis Cook's essay points out, orthodoxy among the Far Eastern religions prominently includes non-realism.) But this assumption in the West was challenged in the modern period, first with respect to general developments in epistemology in philosophy, then within theology itself.

The foundations for non-realism as a viable philosophical alternative in the modern era were laid – quite inadvertently – by Descartes. By taking the self as the epistemological starting point, together with the turn to reason alone and the rejection of the authority of the Church as a proper basis for philosophical investigation, Descartes provides the grounds for the idea that the *human* mind contributes to the very content of what is perceived and so known. As the Continental Rationalists and then the British Empiricists struggled back and forth with the question of the relation between our ideas and 'the world', the new approach Descartes had set out culminated in Kant's transcendental idealism, a reaction to – or attempted middle course between – Rationalism and Empiricism. For Kant, the human mind did not just contribute to the way we see things, it *determined* the way we see things by determining the very conditions for perception. By the twentieth-century, this new turn in philosophy has become foundational to views as disparate as those of William James, Wittgenstein and Heidegger, influencing a host of philosophers from C.I. Lewis, Norwood Hanson and Thomas Kuhn to a whole Wittgenstein tradition, and to Richard Rorty.

The epistemological movement represented by Kant and those who followed him flowered into a non-realism about religion in the work of such seminal thinkers as Ludwig Feuerbach (discussed below in Jack Verheyden's essay) and Nietzsche. Epistemologically, Nietzsche held that there were 'no facts, only interpretations'; regarding religion, he was a non-realist. Others were to follow, though with different perspectives: importantly, Marx in political philosophy, and Freud in philosophical psychology.

It is important, though, not to confuse the realist/non-realist debate in *religion*, with other current debates about realism vs. non-realism in epistemology or metaphysics. There is, for instance, the current debate between naive realism and critical realism in metaphysics and the philosophy of science. But while the realist/non-realist debate in religion is related to these more general debates, its singular focus sets the parameters of the debate: what is the ontological status – if any – and what is the meaning – if any – of a transcendent divine reality?

The essays in this volume fall into five natural divisions. The first essay by John Hick delineates basic boundaries for the religious realist/non-realist debate. In the second section, the essays by Jack Verheyden and Don Cupitt set out the position of theological non-realism, while realists offer their response. In the third section, the question of whether this division between religious realism vs. non-realism is a false dichotomy is raised by the essays of D.Z. Phillips and John Whittaker, with the respondents arguing that the dichotomy is real and the debate crucial. Then, the essays by Brian Hebblethwaite, Paul Badham and myself in the fourth section defend theological realism, while here non-realists offer their response. Lastly, in the fifth section, Phillips and Hebblethwaite provide a final overview, not only of the general issue, but taking the specific realist and non-realist views articulated in the volume into account.

In the first essay, the discussion begins with Hick's explication of the issue between religious realists and non-realists, concluding with a positive appraisal of the realist position. To Hick's mind, this is a genuine either/or issue, for it concerns one's view of the very structure of the universe. He defines three positions: the naive religious realist assumes that 'divine reality is just as spoken about in the language of some one tradition,' the critical religious realist holds that there is a transcendent divine reality but that it is only understood via the enculturated, and so ever changing, conceptual schemes of humans, and the non-realist holds that there is no transcendent divine reality existing *in any way* independently of humans.

As Hick points out, religious non-realism is not the same as anti-religious interpretations of religion – though both are atheistic. Anti-religious views like those of Nietzsche, or Freud, or Marx, or the more modern views of A.J. Ayer or Paul Edwards, reject religion as worthless if not destructive – a delusion. Contemporary religious *non*-realists, in contrast, feel that there is great value in religion, even if there is no transcendent, divine referent.

Hick concludes his essay with reasons for preferring religious realism over non-realism. Non-realism is elitist, for only those with the capacity to understand their essential autonomy and achieve enlightened self-awareness enjoy the salvific power of religion. There is no self-subsistent God to bring salvation to the less capable. Further, on Hick's account, non-realism is pessimistic, while religious realism is optimistic. As William James, a realist whom Hick quotes with approval, said, '[religion] says that the best things are the more eternal things, the things in the universe that throw the last stone, so to speak.'[1]

In Part Two, the non-realist view is presented, first in the classic position in the West of Ludwig Feuerbach, then in the contemporary view of Don Cupitt, and finally through the Eastern perspective of Zen Buddhism. Jack Verheyden points to the remarkable intersection in Feuerbach's work of the centrality of religion (to deny religion is to deny the human) *and* a radical opposition to the traditional referent of religion: an independent, personal God. Verheyden details the roots of Feuerbach's thought – philosophically in Kant and then Hegel, theologically in Luther and then Schleiermacher – Feuerbach then arriving at his own view that materialism must overcome spiritualising (I sense, therefore I am) so that, *vis-à-vis* religion, God becomes an idealised projection of universal humanity. Thus, religion is really the human in relation to itself. Verheyden concludes by critiquing Feuerbach for his limited *internal* (note the Cartesian parallel) approach to religion, overlooking the sort of response Luther could give that the word comes from *outside* the believer's heart. Myra Moss extends Verheyden's analysis by looking at the work of Marx and Engels (and even Feuerbach's influence in Freud). She concludes that Feuerbach was an epistemological realist, not an epistemological idealist, raising the question whether the debate about God has moved away from metaphysics and God's ontological status, to epistemology.

In his spirited paper, 'Anti-Realist Faith', Don Cupitt, a foremost religious non-realist, sees his own religious non-realism as a natural evolution within the general move toward non-realism over the past two hundred years: 'We are all of us non-realists nowadays.' Drawing on the Kantian revolution and its lineage through Hegel, Nietzsche, Marx and now the Wittgensteinians and the Structuralists, Cupitt delineates the contrast between the traditional (Western) goal of attaining absolute truth and the 'modern' perspective, one which is historicist, linguistic and ultimately relativistic. Indeed the mark of the modern era is the recognition that 'we make history.' As a general philosophical conclusion, he believes 'in only one continuous but multi-perspectival common world . . . This one world is human, cultural and historically changing.' And 'Religion is wholly inside it, and it has no outside. I don't take realistic view of *any* non-manifest entity.'

In defence of this religious non-realism, Cupitt offers a number of powerful considerations: we give anti-realist interpretations of other religions, so to take the same perspective of our own religion enables us to view other faiths more sympathetically in our global, pluralistic world; while realism in religion amounts to a defence of the status quo, non-realism makes essential religious reform possible; non-realism makes clear our own responsibility for our religious beliefs, for *we* made them; non-realism keeps us from claiming an inappropriate and destructive authority over others; and, looking to the future, non-realism frees us to be fully creative. In response, Stephen Davis develops a strong set of considerations against Cupitt's argument that religious non-realism is superior to realism *on religious grounds*. Davis argues that (a) Cupitt offers only a parody of objective theism because many theological realists do not hold that Christianity or the biblical message is timeless, or that the oldest version of the faith is the best; (b) Cupitt's position seems self-stultifying for if we can only know things as they seem (perspectivalism), then we cannot know that this view is itself true; and (c) the essence of religion is not just being 'spiritual', but that God calls us. Finally, the real challenge, Davis suggests, is this: Did we create God, or God us? Realists, like Davis, hold the latter.

The essay by Francis Cook is particularly interesting in placing the religious realist/non-realist debate in the context of Eastern religion. He argues in 'Zen and the Problem of Language' that there is a long tradition of religious non-realism in the great East Asian traditions, running from Indian Buddhism through Zen. The seminal Buddhist concern with language comes from the notion that humans, through language, superimpose something on reality which it does not possess. And the particular Zen contribution to this view is that positive predication is misguided because it inherently rules out everything else that a thing can be experienced as. Cook thus sees Zen as a liberation from enculturation – a need now acutely facing the West, and Western religions. Much like Cupitt, Cook concludes that the realist/non-realist debate in religion is not the either/or of *either* referring to real, divine entities, *or* of the death of religion. Rather, as a middle way, a satisfying religious life can be found in the transcendence of realist language. This for Cook is the lesson Zen can bring to the West. For if we do not criticise our realist language, nihilism will be the only alternative.

Interestingly, not only John Whittaker and John Hick, but even Don Cupitt disagrees with Cook's analysis. Whittaker questions whether Zen might not be making comparable claims to those found in Western theism, except that the use of concepts is rejected. For Zen, like the great Western religious traditions, uses language – albeit negatively – *for* soteriological reasons. Hick in effect extends this point by arguing that the Zen view of language – emptiness – does not preclude religious realism. However a word is used, it must stand for something, and to say that everything is contingent is, to that extent, to speak realistically. And Cupitt extends this critique even farther by suggesting that language cannot be wrong *in toto*, and indeed that Christians and Buddhists can come closer together if they take language seriously: Buddhists helping explain the nature of language (its essential enculturation) and Christianity helping to add an ethical dimension.

Now, the inconclusiveness of this back-and-forth between the non-realists and realists raises a question: is the debate specious? Though in different ways, both D.Z. Phillips and John Whittaker make this claim in Part Two.

Contemporary Christian non-realism is often thought of as divisible into two major, alternative formulations. The more directly Wittgensteinian view – which would be exemplified by D.Z. Phillips – understands God as a linguistic element, offering a *descriptive* account of religion as non-realist, whether or not this has always been understood within the tradition. Others, like Don Cupitt as we have seen, understand God as a human spiritual ideal, and suggest a *prescriptive* account: where once God was understood as a transcendent entity, now talk about God should be understood as talk about human hopes, aspirations and ideals. But, while Phillips is thus perceived as a non-realist by his critics, Phillips casts his own view in an entirely different light.

Following a Wittgensteinian interpretation, Phillips holds that realism and non-realism are *equally* confused. Consequently, to reject realism does not make one a non-realist. For Phillips this is the wrong 'grammar' for understanding belief in God. He provides a detailed argument against the views of Roger Trigg and Terrence Penelhum that beliefs need an 'object' which is independent of practices. On Phillips' account, the realist holds that one believes things true, then is committed and acts accordingly. But this leaves out the 'mode of projection' which relates belief to its object. Indeed, while realists charge non-realists with being reductionists, it is realists, says Phillips, who are reductionists since they separate belief from God, having separated belief in God from religious practice. Hence, 'really believing' in God has to do with confession, practice and the fruits of belief, and the (ontological) issue of realism vs. non-realism is specious.

Alfred Louch, and then John Hick and Don Cupitt, take up Phillips' proposal that on a Wittgensteinian view neither realism nor non-realism have to do with the issue of religious belief. Louch, while siding more with Phillips, offers a balanced assessment of the differences between John Hick's and Phillips' views. The dispute, he argues, is not over whether God is an entity (as Hick suggests), but over whether one who holds a view like Phillips' can properly say he or she believes in God when they *do not* think God is an entity; the question is whether the belief is sincerely held. So on Phillips' side, Louch agrees that beliefs about God are not hypothesis, and on Hick's side Louch argues that Phillips' position is, from a realist standpoint, a 'cheap way' as it were of 'claiming the right to religious belief: all you have to do is show how your prayers, hymns, chants, and sacrifices hang together, requiring no authentication outside of chapel.' Taking the realist/non-realist discussion found in the essays in the present volume as an example, Louch concludes that the very discussion is a religious practice: more generally, 'some worship through song or prayer, others through argument.'

In his response to Phillips, John Hick says that realists can agree that if one believes in God, one acts in a certain way. He suggests that the real issue, then, is whether belief in God is *true*: realists saying that it is and non-realists disagreeing. And Phillips is discussing a *different* issue, i.e. whether belief involves commitment. While not agreeing with Hick's realism, Don Cupitt agrees that Phillips has not addressed a central issue. For Cupitt it is part of the task of philosophers to change things – to point out, for example, that whereas someone may be a realist in their faith, friends may feel that they are really non-realists, and (with encouragement) eventually the believer should change his or her life accordingly.

In 'Religious Beliefs, Their Point and Their Reference' John Whittaker, like Phillips, argues that the religious realist/non-realist debate is specious. While he basically agrees with the Wittgensteinian view of Phillips, Whittaker allows that religious belief might be true. The defect of religious realism, as he sees it, is that it tries to be descriptive, rather than evaluative (or what he calls 'teleological'), yet the point of religious belief is its implications, not some factual success. Hence, belief in God is not ontological. John Hick replies that Whittaker fails to distinguish two senses of 'teleological', and consequently fails to show that the realist/non-realist dispute is misguided. Hick argues that 'telos' can either denote a future end or a supreme value. Religious realists in effect employ both senses of the term, while non-realists only employ the latter, evaluative sense. Thus, Whittaker (and Phillips) hold that theistic belief must be either metaphysical, or value-laden. It cannot be both. But for the realist, the notion of a metaphysically real God *is* evaluative; the belief does affect one's whole life. On Hick's reading, Whittaker (and Phillips) have failed to address the actual position of the religious realist.

So the important question of whether the realist/non-realist debate is specious is raised and debated, but, as we might expect, not settled. Having already looked at the non-realist position, this brings us to Part Four, the defence of religious realism.

We begin with Brian Hebblethwaite. As Hebblethwaite notes, Cupitt's position is that ethical and spiritual considerations *require* the rejection of objective theism, and yet the very strength – the very 'novelty' – of his view is that out of this negative criticism of traditional theism emerges a paramount ideal of disinterested love. Hebblethwaite argues for objective theism through a consideration of the ultimate religious, intellectual and ethical inadequacy, as he sees it, of a religious non-realism like Cupitt's.

As 'religious inadequacies', Hebblethwaite questions whether the Church can be sustained and worship can remain meaningful without their traditional referent – a self-subsistent God. Further, he suggests that the very heart of Christianity is the idea of a *relation* with God, and correspondingly that God alone can bring salvation. Finally, he argues that Christianity need neither be immature, as Cupitt characterises it, nor need it fail to do full justice to religious experience: indeed, he suggests, it is only in the appeal to rational argument that one finds in objective theism that the full power of religious experience can be realised. Regarding the 'intellectual inadequacies' of Cupitt's position, Hebblethwaite points to the apparent self-stultification of disowning any metaphysics, while appealing to 'life-energy', and then to materialism as the only way to account for the evolution of mind and values. *Vis-à-vis* 'ethical deficiencies', Hebblethwaite argues against Cupitt's notion that humans alone must create values – for ethics is *not* optional – and he suggests that rather than being egoistic, theological realism enjoins us to focus away from our own egos.

Finally, Hebblethwaite defends theological realism by suggesting that Christian philosophy must have its own agenda, and not be a mere follower of the philosophical currents. If nothing else, the history of philosophy is replete with false steps, and one must decide which philosophical turn is best for Christian philosophy, not which is now most popular or prevalent. And, in Hebblethwaite's view, only objective theism can guarantee reality and objectivity. Cupitt, however, responds that Hebblethwaite has simply rejected decades of recent work in philosophy and theology. First, facts do not come independent of our (later) interpretation: there is interpretation 'all the way down'. And second, what history has shown, Cupitt believes, is that the more realist one's conception of God, the more anti-Christian one's views of morality. This point of contention is taken up in the next paper.

In 'Realism, Non-Realism and Atheism: Why Believe in an Objectively Real God?' I try to set this debate in a wider context. A principal impetus for theological non-realism is its focus on ethical considerations. Yet I think there are no irrefutable grounds supporting either realism or non-realism, and (as for example Hick also acknowledges) non-realism *is* appealing precisely because of this sensitivity to the ethical. For we live in an age when the transcendent God has become unavailable. And as the non-realists see, the question is not whether God *is* but *what* God is. The answer must speak to contemporary concerns, especially ethical concerns.

After noting a number of philosophical and religious reasons which tend to support the turn to religious non-realism, I argue for a modified theological realism. First, I suggest that the fundamental point of disagreement is over the question of sufficient reason, non-realists claiming a non-metaphysical account of God is sufficient, realists claiming the meaning of monotheism is insufficiently explained without ontological reference to God. But this in turn amounts to the question whether *any* religious commitment is plausible in our pluralistic, secular age, a question that encompasses the atheist as well as religious persons (realists and non-realists alike). Within this wider context, I then argue that three features of realism can meet non-realist criticisms. True, matters of faith should be decided in terms of the meaning of life, but the realist can hold that God is *phenomenally* real, not just an unavailable noumenal God. Second, realism better supports the use of reason as central to the religious life. Third, a modified theological realism which *recognises* our historicity would not, on the one hand, reduce religion to morality, and yet it would be inherently theologically humble (a lesson Cupitt and others have driven home). June O'Connor draws out the parallels between my view and John Hick's. She feels that non-realists will find neither Hick's appeal to a transcendent Reality, nor my appeal to a more immediate phenomenal divine reality, convincing. And the charge that non-realism tends to reduce religion to morality is one that she thinks non-realists like Cupitt can accept. She does feel though that the emphasis on autonomy in Cupitt, which my essay – but also those of Hebblethwaite, Badham and others – points out, is a danger, not an advantage of non-realism. For, she argues, we need freedom *through* community, and this must be based on a fundamental (communal) trust.

Paul Badham takes up the defence of theological realism by agreeing with Cupitt that all Christians are non-realists to some extent. But he holds, as Hebblethwaite does, that one's relationship with

God is at the heart of Christianity. And like Hebblethwaite, he argues that the practice of religion – especially worship – assumes religious realism, not only in the Christian, but in the bhakti tradition in Hinduism, within Sikhism, and, clearly, in Islamic worship. Badham sees the central question as 'What difference does belief in God make?' (not unlike the 'presumption of atheism' which I address in my essay). He suggests two things: (a) that a *personal* relation to God transforms the believer, and (b) there is hope for continuation of this relationship after death. Of most value here is the sense of the presence of God, which for Badham can only be realised by Christians if they can believe in the objective reality of God.

Both Phillips and Cupitt offer a response to Badham. Phillips argues that realists like Badham are caught in a dilemma. The specific examples of belief in God which Badham offers only make sense in the context of religious experience, but the religious life is supposed to depend on beliefs about God which have a sense even outside any religious context. If beliefs about God are what *justify* the religious life, then those beliefs are vacuous since they are cut off from the only thing which would give them sense – the religious life. Cupitt points out that realists like Badham typically argue that non-realism is like atheism and therefore is religiously inadequate. But Cupitt turns this charge on its head: for him, the religious person is called to be nothing, so God must be Nothingness. Therefore only non-realism is religiously adequate.

Lastly, in Part Five, one religious non-realist and one religious realist take up a final overview of the debate. In 'Great Expectations: Religion, Ontology and Religion', Phillips argues that each of the realists, and even Cupitt as a non-realist, work from the mistaken assumption that language *refers to reality*. But language does not refer to anything. Hence, while he accepts my argument that if religious beliefs *do* refer to facts this would not rule out the role those beliefs play in people's lives, he argues that it must be shown that reference to God *is* reference to an object. Similarly, he agrees with the importance of taking into account different conceptions of reality – a relativist orientation which Cupitt and I share – but he thinks that for the realist like myself this degenerates into thinking about religious and non-religious beliefs, and realist and non-realist views, as competing hypotheses (a position which, we have seen, Hick also holds). For Phillips, philosophy simply is not metaphysics.

Hebblethwaite offers 'Reflections on Realism vs. Non-Realism', saying that Phillips fails to show convincingly that there is no real issue here (Cupitt of course assumes that there *is* a crucial question at stake). Hebblethwaite suggests that religious realists need to show *vis-à-vis* Phillips' position that there is a *possible* objective ground for religious belief, and *vis-à-vis* Cupitt's position that such a ground is required by the evidence. He then offers the provocative idea that the evidence needed is not just that of religious experience, but also that of rational argument (e.g. a design argument for God's existence) and, importantly, revelation. And *this* he feels, coming full circle, not only substantiates the realist response to Cupitt and Phillips; it also offers a stronger support for realism than the sort John Hick, though himself a realist, has offered.[2]

I wish to thank each of the authors of the papers in this volume for their genuine dialogue and willingness to approach the opposing position of others with care and seriousness. The principal papers and responses were originally presented at the ninth annual Philosophy of Religion Conference at Claremont Graduate School. The papers were then rewritten in the light of comments, a number of the conference participants wrote additional replies to the principal papers, and both D.Z. Phillips and Brian Hebblethwaite wrote overviews of the central issues in the volume, which appear here as Part Five.

It is a special pleasure to have the opportunity to edit a volume where many of the authors are friends, both theological realists and non-realists. I am especially grateful to John Hick and Steve Davis not only as friends and fellow travellers in the philosophy of religion, but as the two individuals who were most instrumental in the success of the original conference, and who generously gave their support for the present volume. I wish to thank Claremont Graduate School where I was a Visiting Scholar while working on this volume. Anita Storck, Department Secretary for Religion and Philosophy at Chapman University, provided invaluable help and understanding throughout the editorial process. Finally, I am grateful to my wife, Jean, whose unwavering support has made this book, like so many other projects, both a success and a delight.

Joseph Runzo
California, 1991

Notes

1. William James, *The Will to Believe and Other Essays*, 1905, pp. 25–6.
2. As an example of Hick's defence of religious realism on the basis of religious experience, see for example Ch. 11 of John Hick, *An Interpretation of Religion* (London: Macmillan, and New Haven, Conn.: Yale University Press, 1989).

Part One
Realism versus
Non-Realism

1

Religious Realism and Non-Realism: Defining the Issue

JOHN HICK

I

The debate between realist and non-realist understandings of religious language exposes the most fundamental of all issues in the philosophy of religion today. I say 'today' because although logically this issue is basic in a timeless sense, it has only come to be generally seen as an issue at all during the last hundred and fifty or so years – roughly since the pioneering work of Feuerbach – and has become sharply focused within the Western religious consciousness only during recent decades. Throughout the previous centuries, and indeed millennia, religious self-understanding has been implicitly or explicitly realist – perhaps the only significant exception being within one strand of what we now see to be the highly variegated Buddhist tradition. But today there are confident non-realist interpretations of Christianity and Judaism as well as Buddhism which make a wide appeal within our contemporary industrialised, science-oriented, de-supernaturalised Western societies.

Philosophical discussion cannot, in my view, settle the debate between religious realists and non-realists. It can, however, help to make clear what the issue is, and this is the limited task to which I am now setting myself.

I shall proceed for the most part in terms of the Judaeo–Christian–Islamic monotheism which has provided the framework of the Western debate thus far, but with reminders from time to time that the same basic issue arises for the Eastern traditions.

II

The first point to be made is that it would be inappropriate to speak of realism, or non-realism, across the board, as though one is obliged to be consistently realist, or consistently non-realist, in the interpretation of all types of language – perceptual, ethical, aesthetic, poetic, scientific, religious. There are in fact probably no pan-realists who believe in the reality of fairies and snarks as well as of tables and electrons; and likewise few if any omni-non-realists, denying the objective reality of a material world and of other people as well as of gravity and God. Thus we are not confronted by two logically indissoluble packages – or even by invariable correlations. As a witness to this fact, Berkeley was an idealist in relation to the physical world and a realist in relation to God.

We would therefore do well not to get our contemporary realist/ non-realist debate concerning religion confused with other realist/ non-realist discussions. It is quite distinct, for example, from the medieval dispute between realists and nominalists. This concerned the status of universals – goodness, redness, roundness, etc. – the realists holding that these exist independently of our conceiving them, as transcendent Platonic forms, and the nominalists the contrary. This is a quite distinct issue from the one with which contemporary religious realists and non-realists are concerned. The latter are free to take either or no side in the medieval debate. Some religious non-realists will also be non-realist about universals and logical and mathematical entities and truths. But others will be non-realist only about the objects of religious discourse. Likewise, religious realists can equally well be either realists or nominalists in the medieval sense. Some (such as Richard Swinburne, for example) are inclined to be realists in relation to at least some universals and to logical truths, while others (such as myself, for example) are inclined to be non-realists at that point.

Our current religious debate has borrowed its terms from Western epistemological discussions that were at their height in the first half of the present century. The general realist view was that in sense perception we are in touch with an environing world that exists independently of all perceivers. The polar opposite was the idealist view that the perceived world exists only as a series of modifications of our own consciousnesses: to be is to be perceived. Realism then divided into naive realism, holding that the world is just as we perceive it to be, and critical realism, holding that there is an important subjective contribution to our perceiving, so that the world as we experience it is a distinctively human construction arising from the impacts of a real environment upon our sense organs, but conceptualised in consciousness and language in culturally developed forms.

III

Although the issues in the philosophy of religion and of sense perception are logically independent, the distinction between naive and critical realism in relation to the world has its equally important analogue in religion. As regards sense perception, I am thinking of the kind of critical realism that was represented by such American philosophers as R.W. Sellars, Arthur Lovejoy, A.K. Rogers and J.B. Pratt. They took full account of the conceptual and interpretative element in sense perception, and regarded our ordinary perceiving as a complexly mediated awareness of a real physical world of which we, as bodily organisms, are part. They held that the sensory content of which we are directly aware (or, as they often said, which we intuit) is private to the perceiving consciousness, but that by means of this we are nevertheless able to live successfully in a real physical world which transcends our own consciousness. Thus Sellars, for example, wrote passages such as the following:

> Perceiving involves more than sensing . . . There is belief, construction and interpretation, all this leading to what is taken to be the awareness of things . . . [We need] to distinguish between the intuition of the sensory appearance, which alone is given, and the denotative selection of a thing-object which is believed in and characterised . . . In short, all sorts of facts about the thing perceived . . . influence our perceptual experience . . . Attitudes, expectations, memories, accepted facts, all operate interpretatively . . . There is, if you will, stimulus and complex interpretative response.
>
> (R.W. Sellars, 'A Statement of Critical Realism', *Revue internationale de philosophie*, Vol. I (1938–9), pp. 474–7)

Since the time, two or three generations ago, when the critical realists were writing we have become even more conscious of the subjective interpretative contribution to all awareness of our environment, including that ultimate environment – if such there be –

of which the religions speak. There is of course still, and probably always will be, a naive realism in religion as in sense perception. The ordinary unsophisticated person, who has not been troubled by the sorts of questions that philosophers raise, is a naive realist in relation to the physical world – though probably without having encountered either this notion or its alternatives. He or she simply assumes that the world around us is as it seems to be; and likewise the ordinary unsophisticated religious person, of whatever tradition, has normally been a naive religious realist. Just what is believed in this way is of course almost endlessly variable, for naive religious realism is not a creed but a way of thinking – namely, assuming that what is spoken about in the religious language that one has learned is just as described in this language, understood literally. And by 'literally' I simply mean 'straightforwardly, rather than as metaphor or myth'. It may very well be that, as many argue today, the literal and non-literal uses of language are not distinct in kind but rather form a continuum of legitimate usages. But a continuum can contain large differences and there is often a large difference between, for example, understanding a biblical story literally and understanding it as myth. Thus a naive Christian realist might, on reading Chapter 3 of the Book of Genesis and treating it as authoritative, believe the human race to have consisted originally of a single pair, who lived in a locality called the Garden of Eden until they were expelled for disobedience. In contrast to this, a critical Christian realist might regard Genesis 3 as a mythic story picturing the state of moral and spiritual disorder into which each generation is born. Or again the naive Christian realist may perhaps think of God as a great superhuman person looking down upon us from the sky. A contrasting critical religious realism can take a number of forms. The form which I favour myself thinks of, say, the Jahweh of Israel as the particular historical *persona* that has been jointly formed by the universal presence of the Real and the culturally unique thought-forms of the Jewish people. The Jahweh *persona* developed over the centuries from the tribal warrior god of the earliest layers of the tradition to the Holy One, blessed be He, of rabbinic Judaism. Both divine presence and human projection have accordingly been at work in the formation of the figure of Jahweh; and likewise of the heavenly Father of the New Testament, of the Allah of the Qur'anic revelation, of Shiva, of Vishnu, and so on; and again – looking further afield – in the formation of the various *impersonae* of the Real – Brahman, the Dharmakaya, the Tao, and so on.

If we distinguish – as we should – between, on the one hand, the psychological, anthropological and social insights of the psychologists, anthropologists and sociologists of religion, and on the other hand the naturalistic presuppositions which have so often accompanied them, the former (though not the latter) can be fully integrated into a contemporary religious realism. This can readily accept, to take a simple and basic example, that God thought of as the heavenly Father is manifestly a conception of the divine in human terms, but will reject the naturalistic dogma which authorises the inference in the minds of many social scientists that the heavenly Father is *nothing but* a human projection.

Thus a critical religious realism affirms the transcendent divine reality which the theistic religions refer to as God, but is conscious that this reality is always thought and experienced by us in ways which are shaped and coloured by human concepts and images. We see the Real always and only through the spectacles of our distinctive religious categories, and these, as we are acutely aware today, vary significantly from one culture to another.

Thus critical religious realism differs importantly both from the naive religious realism which assumes that the divine reality is just as spoken about in the language of some one tradition, and from the religious non- or anti-realism which rejects the idea of a transcendent divine reality existing in addition to and independently of we human beings.

IV

It is time now to specify further the non-realist religious point of view. This also can take a wide variety of forms. But centrally it interprets religious language, not as referring to a transcendent reality or realities, but as expressing our emotions, or our basic moral insights and intentions, or our way of seeing the world, or as referring to our moral and spiritual ideals. The premise, either open or concealed, that lies behind the non-realist understandings of religion is the naturalistic conviction – or indeed faith – that the realm of material things and living organisms, including the human organism with its immensely complex brain, is the only realm there is, and that God exists only as an idea in the human mind/brain – *in mente* but not *in re*. The classic statement remains that of Ludwig Feuerbach, whose *Essence of Christianity* was first published in German in 1841.

He held that the idea of a loving God is a projection onto the cosmos of our ideal of love. The heavenly Father is love personified and deified in the religious imagination. Today Feuerbach's spiritual descendants likewise start from a denial of 'objective theism', i.e. of the conviction that God is a reality *a se* whose existence accordingly does not consist simply in being conceived or imagined by human beings. They then develop their alternative account of religion, which moves along one or other of two paths. For some, strongly influenced by Wittgenstein, and represented here by Dewi Phillips, God is not so much an idea in our minds as an element in our language, the central element, indeed, of the realm of theistic language. This is in turn one dimension of something more many-sided, namely the theistic way or form of life. From this point of view, that God exists means that the concept of God operates effectively in the distinctive expressions and communications of religious people. For others, of whom Don Cupitt is a leading representative, God is an imaginary personification of our spiritual ideals. These ideals have intrinsic validity and are to be served, and served with all our strength, for their own sake. However, the imagined God figure, although sometimes giving psychological reinforcement to these ideal requirements, has also operated in all sorts of restricting and harmful ways and is today better discarded. Whereas Phillips has not, in his writings, emphasised the negative implications of this position, Cupitt has been anxious to have us all face them so that we can proceed to live consciously in a post-realist religious world.

It is important, in line with that last phrase, to recognise that these contemporary non-realist accounts of religion constitute religious, not anti-religious, interpretations. Although in an important sense atheistic, they differ from the atheism of such philosophers as A.J. Ayer, Antony Flew, Paul Edwards and many more, who reject the whole realm of religious language and practice as, at best, the experience of a delusion and hence as valueless or, less favourably, as positively harmful. In contrast to this the stream that runs from Feuerbach through such thinkers as Santayana, Dewey and Randall in the United States, and Julian Huxley, R.M. Hare, and now Dewi Phillips and Don Cupitt in Britain, sees religious language as expressing something of great value, even though its value is fundamentally different from that which religious people have generally supposed. A good way to bring out the positive character of non-realist religious thought is to note the analogy with Kant's move in making ethics autonomous. For Kant, the claim of morality upon us has an intrinsic authority, not dependent upon any external source or power, not even God. We are to do right simply and solely because it is right. Action to gain a reward or avoid a penalty is sub-moral. Analogously, the non-realist religious thinkers are saying that the religious life, including its distinctive language and practices, has intrinsic value and authority. It is to be engaged in for its own sake as inherently the best way to exist, and its value does not depend upon any factor or circumstance beyond itself. The activity of 'worshipping God', for example, does not gain its value, even in part, from there being (objectively) a God to be worshipped. Rather, in 'worshipping God' we are celebrating the ideals which we have personified and deified in our own imaginations. The reality of God is the reality of our ideals, and the 'life of God' consists in the living out of these ideals. And so we find that the religious non-realist can use the whole range of religious language, and can participate in the established liturgies, recite the creeds and prayers, listen to the scriptures, sing the hymns and receive the sacraments, but all within the invisible brackets of the belief that this activity is an autonomous end in itself, rather than a response to an ultimate transcendent reality in relation to which lies our final good.

What has led the religious non-realists to this radical reinterpretation? Negatively, they have been persuaded of the validity of the twentieth-century positivist critique of religion. They regard talk of God, or of eternal life, understood realistically, to be either meaningless or utterly implausible. Thus the first chapter of Phillips' *Death and Immortality* echoes closely Antony Flew's arguments against any form of survival of bodily death – as indeed Flew has pointed out. And Cupitt's rejection of the idea of God, realistically understood, echoes that of many contemporary sociologists and psychologists, who assume without argument that God is wholly a projection of the human imagination. This naturalistic assumption of much of the social science community is all the more powerful for operating as an unquestioned dogma which renders inaudible the counter-arguments propounded today by such considerable figures as, for example, Richard Swinburne, Alvin Plantinga, William Alston and many others.

Nevertheless it is in this area – in the perennial debate between (realist) religion and naturalism – that the main argument has to take place. For only if there are good reasons to reject realist religion is there any need to develop a non-realist alternative. Having pointed this out, however, I am not going to proceed with that debate here.

For the distinctive contribution of the non-realist religious thinkers has not in fact been in this area: here they have simply merged with the widespread contemporary rejection of the idea of the transcendent, and evidently feel little need to offer arguments in support of it. (Even that opening chapter to which I referred in Phillips' *Death and Immortality* is little more than perfunctory.)

The other and more positive consideration behind religious non-realism is the sense that the religious life, as a totality which includes a language and its correlative practices, is not an aberration but on the contrary perhaps the most valuable and ennobling aspect of our human existence. The thinkers we are considering therefore want to retain the religious life, and they seek to do so by emptying it of its to them unacceptable cosmic and metaphysical implications. They accordingly reject the conception of religion as the varied range of human responses to the Transcendent, and reinterpret it as a purely human activity, having its value as an end in itself.

V

Before seeking to evaluate this non-realist proposal we must isolate the central issue, and to that end we need to strip away other associated issues which might be confused with it. One such issue, which figures prominently in some of the literature, concerns the autonomy or heteronomy of ethics. Some of the most eloquent polemics in the non-realist literature attack the basing of morality upon the hope of divine rewards or fear of divine punishment, whether in this life or in a life to come. The authors make the point that action so motivated is not genuinely ethical, and drew the conclusion that a realist belief in God substitutes self-regarding prudence for authentic morality. And it must be admitted that this has happened on quite a large scale in the history of religion. The nineteenth-century Archdeacon William Paley – who has in the late twentieth-century embarked upon a second career as one of our standard sources of erroneous views – wrote that virtue is 'the doing good to mankind, in obedience to the will of God, and for the sake of everlasting happiness' (*Moral and Political Philosophy*, 2nd edn, 1817, p. 36). But this is today something of a museum piece. Most critical religious realists accept Kant's view of the autonomy of ethics, holding that we are so constituted (and, ultimately, divinely constituted) that morality is intrinsic to our nature as social beings. And indeed long before Kant religious thinkers were teaching that we should love God for God's sake and not for any hope of reward. Both the Muslim Rabia and the Christian St Francis Xavier have been credited with the prayer: 'O God, if I worship thee for fear of hell, burn me in hell; and if I worship thee in hope of paradise, exclude me from paradise; but if I worship thee for thine own sake, withhold not thine everlasting beauty.' And, earlier still, it was Plotinus who said, 'If a man desires the good life except for itself, it is not the good life that he desires.' I suggest, then, that whilst the autonomy of the moral life may still be an issue between religious non-realists and some naive religious realists, it is not the issue that they have to debate with contemporary critical religious realists.

Nor, I suggest, is another topic that is much stressed in some of the non-realist literature, namely the socially conditioned and culturally relative character of all religious phenomena. That, for example, settled agrarian societies in the ancient world tended to think of the divine in female terms, and nomadic herd-keeping societies in male terms – together with a hundred and one other correlations between the circumstances of human life and the religious practices and beliefs that occur within them – has been a matter of increasingly public knowledge since at least the work of Max Weber. This knowledge does indeed tend to undermine a naive religious realism, but it is fully accepted by modern critical religious realists. This, again, is not the point at issue between them and religious non-realists.

VI

What then is the real issue? It concerns the nature or structure of the universe in which we find ourselves. Is this, from our human point of view, good, or bad, or indifferent? Whereas pre-axial (or, in Eliade's terminology, archaic) religion was centrally concerned to keep human life on an even keel, enduring or enjoying it as it occurred, post-axial religion, embodied in what we call today the great world faiths, is centrally concerned with salvation – with the transformation of our human situation. It sees ordinary human existence as radically defective: as a fallen life in a fallen world, or as immersed in egocentric illusion and pervasively subject to *dukkha*. But it proclaims at the same time a limitlessly better possibility, and teaches a way to receive or to attain it – for some have found that it is given from beyond and others that it ripens from within. According to the great traditions, each human being is able sooner or later to go through the gateway of transformation, entering the kingdom of God or attaining moksha or nirvana. And these traditions proclaim, in terms of their very different conceptualities, that the structure of the universe is such that this limitlessly better possibility is actually available, and can even be entered upon now. For the transcendent Real towards which the religions point is not an entity or a person that might be directly observed or encountered, but that source or ground of everything, including the experienced deities and absolutes, in virtue of which the universe is, from the point of view of we human beings, ultimately benign or gracious. And so – according to the great post-axial religions – to live consciously in relation to that ultimate Reality in which is our final good is not to nurture an empty hope or a sustaining illusion, as the naturalistic thinkers believe, but is to be living in accordance with reality. In thus affirming the good, or to-be-rejoiced-in, nature of the Real, the great world faiths are forms of cosmic optimism. This ultimate optimism is, however, linked with an immediate pessimism which sees our ordinary existence as in desperate need of radical transformation. It is true that within each tradition, taken as a vast historical totality, there is also a subsidiary strand of ultimate pessimism. In Christianity this has taken the form of belief in a hell in which many – indeed, according to St Augustine (*Enchiridion*, 24, 97), a majority – are to be eternally damned. And it is implicit within that modern development within Buddhism (represented here by Frank Cook) which rejects the traditional belief in a long series of rebirths leading eventually to universal nirvana, so that only for those few who are fortunate enough to be able to attain or at least approach nirvana in the present life can the universe be said to be truly good. But from the standpoint of the normative interpretation of religion which I have adopted here, these strands of thought run contrary to the central and dominant message of their respective traditions.

Now the cosmic optimism of the great world faiths depends absolutely upon a realist interpretation of their language. For it is only if this universe is the creation or expression of an ultimate overarching benign reality, and is such that the spiritual project of our existence continues in some form beyond this present life, that it is possible to expect a fulfilment that can justify the immense pain and travail of the journey. If, on the contrary, such notions as God,

Brahman, Dharmakaya, rebirth, eternal life, are figments of our imaginations, we must face the grim fact that the marvellous human spiritual potential will only be fulfilled to the very fragmentary extent that it is in fact fulfilled in this world – none at all in some, a little in most of us, and a great deal in a very few. Thus a non-realist interpretation of religion inevitably entails a profound cosmic pessimism. From the point of view of a fortunate few it constitutes good news, but from the point of view of the human race as a whole it comes as profoundly bad news.

The issue between religious realism and non-realism, then, is the issue between two fundamentally opposed conceptions of the nature of the universe as it affects our human existence in its world-wide and history-long totality. The non-realist faith starts from and returns to the naturalistic conception that we are simply complex animals who live and die, the circumstances of our lives happening to be fortunate for some and unfortunate for others. Probably half or more of the children who have been born throughout human history and pre-history have died in infancy, their potentialities almost entirely undeveloped. Of those who have survived to adulthood great numbers have lived under oppression or in slavery, or have experienced many other forms of suffering, including anxious fear of starvation or of slaughter by enemies. And amidst these harsh pressures the human potential, of which we glimpse aspects in the saints, artists, thinkers and creative leaders, has only been able to make a very small beginning towards its fulfilment in the great majority of human lives. If the naturalistic vision is correct, that potentiality can never be fulfilled in the great majority, for at death they have ceased to exist. And it would be utopian to expect that our situation on this earth is about to become radically better. Thus the non-realist forms of religion, presupposing this naturalistic interpretation of the human situation, abandon hope for humankind as a whole. However, one seldom sees any awareness of this in the writings of our non-realist colleagues. They could, in my view, learn at this point from Bertrand Russell, who faced unflinchingly the harsh implications of his naturalistic philosophy – as in this well-known passage:

That Man is the product of causes which had no prevision of the end they were achieving; that his origin, his growth, his hopes and fears, his loves and his beliefs, are but the outcome of accidental collocations of atoms; that no fire, no heroism, no intensity of thought and feeling, can preserve an individual life beyond the grave; that all the labours of the ages, all the devotion, all the inspiration, all the noonday brightness of human genius, are destined to extinction in the vast death of the solar system, and that the whole temple of Man's achievement must inevitably be buried beneath the debris of a universe in ruins –all these things, if not quite beyond dispute, are yet so nearly certain, that no philosophy that rejects them can hope to stand. Only within the scaffolding of these truths, only on the firm foundation of unyielding despair, can the soul's habitation henceforth be safely built.

(*Mysticism and Logic*, 1918, pp. 47–8.)

The language here is somewhat florid, as indeed Russell himself noted in a letter some forty years later. But, he added, 'my outlook on the cosmos and on human life is substantially unchanged' (*The Autobiography of Bertrand Russell*, Vol. III, 1969, pp. 172–3). And this, surely, is where an intellectually wide-awake religious non-realist should start. He or she can then rejoice with the elite few whose heredity or environment or both are such that they are able to attain to personal blessedness, purity, the eternal quality of life, moksha, nirvana, satori, before death extinguishes them. But if they are deeply concerned for their less fortunate fellows they may well conclude with Omar Khayyam:

> Ah Love! could thou and I with Fate conspire
> To grasp this sorry Scheme of Things entire,
>   Would not we shatter it to bits – and then
> Re-mould it nearer to the Heart's Desire!

In contrast to this, the great world traditions see the universe as, from our human point of view, ultimately good. As William James put it, religion 'says that the best things are the more eternal things, the things in the universe that throw the last stone, so to speak' (*The Will to Believe and Other Essays*, 1905, pp. 25–6). This does not mean that present pain and suffering, injustice, unfulfilment and tragedy are not appallingly real. But it does mean that they are not the universe's last word. The total process of the universe, whether visualised in Judaeo–Christian–Islamic or in Buddhist or Hindu terms, has at its heart a Reality that is conceived as the limitless love or grace of God, the being–consciousness–bliss (satchitananda) of the Brahman which lies in the depths of our own being, or the infinite outflowing compassion of the eternal Dharmakaya.

I do not believe that it is possible, on the basis of our present limited experience, either to prove or to disprove the truth of this religious vision, construed in a critical realist way, nor even to show it to be either overwhelmingly probable or improbable. The universe can be interpreted in both realist-religious and in naturalistic terms, the way that one interprets it philosophically reflecting the way that one interprets and inhabits it experientially. The non-realist understanding of religious language becomes an option if one has entered into the widespread contemporary naturalistic state of mind. And the basic disagreement with religious realists occurs at that point. I cannot pursue this fundamental issue here. This paper aims only to make clear what the central question is. And my contention is that the debate between religious realists and non-realists is a new form of the old debate between religious (which has in the past always meant realist religious) and naturalistic interpretations of the universe.

VII

Let me ask in conclusion, however, whether we are really faced with an either/or choice between religious realism and non-realism? May there not also be intermediate possibilities? I think not. There can be endlessly different and endlessly complex and subtle variations on either theme, no doubt with all manner of new options yet to be developed. But in the end they will all fall on one or the other side of the distinction between naturalistic and supra-naturalistic understandings of the universe. Unfortunately we lack both an agreed and an agreeable terminology for this distinction. 'The natural and the supernatural', which was the title of a famous book by John Oman published now more than fifty years ago, is no longer in vogue. In addition to natural/supernatural and natural/supra-natural we have natural/transcendental and natural/non-natural. None of these is, I think, entirely felicitous. So we have to speak infelicitously. Using the term 'non-natural' Robert Adams has defined a non-natural fact as 'one which does not consist simply in any fact or complex of facts which can be stated entirely in the language of physics, chemistry, biology, and human psychology' (*The Virtue of Faith*, 1987, p. 105). We should I think add to the naturalistic languages that of sociology. The crucial question, then, concerning an understanding of the universe is whether it includes or excludes reference to any (putative) non-natural facts or realities. In the non-realist interpretations all such apparently non-natural realities as God, Brahman, the Dharmakaya are describable entirely in psychological and sociological terms. They are held to refer to ideas in our minds and/or to modes of human behaviour, including linguistic behaviour. In realist interpretations, on the other hand, (some of) these 'transcendent realities' are non-natural, not describable entirely in physical, psychological or sociological terms. According to critical realism they are indeed all phenomenologically describable in the terms provided by the anthropological sciences, for religious experience, as a psychological phenomenon, is constructed from the same (culturally variable) elements as the rest of our experience. But it is held to be at the same time, and in varying degrees, a cognitive response to a non-natural reality or realities. Non-natural or supra-natural reality is impinging upon us, though the form that it takes in our conscious thought and experience depends upon the concepts and images with which our minds are furnished.

And whether religious language is entirely about natural realities, wholly describable in physical, psychological and sociological terms, or is also about non-natural realities mediated through human concepts, does seem to be a matter of genuine contention. We seem to be faced with a real either/or which there is no point in concealing.

Part Two
Religious Non-Realism

2

Ludwig Feuerbach's Philosophy of God

JACK VERHEYDEN

The philosophy of the nineteenth-century writer, Ludwig Feuerbach, is noteworthy by the centrality of the role religion plays in his thought, on the one hand, and the opposition asserted to the traditional divine referent of religion in Western religions and philosophical thought, on the other hand. It is this peculiar combination which distinguishes Feuerbach as a philosopher of religion. It would be very difficult to find another Western thinker who so vigorously and with such thoroughness elaborates both of the positions stated above. The originality and the power of his contribution resides in his development of the juxtaposition of the profound importance of religion in human life with a sustained attack on the reality of the deity of traditional religion.

There would have been little or no originality in asserting that the gods are illusory and anthropomorphic productions of worshipping religious people, for instance. Such statements can be found in ancient writers. And taking a stand in opposition to God both religiously and philosophically had been a prominent feature during the era of the Enlightenment prior to Feuerbach, and to representatives of atheism subsequent to his era of the mid-nineteenth century. Then, certainly, there have been numerous adherents of the fundamental importance of a religious relation to deity for human life. But one does not normally meet adherents of the latter group who belong also to the former. Ludwig Feuerbach is such a man.

Feuerbach is distinguished in his peculiar stance by the fact that as contrasted with most opponents of theology he knows so much more about the subject matter of religious life and theology than do other opponents. The lines that follow will concentrate on Christianity, not because Feuerbach's thesis on religion is confined to this topic, but because it was the focus of his writings. If at times his position, as delineated here, appears limited by this focus on Christian subject matter – and I assume that such limitations there must be – it is also indicative of the power of his position. He has evidently spent a considerable effort in studying the history of Christian thought. It is hard to object that his familiarity with his subject matter is superficial.

Ludwig Feuerbach began his university studies as a theological student at the University of Heidelberg in the 1820s but found that Berlin was where he wanted to study, with its famous incumbents, Hegel and Schleiermacher. He soon was drawn to the field of philosophy as a student of Hegel. His advanced work in philosophical study was done explicitly as a dedicated Hegelian. He came to depart from the foundations of this philosophical orientation but retained much of the idealistic framework even in his new philosophy of materialism.

THE PHILOSOPHICAL BACKGROUND

In approaching Feuerbach's position on the human religious relationship to God, there are some broad philosophical considerations regarding his historical context that are helpful to have in mind. Feuerbach's education in the first third of the nineteenth-century in German territories meant that for him as for so many others in that era the philosophy of Immanuel Kant and post-Kantian idealism set the issues of conceptual reflection. When Feuerbach comes to the final breakthrough to his so-called new philosophy in 1841 with *The Essence of Christianity*, he says that his work has its ' . . . necessary logical basis in history', and 'The reader, therefore, who is unacquainted with the historical facts and ideas presupposed in my work, will fail to perceive on what my arguments and ideas hinge . . .'[1] The interpretation of Kant and post-Kantian idealism is as complicated a half century of philosophical history as perhaps can be found. But Feuerbach's warning above requires that some attention be paid to how he views this philosophical history as presuppositional for his position.

Kant's critical philosophy 'ended' for philosophers of this era the type of argumentation for God on the basis of the existence and empirical constitution of the natural world. 'Knowledge' was not a word appropriate for theoretical conclusions about the existence of the divine being for Kant. The existence of God could neither be proved nor disproved by any theoretical means in continuity with logic and science. Rather, God and immortality could only be affirmed on the basis of certain requirements of human moral willing. Our human interest in the rational completion of moral life can rationally lead to the postulation of God and immortality. The existence of God is decided by the human agent's moral interests in the harmony of a virtuous will and happiness, not by disinterested and impersonal scientific inference. It is not a passive acceptance of the givenness of God and an immortal state, but rather the active human willing which is crucial for these subjects.

For Feuerbach, we will note that Kant points to God on the basis of a human will's interest in happiness.

Kant's tripartite critical philosophy and his interpretation of religion, the four major phases of his philosophy, called forth in some of his successors an interest in understanding where the unity of Kant's thought lay. For instance, what is the relationship of the transcendental unity of apperception, the epistemological subject of the first critique, to the free self-consciousness belonging to the moral actor of the second critique? J.G. Fichte thought he grasped the deeper unity of Kant's philosophical programme in his philosophy of the transcendental 'I' which is at the root of the various fields of cognition and experience. The limitation on knowledge posited by Kant's thing-in-itself was overcome by the activity of this absolute I in Feuerbach's eyes, who in his idealist days agreed with Fichte not only on this but on most matters.[2]

Fichte's subjective idealism, classically expressed in his *Wissenschaftlehre*, attempted to carry out this union of the theoretical and volitional principles of the Kantian philosophy. Kant has convincingly shown the world constructing nature of the mind in knowledge, and Fichte intended to bring the spirit of this contention to its completion. Kant's transcendental unity of apperception refers not to the empirical individual knower but a transcendental structure in which the knower participates, that is, all individual knowers have this in common. So Fichte in his exploration of the deeper root of transcendental philosophy contrasts the individual 'I' which always exists over against the 'not-I' with a transcendental absolute I. The latter is universal and transcends the oppositions of reason and sensibility, I and not-I, spirit and nature, etc. As a result, Fichte held that the world is not only ordered by reason, as in Kant, but it is produced by the active willing of the absolute I. The natural world is constituted by the transcendental I as the field of its free, ethical action. It provides the material opportunity for human fulfilment of duty.

As a sometime holder of such a position Feuerbach sees that this means that all reality is originally and fundamentally spiritual. He can read Fichte saying, 'Our consciousness of a reality external to ourselves is thus not rooted in the operation of supposed external objects; . . . it is rather the necessary faith in our own freedom and power, in our own real activity . . . which lies at the root of all our consciousness of a reality external to ourselves . . .'[3] Furthermore, in knowledge of supposed external objects Fichte said we perceive not something external at all but only ourselves and our own condition.[4] The effect of Fichtean idealism is to emphasise, without limit it would seem, the productive power and reality of the knowing-acting subject. Feuerbach will break with the idealist contention that reality is primarily spiritual, but the robust power of expressive subjectivity will remain, and basically he appears to continue to hold that in knowing objects we only know ourselves and our own condition. Certainly, such a contention will be true of a divine 'object'.[5]

Fichte became embroiled in the atheism controversy of 1798 with his associate Forberg because of holding that it is the spiritual world of the moral order that is divine, and that to specify God by the use of words such as 'personhood' and 'consciousness' was to attempt to finitise the infinite. God became an acute definitional problem for Fichtean thought. The issue of the relation of predicates of God's nature to the divine being is raised by sharply by this controversy surrounding Fichtean idealism. Also, Feuerbach came to see that the theological doctrine of God's will is really only the free transcendental human will of the absolute I.[6]

Feuerbach saw in Hegel the consummation of the type of idealism elaborated by Fichte. They share idealism's move to overcome dualistic oppositions by a principle immanent in the subject. The Feuerbachian background in Hegelian thought is, of course, extensive and many-sided given Feuerbach's early study and identification with it. I will only lift up three features of Hegel's thought which are useful in approaching Feuerbach. Certainly, there are several others that could be utilised.

First, there is a great emphasis in Hegel's thought on the unity of God and the human world. Idealism's drive to overcome oppositions by an immanent participation is present in Hegel with a striking and forceful affirmation of the togetherness of the finite and the infinite. They are not to be externally related, but the finite is an aspect, a moment, a part of that which is infinite. Indeed, Hegel said that without the world God would not be God. In some places in his writings he indicates that human knowledge of God is God's knowing of Himself. This type of reflexive expression Feuerbach can adapt to say that human knowledge of God is humanity's knowledge of itself.

Second, Hegel's view of reality is the unfolding of the absolute concept, the dynamic unity of thought and being. Hegel's terminology cascades through various levels but the origin and movement of reality is spiritual, and as it unfolds it objectifies itself. This objectification is an 'othering' of spirit in a variety of ways, it seems, in Hegel's philosophy and it would mislead to collapse them all into a single meaning. But one aspect of this movement involves an estrangement of spirit from itself in the very externalising by which it individualises and posits itself outside of itself in self-differentiation. Spirit then needs to move forward to a new sublimated unity which overcomes the moment of estrangement or alienation. This idea of objectification and its psychological consequences of alienation is drawn upon heavily by Feuerbach.

Third, Hegel's philosophy attempts to understand truth as it historically unfolds. History is a realm of development in time. Things progress to higher levels historically. In Hegel's *Lectures on the Philosophy of Religion*, present in transcript form while Feuerbach was a student and then published in 1832, Hegel traces the movement of human religious life through different levels of religions of nature in the primitive state, to China, to India, then transitionally through Zoroastrianism, Syria and Egypt. Development reaches a new spiritual breakthrough in the religions of Judaism and Greece, and, to an extent, also Rome. Finally, this religious development attains an absolute and consummate form in primitive Christianity. Spirit becomes objective to itself and the concept of religion which is the unity of God and the human, attains realisation. The symbols of the various religions, therefore, manifest moments of the movement of Hegel's philosophical categories. Feuerbach appropriates this developmental approach but he does not terminate it with New Testament Christianity.

THE THEOLOGICAL BACKGROUND

While Feuerbach's philosophical lineage is most crucial in order to perceive on what his arguments hinge, to refer to his statement above, there are certain theological ideas which are also influential, and some reference more briefly will be made to them. While mention has already been made of Feuerbach's focus on Christianity, his theological background more specifically is the Lutheran tradition. Feuerbach does not confine himself to interpreting Lutheranism by any means, but there are certain matters stressed in Lutheran tradition to which Feuerbach appeals in making several of his points. He has studied Luther's writings extensively, more than any other Christian theologian by far. One of Feuerbach's smaller books is on *The Essence of Faith According to Luther.* At the centre of Luther's theology, and consequently, also of the tradition deriving from him, is the contrast of law and gospel. The Reformation inaugurated by Luther meant to contrast sharply a salvation resulting from God's free grace with one in which human works cooperated by achieving merit. The law of God is a hammer which exposes the depth of unrighteousness in human beings and directs people to look beyond their own bondage to sin toward the same God whose wrath they deserve. On the other hand, the gospel is the announcement and bestowal of God's justifying grace for those who truly recognise their own lack of goodness and cast themselves on the resources of God alone. Luther's message is one that exalts God as the one alone to be honoured and glorified, while human being is spoken of in language that emphasises its 'totally depraved' state in the most forceful expressions. An example is: 'To God alone belong justice, truth, wisdom, strength, holiness, blessedness, and everything good. But our lot is injustice, folly, lying, weakness, and everything evil, all of which is proven superfluously in Scripture.'[7] The radicality of this contrast is not lost on Feuerbach.

A second implication of Luther's theology concerns his striking concentration on the suffering humanity of Jesus Christ as the relevation of God's grace. At times Luther will say that 'God will not and cannot be found except through and in this humanity.'[8] The love of God, the God that we can trust for ultimate good, is present for us in the humanness of Jesus Christ. There is no other God than that God called Jesus Christ.[9] For Luther this meant that theology should be a theology of the cross as contrasted with a theology of glory. A theology of the cross recognises God in the shame and humility of the cross. God is hidden in suffering. On the other hand, a theology of glory attempts to know God from His works in creation. The natural theology tradition of the Middle Ages could easily become a theology of glory.

Another feature of Luther's theology is closely connected with this veiled revelation of God. He contrasts God as known in faith *pro me*, for me, and for us, with God in Himself, the absolute God, the naked God. God only meets us when He is not clothed in majesty. Feuerbach concludes that God is, then, a being for us.[10]

Lutheran doctrines were not the only theological background for Feuerbach. He had studied with the Reformed theologian, Friedrich Schleiermacher, a controversial figure in his time because of his approach to Christian theology through an analysis of what he calls 'immediate self-consciousness'. Human self-consciousness in its immediate experience includes both consciousness of the world and consciousness of God united in a specific manner in every human being. This God-consciousness is rooted in a feeling of unqualified dependence which contrasts with and provides the unity for the relative freedom and relative dependence entailed in the self's relations with the world.[11]

Following this method, Schleiermacher held that Christian doctrines are accounts of human states of self set forth in language. Schleiermacher did not exclude statements about God's being in theological doctrine, but he did insist that such statements are derivative from basic doctrines which are descriptive of human self-consciousness. In consequence, Schleiermacher's theology appears more immanental than transcendent in its general cast concerning the nature of God. And he clearly emphasises the importance of moods and affective human states of consciousness as prior to intellectual ideas. Feuerbach is certainly indebted to Schleiermacher on this point.

Finally, Feuerbach has a background both philosophical and theological in the biblical criticism of David Friedrich Strauss. The latter writer's *Life of Jesus Critically Examined* in 1835 was the inauguration of so-called left-wing Hegelianism.[12] The furore set off by this book was not because of the utilisation of the methods of historiography in investigating the New Testament. This had been present for several decades. Rather, it was Strauss' contention that so much of the New Testament is not actual history but rather the mythical production of the pre-scientific primitive Christian mind that fuelled an explosion. It was the myth-making mind that insisted on seeing Jesus in continuity with Old Testament rubrics that created much of the 'history' in the New Testament, for instance. Strauss saw the modern mind as beyond myth. Furthermore, Strauss said that while the New Testament asserts the incarnation of God in the individual man, Jesus of Nazareth, the Hegelian conceptual truth of this mythical framework is that God is incarnate in the human race universality and not in any individual. Feuerbach's thought is in direct continuity here with that of Strauss on both counts, that of a mythological representation of a religious reality that is not 'real' for scientific conceptual thinking, and a universal essence of the human as of signal importance in the proper interpretation of Christian ideas. Feuerbach, however, is concerned with the reality of the being of God rather than New Testament history and the location of incarnation.

THE NON-REALISM OF FEUERBACH

The title of this section is ironic because Feuerbach presents his new philosophy of *The Essence of Christianity* as precisely one that is realistic and opposed to the imaginary fantasy of traditional religion and philosophy.[13] Feuerbach was a historian of modern philosophy before he moved to his new position. He sees modern philosophical reflection as begun in Descartes' *cogito ergo sum*, and what is wrong with modern philosophy is already indicated in this phrase. Nonmaterial thinking is taken as the key by which to understand reality. This is a spiritualising move which determines the course of subsequent philosophical thought. There has been a steady movement in this history of philosophy that transforms theology and the spiritual being about which it is concerned into the reason of the human. Fichte and Hegel have carried such a transformation through to its culmination, Hegel attaining the final point here. This course of modern philosophy has been the negation of theology, but it is a negation of theology which is itself hiddenly theology and therefore is in contradiction to itself. It makes spiritual reason the origin of reality, it says that which is spiritual is the most real. That is why it is still a theology, even though in a non-theological form. To criticise the philosophy of idealism as consummated in Hegel is to criticise theology and to criticise traditional theology is of a piece with the criticism of Hegelian idealism.

Not *cogito ergo sum*, but *sentio ergo sum* is Feuerbach's watchward in his new philosophy. I sense, therefore I am. Materialism must overcome the spiritualising of theology and idealism. The human should recognise that reality is mediated through the senses. Sensory perception is prior to thought so that philosophy's attempt to approach reality through thought as primary and the spiritual as originative reverses the real nature of things. To posit matter as ultimately real and originative is the same as saying 'There is no God.'[14] What is encountered through the senses is not limited to man. Light, for instance, also affects animals, plants, inorganic substances so that in determining what light is this generality must be taken into consideration. But, the issue stands otherwise with God. There is no sensory relation and so God is a secret of the human only.[15]

It is this materialistic reversal which separates Feuerbach from every aspect of his philosophical and theological background mentioned above. The continuities are strongly there but this materialistic framework provides a new meaning for them. Since God is a secret of the human Feuerbach offers an analysis of what God is in relation to human being. It leads him to an intense consideration of religion in human life. In speaking of his writings, Feuerbach says: 'All have strictly speaking only one purpose, one intention and idea, one theme. This theme, of course, is religion or theology and everything connected with it.'[16]

In carrying this theme out, Feuerbach says he is going to let religion itself speak, something that he thinks speculation, both philosophical and theological, do not accomplish. Speculation makes religion say only what speculation has itself thought and can express better than religion, religion meaning the concrete aspirations of the hearts and factual practices of worshipful people. Here Feuerbach presents his standpoint as one defending the interests of religion against abstract and ethereal exponents of pure intellect. Religion is basically *sensuous*, something that the traditional philosopher as well as the theologian by the bent of their intellectualising continually abuse.

Yet, on the other hand, Feuerbach needs to correct religion himself. He knows the secret of religion in a manner that religion does not recognise correctly. The intention of religion, its own supposition, is one thing, but its heart, its essence, its true reality is something else.[17] Here Feuerbach's standpoint means that he is a critic of religion, viewing religion as a dream of the human mind – a sensuous, concrete dream, to be sure – from which man needs to be awakened in order to attain clear self-consciousness.

This last word indicates like so many early nineteenth-century German thinkers that Feuerbach is an analyst of human self-consciousness. Since God is a secret of the human only, that which differentiates the human from the animal must be the locus for

religion and its subject matter. Feuerbach contends that this difference of the human resides in the capacity of self-consciousness to
become objective to itself. The human has an internal relation to
itself, it can make itself its own object. But the object in the self
relation is not just oneself as an individual as might be the case with
some twentieth-century existentialist phenomenology, rather it is to
the species of the human. Animal consciousness, Feuerbach supposes, receives the deliverances of sensory perception and judges
things according to outward signs, but it does not make its essential
nature an object of awareness. Because man does do this, it is more
consciously individualised as an 'I' and is universalised in consciousness of the object. While this object at base is generic humanity, Feuerbach thinks it also provides the possibility for human
thought to extend to universalise other particulars in the knowledge
of science.

   This natural self-objectiveness of human consciousness is extremely
important for Feuerbach's philosophy. He elaborates it in a variety
of ways, more than can be explored here. It means that a human
being is in itself at once both I and thou, that is, there is a relation to
the other that is constitutive of human self-consciousness. Thought
is always thinking with another and is socially mediated. Feuerbach
indicates that this has its sensory basis in the sexual differentiation of
human being, into woman and man. But Feuerbach's interest here is
not the exploration of the sexual, but rather that the sensory relation
to the fellow human mediates a relation to the human race in the
individual's self-consciousness. Feuerbach's central thrust continually circles around this interpretation of self-consciousness. As an 'I'
human being is finite and limited. Man wants to be happy, independent of limitations, and to possess power over its existence, but
instead finds itself dependent on the natural world. Human being
knows that it will die, and this means that man is fearful over its
situation. Yet human self-consciousness is not only the 'I' but also, as
indicated, is object related to the human generally. And in this
aspect, human self-consciousness is not limited but, rather, is consciousness of the infinite. The infinite is the infinite nature of humanity itself. Feuerbach thinks the human race extended over time and
space can transcend the specific limitations that pertain to any
individual.

   Feuerbach understands religion in human life in this context.
Without death there would be no religion, but, religion itself is
consciousness of the infinite. It is the consciousness which the hu-

man has of its own infinite nature. And this means that ' . . . in the consciousness of the infinite, the conscious subject has for his object the infinity of his own nature.'[18] Religion, then, is human being's relation to its own nature. Human nature is constituted by reason, by will, and by the feeling heart. To think, to will, to love are the highest powers of man, and when these powers are objectified through human activity it becomes evident to the human what its nature is. Out of such objectifications human being becomes conscious of itself. The consciousness of such objects is the self-consciousness of man. The nature of the human is revealed in this manner in its true essential selfhood. The power that these objectifications have for the human is the power of its own nature. The power of the object of feeling, or of will, or of intellect is the power of feeling, or will, or intellect itself.

Here is a Feuerbachian principle from his analysis of self-consciousness: the object is always the subject's own nature objectified. This applies exactly to representations of God. 'The *absolute nature*, the God of man, is his *own* nature.'[19] Religion as the consciousness of the infinite, the infinity of human nature, is the consciousness of God. The opening lines of John Calvin's *Institutes of the Christian Religion* state that knowledge of God and knowledge of oneself are inextricably intertwined and Feuerbach agrees with this Augustinian tenet. But in Feuerbach's case the consciousness of God and the consciousness of essential humanity are identified. The same objectification that reveals human powers is the presentation of God.

How does Feuerbach explain this identification? Here Feuerbach lifts up the contention already noted that in human being the intellect is not primary. To analyse self-consciousness in terms of reflexive self-objectification and the relation of limitedness and infinitude are conceptually true but these matters are experienced first of all in terms of emotion and imagination in historical humanity. The wishes of the human heart for happiness and security in face of the threat of evil forces gives rise to the imaginative construction of a dream world that represents the capacities, powers and desired ideals of the human race in its infinitude as individualised spiritual beings, and finally as one spiritual being. This involuntary, childlike act of the naive mind wants to have 'all at once' that which pertains to the human nature in all places and future times. The powers of human nature are objectified by the imagination as an individual being *now*. God is this being conceived under the form of the senses, but freed from the limits of sense. As an imagined objectification God differs

from human being only quantitatively; what the latter possesses in
very limited fashion as an individual, the divine being possesses in
endless measure existing at all times, in all places, knowing every
particular thing, etc.

The character of religion, then, ' . . . is the immediate, involuntary,
unconscious contemplation of the human nature as another, a distinct nature.'[20] Religion does not try to make this distinction qualitative and essential. Not only are human emotions attributed to God
such as is evident in the Old Testament's Yahweh, but He even
possesses corporeal properties. Religion is largely beneficial in this
activity of realising the wishes of the heart and providing comfort in
face of the trials of living. 'Hence the nearer religion stands to its
origin, the truer, the more genuine it is, the less is its true nature
disguised.'[21] But things do not stop there for reflection enters and
'what was originally only an emotional impression, an immediate
expression of admiration, of rapture, an influence of the imagination
on the feelings, has fixity given to it as an objective quality . . . '[22] That
is, theology arises and the quantitative difference of the human and
God becomes qualitative, and this is an inexhaustible source of
falsehoods, illusions and contradictions. The rather harmless separation becomes harmful so that fed by theology, religion becomes the
disuniting of the human from itself. Human being sets God before it
as the antithesis of itself. God and the human become conceived as
extremes, God the absolutely positive, the human the absolutely
negative. We recall Luther. Man becomes estranged from its own
humanity, taking away all that is affirmative and good from its self-
understanding and placing it outside of itself in a being thought to
be essentially different. This situation throws religion into contradiction with itself as human being's relation to its own nature.

However, it is Luther's genius to give expression to the most
fundamental truth of religion even in this alienated starting point.
He makes estrangement only a beginning, not a result, a means not
the end of theologically developed religion. Feuerbach says hunger
is pain and torment but its purpose is not in itself. Rather, its goal is
in its opposite, in its own satisfaction. So there is no salvation without need: 'What Luther takes away from you in your human condition, he replaces for you a hundredfold in God.'[23]

God acts for human being and its welfare but Feuerbach concludes that this means that: 'Man completes and satisfies himself in
God.'[24] Christian doctrines are fundamental wishes of the human
heart, and Luther's doctrine of faith has given this its most profound

expression in his account that God is by His very nature concerned with the human, that God does not exist for himself or against us but for us. The religious wish of the human heart is here given its most robust recognition.

Christianity assumes a unique role in the history of human religion according to Feuerbach. It is the religion of the incarnation. Jesus Christ is not a teacher or prophet. He is one in whom God has proved Himself to be a human being. Religion has the character of representing the nature of the human as a distinct being as we have seen. But the incarnation of God in Jesus Christ manifests the truth that God is really human after all. This is the mystery hidden from long ages but now revealed. The truth of religion has come to a new clarity in Christ, but it is the penultimate stage of religious history. The full clarity of the religious consciousness of man comes in the era that realises that the attributes of God belong to the nature of universal and infinite humanity and rejects God as an individual and personal subject.

This contention is the crux of Ludwig Feuerbach's philosophy of God. Christian doctrines of the being and nature of God are fundamentally correct in their account of the divine attributes. These doctrines are false in attributing these attributes to an independent and separate personal being as the repositor of these attributes.

> The idea of deity coincides with the idea of humanity. All divine attributes, all the attributes which make God God, are attributes of the species – attributes which in the individual are limited, but the limits of which are abolished in the nature of the species, and even in its existence, in so far as it has its complete existence only in all men taken together.[25]

The power, the knowledge, the goodness, the justice, the love of God are attributes of the species humanity and are true in this reference. What is false is ascribing them to the being possessing aseity distinct from man and the world.

Feuerbach particularly emphasises love. 'God is love' is a basic Christian affirmation and Feuerbach simply wants to say that 'love is divine', that is, that love is that which is most valuable and worthy of worship. It is in love that human being realises itself for the individual is properly related to the human race in love. 'Is not the proposition, "God loves man" an orientalism . . . which in plain speech means, the highest is the love of man?'[26] Always the principle holds – the human relation to the divine object is the human being's own nature objectified. The objectification is true in terms of the attributes worshipped if they are not transferred to a separated superhuman subject.

This is what enables Feuerbach to evaluate religion so highly. To deny the human is to deny religion, and to deny religion is to deny human being's relation to its own nature, its highest good. The imaginary objectifications of God historically have enabled human being to come to its recognition of who and what it is. In God I learn to estimate my own nature. I have value in the sight of God; the divine significance of my nature becomes evident to me.[27] Without the religious relationship the significance of who I am is lost. I become isolated from participation in the divine life of the potentialities of the human race. The love of God makes me loving; the love of God to me is the cause of my love to God – which is the human race. Religion is crucial for human life for Feuerbach.

Feuerbach's role of defender of religion is evident in his polemic against philosophical speculation and its contradictory union with religion. Not Aristotle's *actus purus* but the suffering God who empties Himself in sacrifice for others, not Spinoza's universal substance but the personal God is the interest of religion. Modern philosophical theology has been all too ready to call into question the predicates of God as anthropomorphisms and espouse in their place some negative principle. But the interests and claims of religion are concrete. Rather than some universal attributes that pertain to some otherworldly principle, 'It is the personal predicates which constitute the essence of religion . . . '[28] That God is personal, the moral lawgiver, the Father of humanity, the Holy One, the just, the good, the merciful – such is the real object of religion.

Despite the fact, therefore, that Feuerbach speaks of his position as atheism because he rejects God as a separate being, he also presses the question as what really constitutes atheism.

> Thus what theology and philosophy have held to be God; the Absolute, the Infinite, is not God; but that which they have held not to be God is God; namely, the attribute, the quality, whatever has reality. Hence he alone is the true atheist to whom the predicates of the divine being, – for example, love, wisdom, justice, – are nothing; not he to whom merely the subject of these predicates is nothing. And in no wise is the negation of the subject necessarily also a negation of the predicates considered in themselves.[29]

In fact, Feuerbach's dedication to the religious standpoint is so thorough that he admits in one respect that the nature of the human generally cannot fully replace God as a distinct being. God is the idea of the human species as an individual being, and this possesses a vitality for feeling, a deeply moving reference that is enrapturing for the imagination. The idea of humanity cannot attain this because it lacks the 'all at once' character that gives the immediate satisfaction which is the life of the feeling heart. God is humanity's intuition of its own nature, and while as a separate individual it disunites the human from itself God also brings a unique kind of emotional fulfilment.[30]

OBSERVATIONS AND CRITIQUE

I have tried to present Feuerbach as straightforwardly in his own terms as I can within the limitations of literary space and have refrained from evaluation in the previous section. His position is sufficiently distinctive in its specifics to enable objections to come from many different types of positions.

It is important to notice the Feuerbachian angle of approach to his philosophy of God. His approach is an internal critique. As contrasted to the lines classically developed by Hume and Kant (in the First Critique) Feuerbach does not attempt to establish the inadequacy of rational argument for the so-called existence of God. Nor does he marshall arguments positively that would require that God did not exist. This type of rational verifiability seems remote from Feuerbach's position on God. His method is to attempt to analyse the religious life itself and the rational articulation of the referent of its worship as it is experienced by religious people. He says that this experience is rooted in emotion and imagination and expresses the need fulfilling wishes of these people. That God is an imaginary objectification is an assertive claim by Feuerbach that is only justified in terms of the overall coherence which he can bring through his internal interpretation to statements about God. But he has a definite propensity to assume more than that, and to indicate that his laying bare the wish of the human heart in its own self-affirmation means that his ontological view of the unreality of God (as distinct from humanity) is justified. In face of that, the statement made by the philosopher Edward von Hartmann – no adherent himself of traditional Western religious thinking on God – is much to the point. Hartmann's objection said:

> His sole original thought is that the gods are projected wishes of the human. Now it is entirely correct that something does not therefore exist because one desires it, but it is not correct that something could not exist since one desires it. Feuerbach's whole critique of religion and the whole proof for his atheism rests nevertheless upon this single conclusion, that is, upon a logical fallacy. If the gods are beings of desire, nothing at all follows from that for their existence or nonexistence.[31]

Hartmann's logical objection is sound, but Feuerbach's 'original thought' is not limited to what Hartmann attacks. This statement of Hartmann's raises the comprehensive issue of what would decide 'the existence of the gods'. So an obvious response to Feuerbach would be a type of interpretation couched in ontological terms that rationally indicated the reality of an ultimate spiritual principle. The theological thinker here could attempt to formulate categories that did not reflect human interests and if such could be found an ostensible referent for religious expression would be vindicated free of all anthropomorphism. Would this be an appropriate and successful reply to Feuerbach's view? Undoubtedly, it would be a relevant factor in the field of discussion. The Kantian restriction on traditional argumentation for God sets the framework for much of Feuerbach's contentions. Overcoming that framework would make Feuerbach's position significantly different. Despite Kant's strictures on natural theology, however, he was not a materialist, and the accomplishment of such a new framework would undercut Feuerbach's materialistic claim. I do not want to imply any underestimation of this aspect of engaging Feuerbach's philosophy of God.

Nevertheless, in reading Feuerbach's major writings on religion in the 1840s the arguments for materialism are quite limited, and while he uses his emphasis on the wishes of the heart to justify the illusory nature of God this is not the dominant theme which he emphasises time and again. His occasional comments on the inappropriateness of the deity according to Aristotle and Spinoza for the life of religion strongly indicates this dominant theme. Aristotle and Spinoza would not qualify as adequate materialists in Feuerbach's philosophy. That is, one could have an ultimate spiritual principle like Aristotle or Spinoza and it would not qualify to change the interpretation of God as the wishful imagination of the heart. The dominant theme for Feuerbach's internal critique of religion is not the existence of God but whether God is as faith holds God to be. The believing heart is directed to the reality of God that graciously comes to the human. The personal love incarnate in Christ, faith, prayer, the life of love, immortality – it is topics like these which Feuerbach explores most powerfully in *The Essence of Christianity* and recurs to again and again. Aristotle and Spinoza on God do not address that kind of issue to Feuerbach's mind. But Luther does! 'As you believe, so you have Him' Luther would say – and so also would Feuerbach. Yet Luther means by such a phrase the coming of God into the human heart. Feuerbach means it as the wishing heart's subjective affirmation of itself. In both, however, God's attitude and activity is 'for us'. Feuerbach's central point in his writing on Christian faith is situated here and is the most difficult aspect of his argument to rebut. The consummating relation of God and the human typically underscores the love of God for the human, and it is this which Feuerbach appreciates. Therefore, he says, why would not human being want to be loved, and therefore imaginatively objectify God doing so?

If a theologian like Luther were to try to answer Feuerbach on this point, it would be through the doctrine of the Word of God in Scripture and proclamation that comes to the potential believer's heart. Feuerbach would find this source outside of the believer a false expression of the disunited deity, but Luther would say that precisely in coming from beyond the potential believer's heart the Word is that which enables the heart to be freed from being merely curved in upon itself.

A response to Feuerbach must meet him finally on his own internal ground of the nature of religion and Christian believing. When a modern reader tires of railing against John Calvin's predestination doctrine or Jonathan Edwards' disdain for human freedom she or he could notice these writers' religious sense of the majestic greatness of God, and that is hard, indeed, to limit to the wishful egoism of the human heart. Friedrich Schleiermacher's intuitive sense of radical dependence on that which is not the world refers the human ever and again to that which transcends Feuerbach's nature and humanity. Rudolf Otto explored how the religious orientation is not the extension of the known and cosily familiar, but is an openness to that which precisely contrasts with such in its being wholly other.

Feuerbach's interpretation of religion must be met with such interpretations as these from the past, as well as those of the present, for his account of the religious dimension is sadly one-sided. But to engage Feuerbach here is not to negate the truth that his side does include. Human need and emotional desire is present imaginatively in religion. Feuerbach can be instructive in what he does see. However, his conclusions overreach his proper footing. One of the most famous phrases in Christian history is Augustine's: 'Thou hast made us toward Thyself and our hearts are restless until they find their rest in Thee.' If that is true there can be a legitimate and inevitable wish of the human heart for the divine – even to be loved.

Theologically, Feuerbach's text is filled with reasoning that seems highly arbitrary. He will say, if God loves the human, is not the human, then, the very substance of God? If God is not indifferent to the beings who worship Him, therefore He is a human God, etc.[32] But this kind of thinking appears terribly forced. Christian theology has usually found there to be some similarity between God and certain human qualities within the context of fundamental ontological dissimilarity. But Feuerbach always seems to take any analogy of God and the human to imply material identification.

The unique power of Feuerbach as an interpreter of religion even while intending to expose its theological inadequacies resides in the ontological referent which he provides for the religious object. There have been writers on the religious since Feuerbach who while rejecting the Christian – or Jewish – doctrine of God held to ideals which embodied some of the predicates of this God. For these interpreters there is no being for their actuality. They are constructions which should guide human living. Now Feuerbach has something in common with this view in its rejection of a traditional God. But Feuerbach differs significantly from such a position with his insistence that the personal attributes of God come to full expression in the nature or essence of the human race. Such has not come about so far but it will in the future. The predicates of God are not only ideals but receive ontological actuality in the unfolding course of the human race.

The profundity of much of Feuerbach's writing is that he can retain some of the religious experiencer's reliance upon a power not its own that brings fulfilment. The confidence of the heart – so important for Luther – is still an ingredient in Feuerbach's interpretation of religious life. The race will bring to realisation the details of the imagination. The religious individual perceives that perfection which pertains to the infinitude of its species.

This grand contention for human nature generally is what caused the left-wing Hegelians, for whom Feuerbach had been the philosophical master, to move away from him. So, famously, Karl Marx said Feuerbach was still too metaphysical and corrected him by social economic structures. The human race no longer played the divine role and so Marx's view of religion was consistently negative as contrasted with that of Feuerbach.

It was left to Max Stirner to press the criticism of Feuerbach most radically in *The Single One and Its Own*. In place of God what do the Young Hegelian friends offer us in their stead, he writes.

> Yet one sees, e.g., by Feuerbach, that the expression "man" is to designate the *species*, not the transitory, individual ego . . . But the species is nothing, . . . Man with the great M is only an ideal, the species only something thought of . . . It is not how I realize the *generally human* that needs to be my task, but how I satisfy myself.

Stirner concludes that he should act for his own benefit and not his neighbour's. To serve humanity is to serve himself.

Feuerbach's identity of God and the human race is rejected here, and the issue raised is one not confined to the debates of left-wing Hegelians of the nineteenth-century. Feuerbach combines an ontological materialism with an ethical idealism by his view of the divine role of the essence of humanity. But if this is too grand a view of the human as Max Stirner – and later Friedrich Nietzsche – thought, how can one continue to affirm the divine predicates of justice, love, etc., as worthy of worship and allegiance? We saw above Feuerbach saying that in respect to God the negation of the subject does not lead necessarily to a negation of the predicates. On the other hand, Stirner draws precisely that conclusion with the possible revision of the term 'necessarily'.

In summation, I will list five types of positions on the status of God that have been referred to in this paper's discussion of Ludwig Feuerbach's philosophy of God in order to distinguish his stance from that of others. It is undoubtedly a rough sketch!

(a) The traditional Christian doctrine of God that affirms God as an ontological subject distinct from and transcendent to the world and humanity. This being possesses predicates of knowledge, freedom, power, goodness, love, etc. (There are important divergences possible within this type.)

(b) The position of idealism such as found in Hegel and Schelling which sees God as immanent in humanity and the world, and consequently, as unfolding and processive. Feuerbach found this position 'a hidden theology' because it was still spiritually realistic. (Again, there are various renditions of it.)

(c) Feuerbach's own position which rejects the transcendent subject of the being of God but retains most of the attributes as the object of religious worship and allegiance. These personal attributes of some knowledge and power, of much justice and love, he ascribes to the nature of the human generally. These attributes are processively unfolding in the world of humanity and will be fully actualised in the indefinite future.

(d) The position that joins Feuerbach in rejecting God as a transcendent or immanent subject of attributes distinguishable from the world and humanity, but holds that divine attributes such as justice and love are ideals produced or discovered by people by which they should live. These attributes do not refer ontologically to the essence of the human as in Feuerbach's position.

(e) The position indicated by Max Stirner which rejects both the divine subject and the divine predicates, producing an orientation that appears nihilistic in terms of the traditional framework of Western religious and philosophical thought.

Notes

1. Ludwig Feuerbach, *The Essence of Christianity* (London: Kegan, Paul, 1893) p. xliii.
2. Simon Rawidowicz, *Ludwig Feuerbach's Philosophie* (Berlin: Reuther und Reichard, 1931) p. 266.
3. J.G. Fichte, *The Vocation of Man* (New York: Liberal Arts, 1956) p. 98.
4. Ibid., p. 37.
5. See Rawidowicz, op. cit., p. 271f.
6. Cf. Rawidowicz, op. cit., p. 270.
7. Cited in Ludwig Feuerbach, *The Essence of Faith According to Luther* (New York: Harper & Row, 1967) p. 34.
8. Cited in Philip Watson, *Let God Be God* (Philadelphia: Muhlenberg, 1947) p. 102.
9. Cited in Paul Althaus, *The Theology of Martin Luther* (Philadelphia: Fortress, 1966) p. 20f.
10. Feuerbach, *The Essence of Faith* . . . , p. 50.
11. Friedrich Schleiermacher, *The Christian Faith* (Edinburgh: T. & T. Clark, 1928) pp. 12–18.
12. D.F. Strauss, *The Life of Jesus Critically Examined* (Philadelphia: Fortress, 1972).

13.   Ludwig Feuerbach, *Principles of the Philosophy of the Future* (Indianapolis: Bobbs-Merrill, 1966) p. 8.
14.   Ibid., p. 33.
15.   Ibid., p. 10.
16.   Ludwig Feuerbach, *Lectures on the Essence of Religion* (New York: Harper & Row, 1967) p. 5.
17.   Feuerbach, *The Essence of Christianity*, p. xxxvi.
18.   Ibid., p. 3.
19.   Ludwig Feuerbach, *Das Wesen des Christentums* (Leipzig: Wigand, 1883) pp. 39–40.
20.   Feuerbach, *The Essence of Christianity*, p. 213.
21.   Ibid., p. 21.
22.   Ibid., p. 217.
23.   Feuerbach, *The Essence of Faith* . . . , p. 43.
24.   Ibid., p. 46.
25.   Ibid., p. 152.
26.   Ibid., p. 58.
27.   Ibid., p. 57.
28.   Ibid., p. 25.
29.   Ibid., p. 21.
30.   Ibid., p. 153f.
31.   Cited in *Werner Schilling, Feuerbach und die Religion* (Munich: Evangelischer für Bayern, 1957) p. 33.
32.   Feuerbach, *The Essence of Christianity*, p. 57; p. 54.
33.   Max Stirner, *The Ego and His Own* (New York: Boni & Liveright, 1907) p. 190f.

On Feuerbach's Conception of Religion as Anthropology

MYRA E. MOSS

In responding to Jack Verheyden's paper, 'Ludwig Feuerbach's Philosophy of God', I will confine my comments to methodological and historical considerations. In conclusion, I will propose several substantive questions.

Among the historical issues suggested by Verheyden's essay were: Was Feuerbach an idealist? If so, in what sense? If not, what were Feuerbach's mature views regarding the ontological status of sense objects and God?

In developing a response to these questions, several definitions and methodological distinctions have proved useful. First, epistemic, as distinguished from metaphysical idealism, is the view that denies 'absolute existence' or existence as a non-object for rational awareness. To restate this description in positive terms: Whatever exists must be conceived in relation to consciousness. Idealist epistemology affirms objects and qualities in their possible and actual relations to consciousness only and denies any object or quality that claims ontological status independently of such relations. Epistemic realism affirms what idealism denies – the existence of objects as independent of cognitive awareness. Second, metaphysical idealism asserts that the clue to the essential nature of reality may be found in the essence of human kind and that it is non-material or spiritual. Third, metaphysical materialism holds that ultimately all phenomena are reducible to matter or material events.

Given these working definitions, how should we interpret Feuerbach's philosophy? Feuerbach's conception of reality as sensible and material allows us to describe him as a metaphysical materialist. Contrary to Hegel, Feuerbach argued that material existence preceded essence. Matter formed the necessary condition or ground for thought. Nature consisted of all those sensuous forces, things and beings which man distinguished from himself as other than human. As a part of nature, human kind was a material being whose capacity for thought and action was a function of its physio-

40

logy. Feuerbach's theory of human nature led to his famous assertion: Man is what he eats.

Was Feuerbach an epistemic idealist or realist with regard to ordinary objects of experience? Despite Fichte's idealist influence, clearly demonstrated in Verheyden's paper, Feuerbach's view of the relations between material being and essence implied that the material world existed independently of human consciousness of it. For him, unconscious nature formed an eternal, uncreated being, ontologically and temporally prior to the emergence of human kind.[1] Material reality transcended our awareness of it and existed not only as an object to some subject, but also apart from that subject.

And finally, what was Feuerbach's conception of the ontological status of God's being? Did the illusory conception of God as an autonomous entity mean that the reality of God was grounded entirely in individual self-consciousness? Does Feuerbach's reduction of the metaphysical being of God to an awareness of the human genus force us to classify him as an epistemic idealist? Perhaps. However, a case can be made that for Feuerbach, the being of God was grounded, moreover, in the essence of human kind, which although material and concrete, was also universal.[2] Thus the object of religious awareness, the metaphysical being of God, became reduced to the perennial reality of man, which due to its ahistorical and universal nature, did not depend for its existence on human awareness. When considered from this perspective, Feuerbach's position represents a form of Aristotelian conceptualism and epistemic realism.

To clarify my interpretation, let us take a look at some of the criticisms raised by Marx and Engels. As early as in the 1845 *Theses on Feuerbach*, Marx praised Feuerbach for resolving religious essence into a human one; but then, according to Marx, Feuerbach erroneously abstracted human essence from historical process, thus presupposing an abstract isolated individual.[3] In the *German Ideology*, Marx and Engels complained that Feuerbach had referred to abstract Man instead of 'real historical man'. Feuerbach took 'refuge in a double perception, a profane one which perceives only the "flatly obvious" and a higher, philosophical one which perceives the "true essence" of things.' Feuerbach did not see how the sensuous world around him is 'not a thing given direct from all eternity, remaining ever the same, but the product of industry and of the state of society . . .'[4] Although an argument based on the *Essence of Religion* can be made that Feuerbach was an emergent evolutionist,[5] nevertheless once a genus appeared, it remained fundamentally the same. So in agreement with Marx and Engels, the Being of Feuerbach's God as grounded in the essence of human nature retained a reality independent of human consciousness.

Feuerbach's denial of traditional theism and affirmation of religion correctly understood was not unique. However, his conception of Christian theology as a projection of humankind, of wishes, dreams and needs, described at times as pathological, does seem to distinguish him from earlier thinkers. Indeed some scholars have claimed that in these respects Feuerbach's philosophy of religion remained unparalleled until the work of Emile Durkheim (1858–1917) and Sigmund Freud (1856–1939).[6] H.B. Acton, for instance, noted some remarkable similarities between Freud's studies of religion and some ideas which Feuerbach had proposed fifteen years before Freud's birth.[7] Although Ernest Jones's authoritative biography[8] of Freud gives no evidence of Feuerbach's direct influence upon Freud, either through his reading or university education, such explanations of the origins of religious thought probably had pervaded Continental culture by the latter part of the nineteenth-century. According to Philip Rieff, privately Freud admitted to remote connections with Kant, Voltaire and Feuerbach.[9]

In conclusion I raise several substantive questions prompted by Verheyden's paper: What are the effects, if any, upon present-day philosophy of religion that derive from the Feuerbachian conception of religion as anthropology? From our perspective, one hundred and sixteen years after the death of Feuerbach in 1872, have we come any closer to conclusively resolving the problem of the ontological status of God's Being? If not, does our failure have implications regarding the possibility of theology? Finally, have metaphysical questions about the Being of God been replaced by epistemic questions of meaning and verifiability?

Notes

1. Ludwig Feuerbach, *Lectures on the Essence of Religion*, trans. Ralph Manheim (New York: Harper & Row, 1967), p. 21.
2. Ibid., p. 122.
3. Karl Marx and Frederick Engels, *The Marx-Engels Reader*, ed. Robert C. Tucker, 2nd edn (New York: W.W. Norton, 1978), 143–5.

4.   Ibid., p. 170.
5.   Feuerbach, *Lectures*, op. cit., p. 94.
6.   Maurice Mandelbaum, *History, Man, and Reason* (Baltimore: Johns Hopkins University Press, 1977), p. 34.
7.   H.B. Acton, *The Illusion of the Epoch* (Toronto: Burns & MacEachern, 1955), pp. 120–2.
8.   Ernest Jones, *The Life and Work of Sigmund Freud* (New York: Basic Books, 1954).
9.   Philip Rieff, *Freud: The Mind of the Moralist* (New York: Viking Press, 1959), p. 24. Also see Marx W. Wartofsky, *Feuerbach* (Cambridge University Press, 1977).

3

Anti-Realist Faith

DON CUPITT

Around two hundred years ago a change came over Western thought. It became much more aware of itself and of its own interpretative and constructive activity than it had been before. Slowly, thinking shifted from being dogmatic to being critical. A whole new realm came into view, as people became conscious of the hitherto hidden apparatus by which we put a construction upon our experience. At first, the rationalists and Kant tried to prove that there was nothing very alarming about the new discovery, because (they said) this thinking machinery of ours is timeless and necessary. They argued that the world *must* be thought in the way that it is thought, so that for these first critical thinkers reality still held firm. But later, as it became obvious that people do in fact see the world and think of the world very differently in different societies and historical periods, it came to be recognised that all our thinking is historically conditioned. Whereas the older dogmatic type of thinking had always tended to go straight from the mind to the cosmos, critical thinking became preoccupied with the variable cultural apparatus that guides the way we perceive and interpret what's out there.

Philosophy did not give up. As before, it fought a determined rear-guard action in favour of necessary truth. Like Kant, Hegel also believed that the difference between science and philosophy is that science is concerned with what merely happens to be so, whereas philosophy is concerned with what must be so. Accordingly he tried to prove that there remains a sort of rational necessity in the way that, living just where and when I do, I must perceive the world as I do. That is, Hegel tried to show that there is philosophical necessity in the process of historical development and in the succession of human cultural forms. As everyone knows, Karl Marx and other historicist thinkers held the same view; but eventually it broke down, leaving a doctrine which has been called perspectivism.

The main doctrines of perspectivism are as follows. There isn't any pure or quite neutral experience or knowledge of reality. In order to have any experience or knowledge at all, you must have a practical slant, an interest, an angle or a perspective which, so to say, makes certain things stand out and become noticeable. To take the simplest possible example, acute hunger may give you an interest in dividing up the world in such a way that the edible stands out from its inedible background. There are indefinitely many such perspectives or angles upon the world – and they are all of them historically occasioned, human and contingent. Some, like certain branches of our natural sciences, are very highly refined. But even the most advanced scientific theories are still human, perspectival, historically evolved and subject to future revision. None of them can claim the sort of dogmatic absoluteness that people thought they had in pre-critical times, when all the most important knowledge was unchanging and came down to us from the past and from above.

So reality has now become a mere bunch of disparate and changing interpretations, a shifting loosely held coalition of points of view in continual debate with each other. Politics is like that nowadays, and so is every faculty in a modern university. So is human reality generally, which is why in modern culture we represent reality to ourselves predominantly through an endless proliferation of perspectival fictions, in the novel, drama and the cinema. We are all of us non-realists nowadays.

The position just described was reached by Nietzsche during the 1880s. He used the slogan, 'There are no facts, only interpretations', and he coined the term 'anti-realism' to describe his doctrine. At the same time, critical thinking was preparing to advance yet another stage as it became aware of language. The new development appears in the United States in C.S. Peirce's doctrine of thought-signs, in Austria in Fritz Mauthner's philosophy of language, and in Switzerland in Ferdinand de Saussure's structural linguistics, but it achieved really wide currency only as the work of Wittgenstein and the French structuralists became known in the 1950s.

Most of the key new ideas about language are by now very familiar. People seem to start by thinking that language is a more or less unsatisfactory dress in which we clothe our thoughts, and that the meaning of a word is an object outside language, as if a word were a label. Because we think there has to be something for a word to stand for, we suppose that the great words of philosophy, religion, ethics and so forth, must stand for unchanging and invisible essences, like the Platonic Ideas. Thus laws, standards, values, concepts and the rest are thought of as being rather like spirits, but impersonal; they are seen as ghostly things that control events. So the popular view of language makes us realists in philosophy and in theology.

The linguist's vision of language is, however, quite different. To him, it is a very large, historically evolving and living system. In effect it coincides with culture, seen as a system of signs. There is no need to go outside language in order to explain it. We are always already within language, and the dictionary is well able to explain every printed mark simply in terms of its relations with other printed marks. A word's meaning cannot be anything external to language because any and every meaning is just a presently held position within a vast dynamic and evolving system of relativities. Since there cannot be any unchanging meaning, there cannot be any timeless truths. The whole world of meaning, which is the true starting point for philosophy, is by its very nature shifting all the time like the prices in a stock market, as human power relations shift.

Like the prices in a stock market, the meanings of words are essentially publicly determined, for a meaning is the resultant of an interplay of forces in the public domain. The philosophers who first saw this, such as C.S. Peirce, quickly grasped that it meant the end of the individualistic approach to philosophy that had dominated the West since the Reformers and Descartes. I cannot determine any meanings all by myself, so I cannot begin my philosophy from myself. Society and the public domain come first. Culture is a system of symbols, and society is a busy communications network. Messages in the various codes are flying back and forth all the time, and we all contribute to the humming activity of the whole.

Concerning the meanings of the symbols used in society's communication code, there is an amazingly high level of agreement. Each one of us is phenomenally sensitive to just what is and is not currently being done with each individual word in present-day idiomatic English, and we are all the time minutely adjusting our own usage in response to social change and new things that we've heard being said. Our desire for mutual understanding and sympathy must be very strong for it to have produced such a refined unanimity as there is among any local group of native speakers on their own home ground.

The comparison that I am drawing between our continual public debate about everything and a market brings out a striking difference between meaning and truth. On the one hand, through our ceaseless chatter we achieve a very high degree of consensus about the meanings of words. On the other hand, in our modern large-scale and highly communicative societies there is no single grand overarching dogmatic truth any longer. All truths, beliefs, theories, faiths, perspectives become just individual stocks in the market. They rise and fall relative to each other as conditions change.

Now comes the point that is hard to grasp: just as there is no sense in asking for the absolute price of something, so there is no sense in trying to step outside the changing human debate and fix realities, meanings and truths absolutely. We have to live and act without absolutes. To take just one example, I personally am prepared to fight tooth and nail for modern evolutionary biology against creationism. But I cannot claim that current evolutionary theory is, in any part of it, objectively, dogmatically and perennially just true. On the contrary, over the generations to come I expect that every bit of current evolutionary theory will be replaced by something different. In this shifting relativistic world of ours, we can still choose our values and fight for them, but our beliefs won't have the old kind of permanent anchorage in an unchanging ideal order.

The point here is hard to express without paradox, but let's try: our modern experience is that there isn't any objective, fixed, intelligible reality out there, such as many be replicated in our language and invoked to check our theories. We now live wholly *inside* our own history, our language and the flux of cultural change. We find that our world isn't made of Being any more, but of symbols and of conflicting arguments. The long-term effect of the critical revolution in our thinking has been to make us so much aware of our own theories, viewpoints and ways of thinking that objective reality has melted away. We haven't got a proper cosmos any longer, only a bunch of chronic disagreements.

Let us now by contrast briefly evoke the traditional religious and philosophical outlook of medieval Christianity. It was Platonic, making a sharp contrast between this changing and corruptible material world below and the eternal controlling intelligible world above. It was pre-critical, so that people made no very clear distinction between culture and nature. They blithely supposed that their own cultural conceptions were part of the natural order of things. It was pre-scientific, and many events were ascribed to supernatural causes. It was also pre-historical, and people's vision of the past was short and very hazy. Life was governed by tradition, a fixed body of knowledge that had come down from the Fathers and from above.

Faith was therefore dogmatic, binding you to a body of truths and a form of life that would remain immutable from the primitive era until the end of historical time.

In such a context both philosophy and theology were oriented towards necessity, changelessness and ideal perfection. For both traditions the goal of human life was to attain absolute knowledge of absolute reality. In that timeless contemplation of absolute necessity and perfection, which religion called the Vision of God, you would find perfect fulfilment and happiness. Thus the old Christian culture was highly realistic in being centred around objective, eternal, necessary, intelligible and perfect Being. Faith was dogma-guided longing for Heaven, and the monk whose way of life anticipated Heaven was the highest human type. The body, time, culture, language, disagreement, history and biological life were all relatively neglected or disparaged.

Now consider how completely we have reversed the traditional outlook of Christian Platonism. The world above and all the absolutes are gone. The whole of our life and all our standards are now inside language and culture. For good or ill *we* make our own history, *we* have shaped our own world, *we* have together evolved all norms to which our life is subject. Religion for us must inevitably be something very different from what it was in the heyday of Platonic realism. Indeed, it is plain that if I am right, then Christianity must be revolutionised to survive.

There are people who still hope that the old order can be restored. For them, there is no intermediate position; the end of dogmatism is the beginning of nihilism. They are terrified by the thought of a world without certainties. They yearn for a society constrained by one absolute truth determined by one absolute power. But anti-realists like me reject their view, and claim that Christianity can and should be modernised. We invoke the symbol of the Day of Pentecost, when God scattered Himself and was distributed as spirit to each individual believer. Just as Truth has come down from heaven and is now immanent within the movement of our various human conversations; just as political sovereignty is no longer wholly vested in a superperson above society but is dispersed throughout the body politic; just as, indeed, the whole of the former world above is now resolved down into the life of this world – so God also is now in each of us.

This discussion has I hope made a little clearer what we mean by a non-realist philosophy of religion. Realists think our religious language tells of beings, events and forces that belong to a higher world, an invisible second world beyond this world of ours. But I believe that there is only one world and it is this world, the world we made, the human life-world, the world of language. To think of language as replicating the structure of some extra-linguistic reality, some world beyond the world of our language, is I believe a mistaken way of thinking of language *anyway*. Every word is more like a tool for doing a job than like a xerox copy of something that is not a word. The only language we can know is wholly human, completely adapted to its job of being the medium in which human life is lived in the only world we have. So we should see religious language in terms of the part it can play in our lives, rather than see it in a mythological way as conjuring up a picture of a second world. For us, there is only *one* world, and it is *this* world, the manifest world, the world of language, the world of everyday life, of politics and economics. And this world has no outside. It doesn't depend in any way on anything higher, and there is no meaning in the suggestion that our cultural beliefs and practices need to be set on any external foundation.

Thus I believe in only one continuous but multi-perspectival common world. In it language and experience, meaning and feeling, nature and culture are fully interwoven. This one world is human, cultural and historically changing. Religion is wholly inside it, and it has no outside. I don't take a realistic view of *any* non-manifest entity. The Word has become flesh, say Christians: that is, the intelligible world must now be resolved back into its manifest basis.

This fully secularised and incarnational vision of things became dominant about two centuries ago. Among the historical events that marked its emergence were the industrial revolution, the democratic revolutions, the Romantic movement, German Idealist philosophy and the rise of the novel. It is emergent in David Hume, but is stated most grandiosely by Hegel. More recently its implications have been spelt out in one way by American pragmatists like Richard Rorty who follow John Dewey, and in another way by Nietzsche and the modern French philosophers who admire him.

These may seem a disparate group of thinkers, but what they have in common is a desire to escape from the legacy of Plato. They are all naturalistic. They reject two-worlds dualism, and in particular they see our life as being so profoundly historical that there can be no sense in the idea that we are subject to the controlling influence of a timeless order. Our language, our knowledge and our morality are human and ever-changing, not cosmic. There's no point in trying to assess them in terms of their relation to just one set of timeless, superhuman intellectual and moral standards.

An example: conservatives sometimes complain that moral or academic standards are lower than they used to be. But the world of two or three generations ago was a different world, with different standards. In their world they measured things by their standards; in our world we measure them by ours. We have no more reason to absolutise their standards than we have to absolutise our own. In fact, we shouldn't absolutise *either* set of standards: instead we should simply recognise that historical change happens and that it demands a continuous reinterpreting and recreating of our standards.

In this way we come to see that our standards and all our supposed 'absolutes' are themselves historical, immanent within language and subject to continual remaking. This has in turn the effect of making certain old ways of thinking no longer possible to us. Consider, for example, 'the Word of God'. Our understanding of what language is has become so fully human, cultural and historical that we now cannot conceive a solitary non-human and extra historical language user. At one time people naively saw God as a member of their own language group. He spoke to them in the tongue of their own place and time. But how shall we put it now? To what language community does God belong? In what dialect and of what period is God's speech, and how in terms of modern linguistic theory do His words have meaning for Him? What instinctual drives power His utterance, and what body has He to vibrate as He produces it?

Just to raise these questions is to realise that a realistic view of God as a language user has long been impossible to us. And as we turn now to the philosophy of religion, I must repeat that I am merely describing the world as it has been this past two centuries. It is the world as ordinary people experience it in their political and economic life and represent it to themselves in the novel, the newspapers and the cinema. It is the way the world is for students of language, the social sciences and history. I cannot say that it is the metaphysical truth of the human condition, because it is how things look after the end of metaphysical truth. No one vision of things can any longer be compulsory. The philosopher cannot claim the authority to act as culture-policeman. Instead he'll have to be something more like an interpreter of the times, who seeks to show *both* the diversity of the possibilities at present before us *and* the family resemblance among all the perspectives and forms of life that are available in some one period, such as our own. So I am not telling you how things are absolutely, but only offering you an interpretation of the way they seem, just now.

It is in that undogmatic and post-authoritarian spirit that we return to the question of realism and anti-realism in the philosophy of religion.

First, we must obviously acknowledge that the majority report of tradition comes down in favour of theological realism. Most believers have thought that supernatural beings and influences really exist, independently of us. They have thought that there is a real God out there controlling world events, who may intervene, assist us by His Grace, answer our prayers and so on; and they have thought that there is a real supernatural world wherein we may go on living after we have died. That surely is how most people have seen matters.

There are, however, two massive exceptions to this generalisation. First, the ancient tradition of Christian Platonism clearly recognised that our words are only human words, and accordingly stressed the descriptive inadequacy of all our talk about divine things so strongly as to be agnostic. Between the third-century and the Reformation, most of the great theologians stood in this tradition. Secondly, the Hebraic and Protestant tradition always saw religious language as being imperative rather than indicative. It tells us how we must think and live, rather than how things are. Its purpose is to govern rather than to inform. These two themes, the negative theology and voluntarism, have between them ensured that throughout the Christian tradition the intellectuals have been much less realistic in their belief than ordinary people.

This has continued to be true in the modern period. The great founders of modern religious thought, Kant, Hegel and Schleiermacher, were all in their different ways anti-realists about God, two centuries ago. Their influence has ensured that most of the long line of Continental theologians since have been anti-realists also, but they used slightly veiled language and their English readers have not understood what has been happening. This was true, for example, of Schweitzer, Bultmann, Neibuhr, Bonhoeffer and Tillich in our own century. The case of church history is also very notable, for fully non-supernaturalist church history began to be written in the Prussian universities in the 1740s, and nobody today complains that it leaves out anything. We seem to accept that purely secular church history tells the whole story.

Furthermore, we habitually put forward an anti-realist interpretation of *other people*'s religious beliefs. Thus, I have at home several small bronze images of Shiva. Ask me, and I can, in principle if not in fact, tell you all there is to know about Shiva and how he is worshipped, and I don't have to leave anything out. I need miss nothing, I can sympathetically explain everything, and I can even join in if I wish. The anti-realism consists in the recognition that Shiva is real only to his followers and within their perspective. If Hinduism vanished from the earth, there'd be nobody left to whom Shiva was real. But, for the present, Shiva lives. The anti-realist can in principle see all there is to see and say all there is to say. Since we have given up ideas of absolute truth and error, we can look down other perspectives without prejudice.

The anti-realist viewpoint has already made it possible for us to view other people's faiths more sympathetically, and to enter into them more deeply, than in the past. How much more then will we profit if we move over to an anti-realist view of *our own* faith!

The reason why we would gain so much is that realism in religion acts as an ideological defence of the *status quo*. It discourages us from attempting to carry through much needed reforms, and even prevents us from seeing their necessity. By suggesting that our religious beliefs were revealed to us by an eternal and objective God, realism makes us afraid to question them. And realism brings with it two other ideas that also inhibit us from thinking. *Essentialism* suggests that Christianity is a timeless, coherent system of thought no part of which can be altered without weakening the whole, and *primitivism* maintains that faith was purest near its point of origin so that we have to keep going back to the past for correction and for legitimation.

All these ideas are surely wrong. To the historian's eye Christianity is not a timeless and coherent system of thought, but a product of history and in continual change. It is a rather loose aggregate or miscellany of ideas from different times and places, many of which are at odds with each other. There is no reason to think that just being old makes an idea more likely to be right. On the contrary, we usually find that very old ideas are now very bad, and need to be replaced. And since critical study shows that despite the myth of immutable truth Christianity has in fact been evolving throughout its long history, there is no reason why we should not now do openly and consciously what our forerunners did unknowingly.

So, indeed, we *are* now doing, for we are increasingly aware of our responsibility for modernising Christianity and getting it up to date. We set about bending the tradition and rewriting history. We seek to purge the cruelty and sexism from Christian symbolism, and we begin to ordain women. By doing all this we now admit that it was we who made our religious beliefs, it is we who are responsible for them, and it is up to us to put them right. In short, our religious beliefs and practices are an integral part of the evolving totality of culture, and must change with it. So we acknowledge that religion is human, historical and cultural all the way through. It could not have been otherwise. Nor does this matter, because if we remember our Bibles we'll recall that the religious system was never *intended* to be an end in itself. It is only a means: eventually it should make itself redundant, because the goal of the religious life is a spiritual state that is beyond all the symbols. So you have to have the ladder to climb, and you have to know when to kick it away. Often, religion fails to liberate people spiritually because they take its teachings too literally and don't know when and how to pass beyond them. In Asian religion it was a well-accepted principle that a particular name of God, or a particular set of worship-guiding images, should be used only for so long as they are helpful, and should then be left behind. People were encouraged to treat their own religious ideas lightly. In the West, unfortunately, our religious outlook has usually been heavy, crude, gloomy and terroristic. The anti-realist point of view offers the prospect of Western religion's becoming a little more sophisticated than it has been in the past. It's about time this happened, because Christianity as we have known it so far has been, frankly, barbarous compared with what it should be. We have been locked into truly frightful excesses of power and guilt, cruelty and sentimentality. We need a clean-up urgently.

Again, anti-realism helps, because now for the first time the believer no longer claims any special cosmic privilege. I am a priest, I practise Christianity in full, and I try to tread the spiritual path. I have found joy in loss, for now there is no remaining respect in which I think that I am in the light and some other human being is in darkness. I have no old-style supernatural or Plato-type metaphysical beliefs. I am as ignorant as everyone else, and I shall die like everyone else. Having no cosmic advantage, I can claim no spiritual authority or power over other human beings, and I have no moral standing for making them feel guilty. As I follow Christ I am now as naked as he is. By the standards of earlier centuries, my views are certainly radically sceptical. God is a guiding spiritual ideal, eternal life is holiness now. We must become radically emptied out and free. And in this state we can learn to practise Christianity a great deal better than in the past. The end of theological realism will at last make possible a Christian ethics which is more than mere obedience, an ethic of productive, world-changing and value-realising Christian action.

We can thus become creative, for the first time in Christian history. In the old scheme of things God did all the creating. God stood on the far side of the world, everything was ready-made for us, and nothing much could be altered. Human beings were not in fact spoken of as creative before the eighteenth-century. Today, by contrast, human creativity confronts the flux. God has moved round to our side, and looks through our eyes. Christian action is now at last liberated. The believer is like an artist. The material we have to work on is our world and our own lives.

Against 'Anti-Realist Faith'

STEPHEN T. DAVIS

Most of us who believe in the existence of God made our peace long ago with the fact that there are intelligent and moral people who do not believe in God. We also know that some of these same people wish to retain certain aspects of the religious life. If Cupitt belongs in this last category (and I believe he does), there is nothing here so far that is particularly threatening to believers in God. But what does seem grotesque is Cupitt's implicit suggestion that his views are superior to belief in God for purely religious reasons.

The stakes here are high. Cupitt's thesis is not a matter of abstruse technicalities at the theological margins. This is an issue about which Christians – scholars and laypersons alike – will care deeply.

Let me offer three criticisms of Cupitt's paper. The first concerns what we might call rhetorical method. Cupitt has an objectionable tendency to offer what I can only call absurd parodies of positions he opposes. It is almost as if being an orthodox Christian, or even a religious realist, is an exercise in sheer buffoonery. Now I take the term 'realism *vis-à-vis x*' to be the view that *x* exists (or does not exist) independently of beliefs about *x*. 'Realism *vis-à-vis* God', then, is the view that God either exists or does not exist quite independently of what anyone believes about God. But as Cupitt depicts realism, it entails all sorts of bizarre intellectual baggage – much of which would only startle most realists.

For example, according to Cupitt, realism entails: (a) that there are unchanging and invisible essences; (b) that there is an invisible higher world beyond this world which our language describes; (c) that meaning is a spirit-being that inhabits a word; (d) that mind is a spirit-being that inhabits a body; (e) that a law of nature is a spirit-principle that controls events by pulling them with invisible wires; and (f) that there are three (rather than the standard two) modalities of truth – 'true', 'necessarily true', and 'absolutely true'.

Now perhaps there are realists who hold these views, but not all realists do or logically must. (a) Some realists believe in invisible essences and some do not (not all realists are Platonists). (b) Some realists posit an invisible higher world, and some do not. (c) I cannot think of anyone – realist or non-realist – who reifies meaning ('a spirit-being that inhabits a word') in the way Cupitt describes. (d) Some realists are Cartesian dualists, but some tend toward physicalism. (e) Most philosophically inclined folk these days realise that natural laws are descriptive rather than coercive. The law of gravity, for example, does not pull apples toward the centre of the earth – it describes the fact that in our experience apples (when left unsupported near the earth) always fall toward the centre of the earth. (f) I do not know what the term *absolutely true* means. I think I have a fairly good grip on what it is for a statement to be true; I also think I know what it is for a statement to be 'necessarily true'; but the modality Cupitt repeatedly criticises throughout his paper ('absolutely true') is mysterious to me. At the very least, Cupitt needs to define what he means.

Religious realism, Cupitt says, includes or entails: (a) that Christianity is a timeless, coherent, and pragmatically immutable system of thought; (b) that the oldest version of the faith is the purest; (c) that biblical and Christian language has timeless, transcultural meaning; and (d) that God's language isn't real human language. As a result of religious realism, Cupitt says, Christianity has become barbarous ('locked into truly frightful excesses of power and guilt, cruelty and sentimentality').

But it surely seems possible to produce coherent versions of religious realism that contain *none* of these items. Aquinas, Schleiermacher, Barth and Tillich all seem to me to be religious realists who would embrace few or none of them. I count myself a religious realist, and I would embrace precisely none of them.

The point is that religious realism is not nearly so ridiculous a specimen as Cupitt implies. In order to demonstrate its implausibility, one must refute realism's most plausible versions, not just the absurd ones. A person can be a Christian realist without being committed to any of the picturesque caricatures that Cupitt dismisses.

My second criticism is that I believe Cupitt's position is self-stultifying, i.e. it refutes itself. If I were to make the statement, *I am unable to produce a sentence of English*, that statement would be self-stultifying. So would be the position of someone who claims to know that *Nothing whatever can be known*.

Cupitt describes sympathetically a position he calls perspectivism, the theory that we cannot know how things are but only how they seem to us. But does he think perspectivism is *true*? If it is true, then in one important respect, we *can* say how things are, namely that we cannot know how things are but only how they seem to us. Thus, perspectivism is self-stultifying. But if perspectivism is not supposed to be true but rather is itself only one among the available perspectives – it is merely somebody's point of view – then why should non-perspectivists take perspectivism seriously? What Cupitt must do is provide a reason why they should do so, an argument that involves no truth claims about perspectivism.

Similarly, Cupitt says, 'There is no single grand overarching dogmatic truth any longer.' I do not know exactly what this statement means, but I do wonder whether Cupitt considers it true. Does he think this very statement is itself the grand overarching truth that we must now respect? His paper certainly gives that impression. 'There cannot be any absolute descriptions of what is going on,' Cupitt also says. Again, I am not sure what the term *absolute* means here – perhaps it just means *true*. But the position that there cannot be any true description of anything (involving, as it does, a purported true description of something) refutes itself.

Later in the paper Cupitt allows that anti-realism is not 'the metaphysical truth of the human condition'. 'No one vision of things', he admits, 'can any longer be compulsory.' But then we wonder what epistemological status anti-realism is supposed to have. If it is just one among many perspectives, why should realists take it seriously? In another place, however, Cupitt seems to argue that religious realism is not only false but necessarily false. 'Religion', he says, 'is historical and cultural all the way through.' And then he adds, 'it could not have been otherwise.'

The point is that Cupitt's position is either self-stultifying, i.e. cannot consistently be held, or else is open to objections along these same lines to which he owes readers an answer.

My third criticism concerns the question of the essence of religion. One of the most intriguing aspects of Cupitt's position (and one that I suspect puzzles many laypersons) is that despite his views he goes right on practising religion. The answer, I think, is to be found in that line of Cupitt's paper where he says,' . . . the goal of the religious life is a spiritual state that is beyond all the symbols.' If spirituality (understood as a certain sort of psychological state) is the goal and heart of religion, then, obviously, one can be a non-realist or even an atheist and still be religious. Indeed, one of my friends – a practising Zen Buddhist – is an atheist, and his level of spirituality is, I believe, higher than mine.

I cannot disprove Cupitt's contention that spirituality precedes doctrine and is what really matters in religion. I can, however, lay on the table my own view. The essence of Christian faith is not a kind of spirituality to which God is logically and causally and (so to speak) teleologically dispensable. It rather concerns a call from God that we respond appropriately to the love of God as it is revealed pre-eminently in Christ. 'Man's chief end', as the Westminster Shorter Catechism of 1643 beautifully says, 'is to glorify God, and to enjoy him forever.' So God (by which I mean a being whose existence is independent of anybody's views about God) is essential to Christian faith.

The point is that the basic issue turns out to be belief in God. So anyone who wants to evaluate the turn Cupitt's theology has taken in recent years must begin by asking: Did God create us or did we create God? Those who believe that we created God and that accordingly there is little point in being religious will be atheists. Those who believe that we created God but that there is still value in being religious will follow a path like the one Cupitt has laid down. Those who believe that God created us and that our highest duty as human beings is to glorify God will be religious realists who will strive to live lives of worship and service.

4

Zen and the Problem of Language

FRANCIS H. COOK

In view of the current debate in the West between those who adopt a non-realistic approach to language and those who attempt to salvage a claim that religious terms refer to actual objective things, it is worth noting that there is an East Asian tradition which has for many centuries maintained a strict non-realistic approach to language. I refer, of course, to Buddhism in its Mahayana form. Though not much has been written about Zen non-realism, there is a literature on Buddhism and language generally. Some articles have been written on the parallels between Wittgenstein and Zen, and there are a few studies of Zen parallels with other thinkers and movements which touch directly or indirectly on language: Heidegger, Buchler and, most recently, Derrida. The centrality of the issue of language in Buddhism has been thoughtfully and carefully presented by Frederick Streng in his study of the doctrine of emptiness (shūnyatā), and an earlier study of the Mādhyamika school by T.R.V. Murti shows the central Buddhist problematic to be that of epistemology and language.

This literature reflects a recognition that Buddhism has always been intensely interested in language. Also, it indicates clearly that the critique of language by Buddhism is very similar to that in the West in recent times. It is interesting to note that to one degree or another, this critique has been a focal concern for probably the entire 2500 year history of Buddhism. Indeed, in order to grasp what Buddhism is all about means grasping the centrality of the problem of language. I would go so far as to claim that the greater part of Buddhist philosophy is about language, directly or indirectly. In the following pages, I wish to say something about Zen non-realistic use of language and to use those remarks as a basis for some suggestions

about what Zen can teach the West with regard to the consequences
of non-realism in language.

From very early time, well before the beginning of Zen in China,
Indian Buddhism has reflected a view that a major problem for
human beings is that we tend rather naively to believe that a word
must have a corresponding referent. In a text from the first century,
the *Milindapañha* (*Questions of [King] Milinda*), which is an extended
discussion of Buddhist teachings by a monk named Nagasena and a
Greek king who ruled north-west India at the time, there is an
important discussion concerning the existence of a 'self' (*ātman*), that
'ghost in the machine' that we all believe we are and which presumably remains self-identical through time. The monk, Nagasena, tells
the king that indeed no such entity exists, to the amusement and
incredulity of the king. 'If that is so,' says the king, 'who practises the
path of the Buddha? Who becomes enlightened? Who accrues merit
or demerit? Who receives alms from householders? Is there in reality
no such person as Nagasena?' Nagasena replies by saying that there
is no real 'Nagasena'. There is only a conglomeration of interde-
pendent, mutually-conditioning material and psychic factors – five
in all – none of which collectively or singly is Nagasena, even though
his mother and fellow monks refer to him as 'Nagasena'. Using the
analogy of a chariot, he says that for instance the wheels are not
'chariot', the seat is not 'chariot', the axle is not 'chariot', and so on
throughout all the parts of the vehicle. Nor are all the parts together
'chariot'. Only when the parts are assembled in a certain way do we
conventionally designate that configuration of elements a 'chariot'.
Thus, says Nagasena, 'chariot' is in fact a 'mere designation', a
'convenient expression', and so is 'Nagasena'.

There are several noteworthy points in this exchange which bear
on the issue of language usage. First, Nagasena is denying that
things are endowed with essences or natures which makes them
what they are and therefore necessarily labelled in a certain way.
There is no 'chariotness' which legitimates the name 'chariot', no
'Nagasenaness' which determines that he must be named 'Nagasena'.
Second, he is claiming that the words we use are no more than
conventions, which is to say convenient indicators that enable the
work of society to be done. We thus agree that we will call this object
a 'chair', so that it can be purchased, we can sit on it, rest, and so
forth. And, in fact, no harm is done when we use words in this way;
indeed, we must use them. The only problem is that we do not use
words in the knowledge that they are mere convenient labels but

rather believe that the words point to things or events which possess natures indicated by the words. Thus, we use the word 'good' in the belief that its referent is essentially good. We speak of 'me' and 'you' not in the knowledge that this is mere convenience but with the canny sense that the words point to things with different natures. We are then in a situation similar to that of Adam in the retelling of the book of *Genesis* by a black preacher (*Ol' Adam and His Chillun*) in which God marches out animals one by one to be named by Adam. 'What is this one?' asks God. 'It looks like a giraffe to me,' says Adam.

Buddhism, whatever its pronouncements regarding the ultimate nature of language, has always agreed that the use of language as a pragmatic necessity is legitimate, that taxonomy is a harmless practice as long as it is not taken seriously. But to use words realistically, in the belief that the word somehow accurately captures the true nature of an event, is confusion and causes great pain for the user and others. Witness the use of the term 'evil empire' in international relations, or 'pushy bitch' in the ongoing war of the sexes. People of education and good will will say that such terms are misguided and prejudiced, not to mention bad spirited, but what of words such as 'good', 'person', 'God', and *nirvāna*? Do they name realities?

Now Zen, which appeared late in Buddhist history, has continued this interest in and critique of language, intensifying, rhetorically if nothing else, the Buddhist conviction that concepts and their verbal expression are totally inadequate for grasping the true nature of things. Thus, Zen is a continuation of seminal Indian Buddhist teachings and approaches concerning language, and the difference between the two is mainly in rhetoric and methodology, because Zen ought to be seen not as any important deviation in central teachings but rather as a distinctly Chinese method of teaching and internalising the teachings. Specifically, it can be seen as a *style* of approaching concepts and words. This style is abundantly evident in the collections of biographies of the great Zen teachers and in the collections of dialogues between teacher and student (*mondō*, lit. 'question–answer'. I am using Japanese pronunciation). These collections show the Chinese style to be iconoclastic, irreverent, mocking, often scatological, intended to shock. When a monk asks Mumon, 'What is Buddha?' Mumon replies, 'A dried shit-stick' (*kan shiketsu*), referring to the ancient use of bamboo spatulas prior to the invention of toilet paper. Another teacher admonishes his students, 'If you utter the word 'Buddha', you should wash out your mouth.' And there is the famous expression which warns in the most shocking manner against using religious terms realistically: 'If you meet the Buddha on the road, kill him.' Finally, there is the teacher who held up his staff before the assembled monks and said, 'If you call this a staff, you deny its reality; if you say it is not a staff, you deny the fact. Now, speak; what do you call it?' Here, in these few samples, there is no abstract discussion, no subtle epistemological or ontological arguments, no display of crushing logic. The approach is direct, colloquial, blunt and earthy. The attempt is to shock the neophyte out of his habitual, stereotyped responses to experience.

Scatological language, apparent non-sequiturs, shouting, kicking, and beating makes Zen appear to Westerners reared in an entirely different form of philosophical and religious behaviour to be a madhouse presided over by the Marx brothers. Indeed, the traditional Zen master has been characterised by one Western writer as half clown, half midwife. However, and this is important to bear in mind, we would be making a very serious error if we do not see all this as existing within the context of a deadly serious conviction that a profound liberation and spiritual self-transformation are both possible for ordinary people and that this liberation is the most important task to be accomplished in one's lifetime. These teaching methods, which were presumably the creation of a series of brilliant Chinese teachers, and which diverged radically from Indian methods of teaching, were employed for but one reason, and that was to cajole, coax, stun, shock or browbeat the student into abandoning his habitual tendency to believe that reality has any relationship at all with concepts, categories, dualisms or the words that encode and express these creatures of the mind.

Despite its unique style, Zen is a continuation of attitudes towards language that originated in India in a group of scriptures with the name *prajñāpāramitā*, 'The Perfection of Wisdom'. They seem to have appeared about a hundred or two hundred years before the Common Era, and their entire purpose was to propound the teaching of 'emptiness' (*shūnyatā*). A condensed form of this otherwise immense literature, the 'Heart of the Perfection of Wisdom', presents the heart or gist of the teaching by saying that the five constituents of being (five *skandhas*) are all empty, and that there are no eye, ear, nose, tongue, body or mind, no sights, sounds, odours, tastes, touchable objects or mental objects, no Four Noble Truths, no old-age, sickness and death, no ignorance and no cessation of ignorance, and no enlightenment or *nirvāna*. To summarise the conclusion in my own words, the sutra ends by saying that when one realises that there is no Buddha or enlightenment, one becomes an enlightened Buddha.

'Everything', says the scriptures, 'is empty,' but what does 'empty' mean, and is it true to say that everything is 'empty'? Fundamentally, to say that something is empty means that the entity or event in question is lacking in independent, autonomous existence. The Sanskrit term I am translating as 'independent existence' is *svabhāva*. *Sva* is 'self', and *bhāva* is 'being' or 'existence'. The term is variously translated as 'own-being' (Conze), 'self-existence', 'independent existence', and so on, but all translations pretty well capture the basic meaning, which is that the discriminandum in question does not exist in and of itself. Rather, it owes its being to something else, usually two or more conditions. Whatever it is we are speaking of, whether it is a human being, a mountain or cloud, the feeling of pleasure, the concept 'pleasant', a flash of irritation, or basic perception or consciousness itself, all come into being, are maintained, and cease to exist *only* due to a multiplicity of conditions. This is true whether we are speaking of objective entities, or so-called natural phenomena or psychic events. This was important soteriologically for Nāgārjuna and other Mahayana Buddhists, because it meant that some cognitive or moral fault of personality was not really an intrinsic or essential marker of personality but merely a temporary occurrence due to conditions. Ignorance could be eliminated with knowledge, greed could be replaced by generosity, and, consequently, the individual need not become obsessively concerned with perceived cognitive and moral flaws or fall prey to the erroneous thought that he or she was *by nature* ignorant, greedy, lazy, proud and so forth.

This way of regarding experience, which T.R.V. Murti called the 'central philosophy of Buddhism', was thus a systematic process of seeing all experiential data as lacking in any independent being due to the fact that each event/actuality existed only as a temporary function of a multitude of environmental conditions. Since there is no single causal or conditioning centre of this process, then in effect, there is only a situation in which all events appear together in mutual conditioning. Hence Nāgārjuna's definitive definition of emptiness: emptiness is conditioned co-arising (*shūnyatā* = *pratītya-samutpāda*). Since it is assumed that only that which exists independently of the other has real being, it follows that nothing can be found which has real being. A further consequence of this is that there is everywhere and at all times only constant change, without anything which undergoes the change.

Sarvam shūnyam means that 'all is empty,' and 'all' means everything without exception. The critique of emptiness applies not only to the external world but also, perhaps particularly, to the interior world of thoughts, ideas, mental images, feelings, categorial schemes and patterns of thought. It therefore applies with special force to language. In fact, it is clear when we read one of Nāgārjuna's works that he was not speaking of the external world when levying his attack. Rather, he was almost completely concerned with our *ideas* about that world. Consequently, when he analyses 'coming' and 'going', for instance, and denies that they exist, he is denying that the idea of 'going' corresponds to some real external event. Ontology is of course implicated in the analysis, but the object is predominantly epistemological. This is as it should be because in Buddhism it is not nature which is the religious and existential problem but rather our idea of it.

What is particularly fascinating in Nāgārjuna is that while his attack is a rather general one in calling into question all concepts and words, he devotes most of his time to showing that even the most sacred terms of Buddhism, along with philosophical categories, are no less empty. He is consequently the pre-eminent reminder to all Buddhists that not only must the individual seeking liberation constantly realise that the key terms of the system have no real, objective referents but that liberation itself is by definition the overcoming of the conceptual, dualistic mode of apprehending experience. Not only the bipolar concepts of 'Buddha' and 'unenlightened beings', 'good' and 'evil', 'bondage' and 'liberation', and 'life' and 'death', but even basic categories such as 'self' and 'other' and 'exists' and 'does not exist' are mere mental constructs (*prajñāpti*) and correspond to nothing outside the mind.

In pursuing the task of demonstrating the truth of the dogmatic assertion of emptiness found in the 'Perfection of Wisdom' scriptures, Nāgārjuna used the strategy of showing that the words we use operate within the context of a kind of language game. He commonly alerts us to the fact that we think, and hence speak, with a kind of binary logic; that is, dualistically. His point, which is based on the assumption that all exists only in mutual interdependence, is that a word exists only because it is opposed to its opposite. As a result, the word 'good' exists because of its opposite, 'bad'. The converse is, of course, equally true. We speak of 'liberation' because we imagine 'bondage'. (What is the opposite of 'orange'? 'Non-orange'.) The real problem then arises when we assume that experience can be truly grasped when this pattern of thought is superimposed on the experience. Thus, Nāgārjuna and his school understood that words, and the concepts they express, exist only relatively to each other within the total game of language. For this reason, the early twentieth-century Russian Buddhologist, Theodor Shtcherbatski, discussed the emptiness doctrine as a 'theory of relativity'. He did not mean 'relativity' in quite the way physicists were using the term at the time, but his label is suggestive to the extent that it indicates the approach to language by the Mādhyamika school. Perhaps a better label would be 'relationality', because Nāgārjuna was clearly saying that any word has only a relational reality within the whole system of words.

Nevertheless, it might be argued, even though we grant that the mind works in such a manner, interpreting experience rigidly in terms of 'yes–no' and 'is–is not', it does not logically follow that reality does not correspond to the pattern. Perhaps we think and speak the way we do because it reflects the way things are, and thus we call something 'good' because that is what it really is. However, emptiness is universal, and therefore events are no less empty, void of any intrinsic natures that would make them *invariably* one thing to the exclusion of every other possibility. 'Good' would always and at all time be 'good' and would be recognised by all rational beings because it can be identified by a marker that clearly indicates 'good'. In fact, this is the position of a great number of people. Unfortunately, when others label it 'not good', the former have no recourse but to accuse the latter of blindness, confusion, error and wickedness. However, this is precisely the locus of the current debate concerning language.

One Zen master (the Japanese monk, Dōgen: 1200–1253) reflected on this tendency to believe that the words we use name real things and concluded that the use of value terms tends to depend on temporary conditions and not that words name anything possessing some intrinsic nature. He uses the example of a young man who lives in a large city and has come to hate the crowds, noise, violence and general turmoil. 'This is bad,' he says, and he moves to the country, which is seen as 'good'. After some months of exquisite boredom, with only bluejays and pines to share his solitude, he can stand it no longer. 'This is very bad,' he says, and returns to the glamour and excitement of the city, which has now become 'good'.

Notice, says Dōgen, that what was originally bad has become good and what was considered for a while to be good has become bad. Dōgen then asks, is city life intrinsically good or bad? What do we mean when we use such terms? Is anything intrinsically what we impute to it when we impose a label on it?

While the above discussion was in terms of value language, Buddhism has always generalised with regard to language. We base action on a rather naive and uncritically held assumption that the reason we use language the way we do is that our words capture essences, the reality of events, and consequently we are able to proceed in our lives confidently in the knowledge that we know what is what. The Buddhist contribution to the debate language is its discovery that reality does not disclose itself in the form of language but rather reality is obscured by habitual, innate patterns of thought and language which are imposed on a reality that is void of what the language names. In other words, we do not discover the real and then name it, we rather impose or superimpose over reality what it does not possess. Buddhist systematic texts refer to this process as *āropya*, which is commonly translated as 'superimposition'. It is a process of *creating* reality rather than *discovering* it. The reality which is so compelling to us that we fight and kill in its name is nothing but mental construction totally lacking in an objective basis. Whatever reality is (*pace* Kant), it eludes thought and language. It is inexpressible (*anirvachanīya*), inconceivable (*achintya*) and ungraspable by thought and language (*anabhilapya*).

This massively negative view of concepts and language appalled Nāgārjuna's Hindu contemporaries, who promptly labelly these Buddhists *nāstikas*: literally, 'those who say "does not exist"', and a fair translation of the term might be 'nihilists'. Nāgārjuna, however, rightfully denied that he was a nihilist, and to the charge that the emptiness doctrine nullified the religious life, he argued that the religious life is only possible because all things are empty. One thing that must be kept in mind is that the Buddhist non-realist approach to language occurs within the context of a salvational system that takes the religious life and salvation utterly seriously. Buddhism as a system of teachings and practices is believed to be a way of life eminently worthy, of supreme value, and the process of emptying out concepts and words is merely the means to the end of a religious life. Consequently, the process of emptying out, which is negative in nature, has the function of making possible a mode of being and action which is quite positive and believed to be the crown of human achievement. In short, there is an important and positive purpose in denying all things.

Another point to keep in mind is that the total rejection of the ultimate validity of language does not mean that the conventional use of language is rejected *in toto*. Decision-making and communication are unavoidable and even necessary for the individual who construes the religious life as a life of unremitting activity in the service of eliminating suffering and delusion in the world, such action being the expression of clarified insight and the self-critical use of language. Language must be used, but not in such a way as to lead to stereotyped responses, illusion, absolutism, narrowness and, of course, craving and loathing. A free and unconditioned response to events, avoidance of emotionality, and total impartiality are only possible when language is used in the knowledge that it is only conveniently and conventionally useful but, in the end, really non-referential. This is nicely expressed in one of the famous passages from the *Vajracchedika Sūtra*, one of the 'Perfection of Wisdom' scriptures:

> The bodhisattva, the great being, liberates all sentient beings, whether born from wombs, born from eggs, born from moisture, or born miraculously, and leads them all to *nirvāna*. Yet, though he does so, in truth no beings are led to *nirvāna*. Why? Because if he entertained the thoughts of 'beings', 'leading', and *nirvāna*, he would not be an awakened being (i.e. bodhisattva) [and thus would not be capable of leading all beings to *nirvāna*]. (Paraphrase of the original.)

The Chinese adaptation of this Buddhism, which we call 'Zen', in the Japanese pronunciation, may be understood as an extremely practical and radicalised approach to the problem of language, a Sinicised Mādhyamika which internalised and expressed the doctrine of emptiness in forms that felt right to Chinese. It would be possible to amass a vast amount of Chinese Zen literature to illustrate how Chinese Buddhists understood the basic Buddhist problematic and how they approached the problem. Any collection of koans is full of examples of Zen teachers trying to drive home for their students the fundamental conviction that concepts and language bind and confuse, blinding us to the true nature of things.

One of the most significant contributions of Chinese Zen to the earlier and more general discussion of emptiness is its tendency to emphasise what we might call the other side of the coin. Indian Buddhist literature tends to deny and negate; all is empty, there are no essence or substances, there is no Buddha, and so forth. They are certainly correct in pursuing this manner of discourse, and some Zen texts use the same approach. However, what we find in Zen texts is a new tendency to hint at what it means to say that something is empty or that words do not adequately grasp reality. The emphasis in this literature is on the multidimensional nature of events, their ultimate elusiveness, their boundless openness to varying ways of experiencing them. And this is the source of the problem with words. When we say that this thing is a 'fan', we automatically restrict it and fail to see that it is also many other things.

This is very nicely shown in a passage from an essay named *Genjō-kōan* ('Presenting Absolute Reality'), by the fourteenth-century Japanese Zen master, Dōgen. He says that if we get in a boat and go out on the ocean and look around, we say that the ocean is 'round'. However, a fish living in the ocean sees it as a 'palace', while celestial beings hovering in the sky high over the ocean look down and see a glittering 'jewel'. The passage concludes with Dōgen saying that the ocean has many other qualities. It is an interesting passage, particularly in context, because it makes several points. First, with regard to the remarks I made above, to label something is to grasp only a single aspect from what may be a vast number of aspects. It is not that the label is totally inappropriate but rather that it limits possibilities. Also, Dōgen is making the obvious point that words are functions of perspective, and this could be personal, ideological or broadly cultural. The problem is that we are not all ocean voyagers, or fish, or celestial beings, and so there tend to be many perspectives, many labels, and, subsequently, dissent and wrangling over who is correct. However, freedom from language is also freedom from a limited perspective, and the resulting perspective of no perspective reveals experience as boundlessly open. This is what emptiness, which means emptiness of any fixed essence, means: when we deeply understand that things lack intrinsic natures indicated by a term, we also deeply understand the 'boundless openness' of each thing. For this reason, some Buddhologists such as Masao Abe have suggested that 'boundless openness' might be a more accurate and meaningful translation of the Sanskrit *shūnyatā* than the more widely used and etymologically accurate 'emptiness'.

There is, consequently, a point to the Zen attack on language, and that is the attainment of liberation, which is of course the stated objective of all Buddhism. However, because of the relationship between language and culture, I would like to go so far as to claim that the ultimate objective of Zen is the attainment of liberation from culture itself. Zen seems to have realised early in its career, as we in the West are becoming increasingly aware, that the realities which seem to us to populate our larger world are simply those realities which a particular culture, and hence our language, *permit*. The crisis of the West in recent decades is the crisis generated by the suspicion that the 'real' or 'true' are not things which are universally fixed and agreed upon, as any linguist knows who studies, say, English, Chinese and Hopi. Even fundamental categories such as time and space, selfhood and nature are understood in very different ways. To become aware of this is to become equally aware of the plurality of definitions of truth, reality, value and significance, and this is what seems to trouble people the most. How to conduct our affairs if we doubt that action is based on nothing more substantial and enduring than tribal habits? The nihilism foreseen by Nietzsche and which has become a problem in our time is the result of our realisation that meaning is not the meaning of the whole human race but only my meaning; values are not engraved on some cosmic bronze tablet but are only the values of an individual born of Protestant, Caucasian, middle-class parents living in Texas in the middle of the twentieth-century; reality itself is not *the* reality but only, as the comedian, Lily Tomlin, says in a recent stage play, 'a collective hunch'.

The reality, meaning and value encoded in the language of a culture and imposed on us by culture are so sedimented in our minds and hearts that they seem not only self-evident to us ('we hold these truths to be self-evident . . .') but have become such integral parts of our lives that any threat to them is as serious, perhaps more serious, than a threat to our flesh and bones, and so we react as if life itself is threated when something like values are called into question. Why else the impassioned outcries when Rorty, Derrida and other like-minded thinkers call into question our most basic assumptions? There is also a corollary scurrying about in philosophical and theological circles to find that grounding position, that unshakeable foundation, that will restore confidence in our ability to detect the real and articulate it. For some people, the issue of the relationship of thought and language is an either-or situation. Either thought and language are reliable instruments and thus a solid basis for life and action, or nothing matters at all. In this context, the emotion-laden term 'nihilism' pops up often, just as it did in the Buddhist–Hindu debates two thousand years ago.

But I wonder often why this scepticism about language should evoke such emotional responses. Buddhism has an answer to this, finding the reason in a fundamental fear and insecurity in people, but I shall not take the time to explain Buddhist anthropology here. I really ask the question rhetorically, because from a Zen perspective, this recent (since Kant?) worry about thought and language is not threatening and an invitation to personal and social chaos necessarily but an opportunity for a profound spiritual transformation. Thus, from my point of view, this recent scepticism in the West is rather late in arriving and still not thoroughgoing and enthusiatic. In other words, Western philosophy and theology have never been as self-critical and self-correcting as Buddhism has been because this has never been seen as an opportunity.

If it be granted that an uncritical participation in culture and a naive use of language are restricting, encourage narrow and provincial views of the world, and limit the full range of potential, surely liberation from culture and its linguistic expression must be seen as positive and desirable. It has long been thought, for instance, that an important function of university liberal education is precisely this cultural self-criticism, with its corollary broadening of understanding and sympathy for other ways of organising experience and for other views of value. This is also a prominent feature of Buddhist–Christian dialogue, as many understand it. Thus, we agree in principle, in many contexts at least, that liberation from culture is a positive and desirable thing. Where we tend to draw back, however, is the point where we are asked to reflect *seriously* on what we mean when we use such terms as 'real', 'true', 'justice', 'human rights', 'God' and *nirvāna*. Approaching what we fear is the black, bottomless pit of Nietzschean *nihilum*, we draw back giddy and nauseated. This reluctance to jump into the pit and see what happens is why I have criticised Western theology and philosophy for being half-hearted.

Yet, we have all the time the historical precedent of Zen as an example of an approach to experience which insists that a radically critical appraisal of culture and language need not be the inception of black despair with its corollary immobilising of the springs of action and creativity, and the proof is the fact of artistic, literary, philosophical and religious creativity in Zen cultures. I do not want to seem to deny that the process of emptying out is a terrible wrenching experience, perhaps frightening and confusing, and, in fact, to remain frozen in that place would make life unendurably bleak.

However, as generations of Zen masters have insisted most vocifer-ously, the emptying out process is not the final resting place, nor the ultimate vantage point from which to assess the world. One *must* move beyond the process of denial in order for the awakening experience to be both genuine and usable, and the further step is said to reveal a deeper and more real value and meaning in experi-ence. Both Zen and its Indian predecessors have articulated this necessary further step in a number of ways. Nāgārjuna, for instance, makes it crystal clear that once one has contemplated the world as empty, one must take the further step of emptying out emptiness (so-called *shūnyatā-shūnyatā*, the emptiness of emptiness). Indian Buddhists likened the perception of emptiness to a medicine which has the sole purpose of curing illness. Once the illness is cured, they said, one does not continue taking the medicine. Nāgārjuna's main purpose was to demonstrate that *all* positions are delusory, whether it is the position implied in a word or a philosophical or ideological position. Since emptiness is also a position, one has ultimately to abandon that position also. No positions!

The Zen equivalent of the Indian approach is found in the well-known saying: 'Before Zen practice mountains were mountains and rivers were rivers. Once I had some insight into the nature of things, mountains were no longer mountains, and rivers were no longer rivers [i.e. they are empty.] Now that my practice has matured, mountains are once again mountains, and rivers are once again rivers.'

Now, here is what is so instructive and valuable to Westerners who have reacted with horror (since the time of Nietzsche?) at the growing crisis of confidence in epistemological certitude, at the grow-ing acceptance of pluralism in all forms, and at the dreaded spectre of cultural relativism. One can, and indeed must, as a really serious person go through the process of emptying out culture and lan-guage, so that one no longer sees mountains as 'mountains'. Then, however, it is absolutely imperative that one once again sees that mountains are 'mountains'. But this does not mean that one simply retraces one's steps back to the first position. I suspect that the bridge one crosses from simple naive affirmation of things to their total denial is a one-way bridge which does not permit a return. A case in point would be something like the move from theism to atheism, or the rejection of the nation state as a source of good. Although the final stage is an affirmation of things, it is nevertheless an *affirmation always mediated by the negation of the emptying process.*

This final stage, in effect, is simply the ability to participate in culture and use language, playing the game, as it were, as a matter of free choice, using the word 'mountain' while all the time knowing that it is not really a mountain. Such a progress from simple affirmation through negation to a final mediated affirmation has been referred to by one Western writer as a process of moving from a naive and uncritical 'beification' to a middle position of 'debeification', to a final position of 'rebeification'. But it can not be overstressed that the ultimate 'rebeification' is always one mediated by negation.

Consequently, the lesson that Zen teaches is that the emptying out of language is not the complete rejection of it but instead a liberating process that frees one from illusion, dogmatism, absolutism and other evils that derive from the uncritical use of language but still permit its use. We thus willingly play the game of culture and language but are at the same time free of them. I think that it would be correct to say that instead of the abandonment of culture and language, the need is really to understand what it means to be a product of culture and to clarify what language is and how it is used.

It would seem to follow from what has been said that the 'higher affirmation' of the third stage entails very important consequences. First, it involves an irrecoverable loss of certainty that any word we use points to a real, corresponding external reality. Second, it involves a realisation, a revelation perhaps, that inasmuch as words express culture, my language can only express my culture. A corollary of this is that since I am unable to determine objectively whose language is the correct one, I am not warranted to be dogmatic in the area of religion, ethics and philosophy. Third, it involves the willingness to live in a world which is ambiguous, indeterminate and insecure. The general consequence is that I realise that the language I use, and the values and meanings which are encapsulated in it, are sheer accidents of time and space and not at all 'self-evident'.

Zen does not see these consequences as a loss. Rather than trivialising or demeaning human life, as I have argued elsewhere, such consequences could pay a major role in promoting a true humanity. Zen, and Buddhism generally, have always held up the individual who has made such an achievement not as a diminished individual but as the perfected human being. The Buddha serves primarily in Buddhism as a model for what can be achieved. And here is my final suggestion concerning Zen's contribution to the language debate. The radical critique of language and culture and the final reappropriation in a clarified form which I have outlined above not only does not imply the abandonment of religion and religious values but rather shows, in the fourteen-century history of Zen, that a fulfilling and satisfying religious life can be found within a framework of transcendence of language and culture. Certainly the rejection of language as it is used realistically is a threat to some kinds of religion. Fundamentalism, or any religion which insists that its symbols have objective referents, exclusivist or absolutist tendencies, or what Tillich called the 'religion of fear', can not tolerate the kind of transcendence of language which Zen teaches. But this does not mean that *a* religious life *per se*, with all it means to the individual, is incompatible with a totally non-realistic use of language. Whatever the stakes are in the realist versus non-realistic debate, the issue is not an either-or one wherein *either* language names real, objective things *or* religion is dead. Some Christians, for instance, have adopted a Buddhist approach to the Christian symbol system and defend their position as being satisfying and meaningful. Yet, any religion which adopts the Buddhist approach is going to be a very different religion.

The Zen approach to language, including religious language, while admittedly negative, has the ultimate function of revealing something eminently positive and valuable. The same may be said with regard to the meaning and values encoded in language. The radical criticism of values means that values which are mere tribal concerns, conditioned and often changing over time are emptied out and rejected as ultimate. But, as with the transcendence of words, the object of this transcendence is the disclosure of something of greater value. Specifically, it is the disclosure of true value, and Zen writers such as Kitarō Nishida have correctly asserted that there is a real, true good which transcends both individual self-interested good and the collective good of the tribe. The same is true of meaning or significance. Christian thinkers, for instance, tend overwhelmingly to affirm the meaning of history, that history is real and that it has significance. Buddhists, on the other hand, deny that history, if it exists, has any meaning or is anything other than a series of accidents. Of course the big question is, who is correct, and how do we know it? I suspect that any Zen person who thought about the matter would have to conclude that the real meaning of events is that they are completely meaningless, in the sense that they do not, in and of themselves, contain the meanings that we find in them. I know that this 'meaning of meaninglessness' has a quaintly paradoxical air about it, but it nevertheless communicates the Zen conviction that the very meaninglessness of events is, if you will, a 'meaningful', positive perception. Freedom is, among other things, freedom from meaning. After all, when a monk asked master Rinzai, 'What is the meaning of Bodhidharma's coming from the west?', referring to the arrival in China of the Indian monk credited with starting the Zen tradition, Rinzai answered, 'If there is any meaning at all, you can never save yourself.'

Zen has maintained its iconoclastic, blasphemous, often scatalogical approach to all language, not excluding the most sacred symbols of Buddhism, throughout its fourteen-century history, in its faithful continuation of the older Buddhist strategy of destroying all dualisms and concepts in so far as they are believed to represent reality. Words are rejected as representing reality inasmuch as they are assumed to express the concepts, dualisms, ideological positions and philosophies. But the object of this was the attainment of a pristine clarity of insight into experience so that life and action would have a truer basis. Zen history shows clearly that a satisfying, liberated spiritual life can be pursued while at the same time denying that the symbol system refers to anything real. Language may be used once it is purified and clarified, as the voluminous literature of Zen attests. Thus, the recent scepticism about religious language in the West is not necessarily the end of the world; it may signify the end of an illusory world, but who can argue that an illusory world is worth saving? How the West will deal with the problem of language is anybody's guess. There is not likely to be a rush *en masse* to Zen for an answer, nor is there any reason why there should be. Zen is a highly effective way of dealing with illusion, and attests with its history that a solution is possible, but it should not be promoted as the only way. There may be other ways of 'climbing out of the black lacquer bucket', but whatever way the West discovers, it cannot involve the very tools and methods now being called into question. But something will have to be done, because the only alternative is widespread nihilism and its personal and social consequences.

Zen, Realism vs. Non-Realism, and Soteriology

JOHN H. WHITTAKER

The first of my two comments on Francis Cook's paper is a question solely about Zen and the second is a question about Zen in relation to realism and non-realism in religion. Perhaps the best way to develop the first is by beginning with Professor Cook's remark that Western philosophers assume that a rigorous analysis of experience etc. provides a firm foundation for action. I don't doubt that some Western philosophers assume this, but we do not all accept it unquestionably, as there are problems involved in deciding questions about how we are to live on the basis of purely factual reports about what is the case. We cannot have a 'firm foundation for action' without making some value judgments; but from a factual description of reality, no value judgments follow. My question is, to what extent is an analogue of this assumption involved in Zen? Does the emptying process of Zen leave one in possession of an *accurate* though *inarticulate* knowledge of the real world, from which implications about selflessness, compassion and the detachment from craving are to be derived? If so, then it might be said that Zen makes an assumption which is comparable to the assumption that we (supposedly) make in the West. The difference is that Westerners think that a knowledge of reality is to be gained by analysis, discrimination and conceptualisation, whereas Buddhists think otherwise. To them, *knowledge* is still the goal but language, instead of facilitating proper understanding, actually hinders it. *True knowledge*, or *prajna*, is attainable only after the discrimination enshrined in language has been transcended. But does one still assume that a direct grasp of reality – something that we might call a post-verbal 'metaphysical' understanding – brings saving implications in its wake?

I would like to pose an alternative view. On this alternative view, all of the things that Zen says about reality, *and* all of the things that Western religion says about reality, are said in virtue of a soteriological intent. Zen *wants* reality to be such-and-such a way because that view of reality can be used to support the *saving* teachings which it offers about selflessness, compassion, right understanding, etc. Since

77

Zen says very little in a positive way about reality, however, perhaps it would be better to say that the *denials* which it makes about the common understanding of objects are made *in virtue of their implications in undermining craving*. Objects are not enduring things *so they cannot be possessed*. The self is not a substantial entity *so there is nothing to be satisfied by craving*. True reality does not confront us when we discriminate *so there is nothing essential to be won by an analytical understanding of the world*. Such things are said because of the *force* that they are meant to have (indicated here by the words in italics).

On this view of the matter, then, the practical knowledge of religious teachings is superior to 'pristine' metaphysical apprehensions which have no practical implications. This is true whether this metaphysical apprehension is couched in language or whether it transcends the limits of description. Either way, the practical aims involved in the representation of reality *govern the discussion used to sustain them*. The manner in which a religion depicts objects, selves, language, etc., is not concerned with abstract truth for its own sake but for the sake of those attitudinal adjustments that will deliver people from isolation, fear, suffering and selfish anxiety. In Zen as in any other religion, the description of the world may be thoroughly fettered by these motives.

I do not mean to deny, of course, that the religion of Zen is built around *experience*. But I am suggesting that the way in which this experience is understood and put to use in the religious life is governed by teachings with a soteriological intent. This intent is not the consequence of a logically prior, religiously neutral, grasp of reality from which practical implications somehow (this never being explained) logically follow. The practical, attitudinal, aspect of understanding is the most prior to Zen intuitions, underived and absolutely basic. It is there behind all the teachings, the experiences, and the meditational practices of the religion.

My first question, then, is, which view more nearly captures the spirit of Zen – the view that its soteriological implications are derived from a prior, metaphysically neutral, grasp of reality, or the view that these soteriological intentions *logically precede and govern* Zen perceptions of reality. That is, does Zen hold that a proper understanding of reality *prior to any method of projection* is required for the religious life, or that its teachings about reality and language are *inseparable* from its own religiously governed intentions?

The indications in Cook's paper seem to favour the second alternative. He notes, for example, that Zen teachings are dispensed as medicine whose sole purpose is to effect a cure, after which they no longer need to be taken – which suggests that these teaching serve to make a point about selflessness, which in being made renders them dispensable. If this is true, and the 'metaphysical' claims of Zen are dispensable, how are we to construe the prior claims that Zen does make? Given the priority of practical intuitions here, do we not have to construe truth in a way suited to these practical commitments?

The idea that there must be *things* in the world for sentences to be true of has dominated Western philosophy; where there are no *things* for sentences to be true of, there are no truths to be formulated. Professor Cook has shown that Zen Buddhism is incompatible with this insistence on *things*, and so it appears that there are no truths which could possibly be uttered in Zen. But doesn't this really mean only that the truths of Zen cannot be represented as if they were descriptive truths about *things*? Zen is built on the conviction that freedom from *dukha* is possible, that craving is the source of suffering, that a life of proper detachment is 'eminently worthy', and that the realisation of selfless understanding is wisdom. These might be called 'axiological appraisals' or 'teleological judgments of ultimate worth' or 'irreducible insights about the possibilities of deliverance'. The difficulty that we as philosophers have in imagining how it can be that such propositions might be true is due to our ineptitude as thinkers, not to the inappropriateness of believing in them. We want them to follow from a neutral metaphysical state of affairs, but this might well be because of the poverty of our philosophical analysis – that and the fact that we are used to conveying evaluative appraisals in the form of descriptions.

In any case, Zen masters agree that there is a good which 'transcends both individual self-interested good and the collective good of the tribe', and this good is the goal which makes religious struggle worthwhile. Zen practitioners believe that *this good exists*, and they would be loath to describe this view as arbitrary or accidental. They cannot present this view as a view about contingent states of affairs – and so cannot be 'realistic' in the sense which Cook assumes. Yet it does not violate the grammar of the word 'true' to express this confidence as a belief in the *truth* of this fundamental, evaluative, stance.

Might not Zen and other religions as well be grounded in such truths as these – not truths to be tested as metaphysical hypotheses but truths to be tested as respositories in which we might or might not find the deliverance we seek? That is my second question.

Zen and Realism

JOHN HICK

Mr Cook has given us a marvellous exposition of the Buddhist view of language and its limitations. But I think that he is under a misapprehension in thinking that in so doing he is arguing against realism in the use of language – although he is certainly arguing against a naive realism. But realism is not the view that there are essences or natures which make things be what they are. It is not the view that there is a 'chariotness' or 'Nagasenaness' or 'Frank Cookness' or 'John Hickness', over and above chariots and Nagasena and Frank Cook and John Hick. Nor is it the view that the nouns that we use, such as 'chariot', 'chair', etc., are other than 'convenient indicators that enable the work of society to be done' (p. 62). When I refer to this as a table I am simply using an agreed verbal symbol for a phenomenon – that is, for something experienced – and the use of the symbol leaves open all questions about what its inner or ultimate or hidden nature is. If someone says that the table is really a swarm of quanta of discharging energy, or that it is a manifestation of *sūnyata*, or a moment within the ceaselessly changing field of *pratītya samutpāda*, they may be right, but we all still all go on calling it a table; and we are using the word realistically, to refer to something that is there, for which our conventional name in English is 'table'. We can continue to use language realistically and fully agree with Mr Cook that 'concepts and their verbal expressions are totally inadequate for grasping the true nature of things' (p. 63).

And if we go on to say, with Mr Cook and with the Buddhist tradition, that nothing has self-existence, or in Western terminology that nothing has aseity, but everything is totally dependent, perhaps dependent upon everything else, we are still speaking realistically – for we are intending to say how things actually are, what the actual situation is.

And so I reckon that Mr Cook's argument against essences, and against the naive assumption that human language captures the nature of reality, is all sound, but not directed against realism.

There is, however, another area in which at least some Zen thinkers, including Mr Cook, are genuinely non-realist, namely in their language about the transcendent. According to the Pali scriptures, Gautama Buddha taught an understanding of our present existence as set within a much larger context than simply our bodily existence on this earth at this time. He taught that we are born many times on earth, creating and then de-creating our *karma*, until at last we attain to the ego-free state of *nirvāna*. Mahayana teaching, within which Zen falls, added that eventually every human life process or project will attain to *nirvāna*, aided by those, the *bodhisattvas*, who have already attained it; and it added also the conception of the eternal *Dharmakaya*, the ultimate reality that is manifested in the heavenly Buddhas of the *nirmānakāya*, some of whom become incarnate as historical earthly Buddhas. Some modern Buddhists, particularly Western ones, interpret all this in a non-realist and mythological sense. That is something for them to argue about with those of their fellow Buddhists who understand it in a realist way. But – and this is the point I want to make about Mr Cook's paper – this issue is not the same as the question whether, as realists can also agree, all human language and conceptuality is ultimately inadequate to reality. I think it is helpful to keep these various issues straight in their relationship to one another.

Can We 'Go Beyond Language'?

DON CUPITT

Both the style and the content of Francis Cook's paper are naturally very congenial to me, but I do query the notion of 'going beyond language'. It is an obviously paradoxical idea, because after all we must still use language to state it. Nobody is going to step forward and describe to us, *in some medium other than language*, the blissful region that lies beyond all words. And in any case, I believe there is no sense in describing a natural language in its proper setting as *ever* being incomplete or inadequate. On the contrary, I affirm the priority, completeness and ubiquity of language, every natural language being fully adequate to the concrete form of life that has produced it and is transacted in it. Language can no more be wrong wholesale than a culture can be wrong wholesale. You know and I know that in the everyday business of life we all understand each other *perfectly* so long as we stick to mundane matters.

Not only is language, in my view, just fine as it is, but I also hold that since the world of language is the human world a Christian should not try to escape from it into some questionable extra-human realm. So I believe that Christianity and Buddhism can draw closer together if Buddhism can only take the linguistic turn. When we both of us accept the post-structuralist view of language, then the Buddhist will see language as a boundless field of insubstantial, shifting, differential semantic relationships. This means that the modern metaphysics of language is in many ways a *Buddhist* metaphysics. At the same time the Christian desire to stress the ethical, intersubjective and radically human character of the world of meaning that we inhabit will also be satisfied. One may glimpse here the possibility of a future convergence.

Part Three
A False Dichotomy?

5

On Really Believing

D.Z. PHILLIPS

It is widely assumed in contemporary philosophy of religion that if a philosopher wishes to give an analytic account of religious belief, one which seeks to clarify the grammar of that belief, he must choose between realism and non-realism. These, it is thought, are the only philosophical alternatives open to him. According to Terence Penelhum, 'Most atheists and agnostics are theological realists, and obviously most defenders and apologists for faith are also.'[1] Most, but not all, for, it is said, on the margins of the dispute between belief and unbelief are those philosophers and theologians who give non-realist accounts of these alternatives. According to realists, the non-realist analyses fail to capture the essence of belief and atheism.

What is the theological realist's account of believing in God? According to Penelhum, anyone committed to realism 'would hold that the supernatural facts which he thinks faith requires must indeed *be* facts for faith to be true, so that if they are not facts, but fantasies (or, even worse, not coherently expressible), then faith is unjustified' (p. 151). The realist admits that faith, believing, has consequences which constitute the commitments which make up living religiously, but he insists, to use Roger Trigg's words, that 'The belief is distinct from the commitment which may follow it, and is the justification for it.'[2] The non-realist's sin, it is said, is to conflate believing with the consequences of believing, so making the realist's conception of belief redundant.

For the realist, the non-realist analyses of religious belief are reductionist in character. These analyses have been arrived at as a result of the alleged difficulties created for belief in the existence of God by the demands of verificationism. Many non-realists concur with this view. They are prepared to admit that realism portrays what faith once meant for people, but argue that this conception of faith cannot be sustained today. In this respect, non-realists are revisionists. As Penelhum says, 'Neither Hare nor Cupitt is claiming

85

that theological realism *has not been* integral to the faith "as it is"' (p. 153). The same could not be said of R.B. Braithwaite and the late Bishop of Woolwich. They all dispense with something, which they admit was once integral to faith, 'in the interest of preserving and revitalising the rest of it' (p. 163). The realist claims that what the non-realist dispenses with is logically indispensable for any notion of belief.

In contemporary philosophy of religion there has been a Wittgensteinian critique of realism. Given the assumption that philosophers have to choose between realism and non-realism, it is not surprising to find this critique discussed in these terms. The criticisms, and mine more than most, are placed firmly in the non-realist camp. According to Penelhum, however, there is one important difference between my work and that of the non-realists we have mentioned. As we have said, they admit that realism had once been integral to faith. But, Penelhum says, 'What Phillips has sought to do, if I understand him correctly, is to present an understanding of religious thought and practice that shows faith *as it is* to be a non-realist phenomenon' (p. 163). Clearly, for Penelhum, this is an audacious claim, and he is astonished and puzzled, I suspect, as to how anyone can advance it. It is bad enough, in his eyes, to claim that we can dispense with theological realism in faith as we know it today. To say that such realism was *never* applicable to faith seems, to Penelhum and Trigg, plainly absurd.

What I shall show in this paper is that Wittgenstein's critique of realism is far more radical than Penelhum and Trigg suspect. They assume, throughout, that realism and non-realism are intelligible alternatives. Their concern is simply with which one gives the correct analysis of religious belief. They are confident about the answer. They do not realise that, for Wittgenstein, realism and non-realism are equally confused. Further, what Wittgenstein is saying is not that realism is a correct analysis of ordinary beliefs, but not of religious beliefs. His view is that realism is a confused account of *any* kind of belief: believing that my brother is in America, that a theorem is valid, that fire will burn me. In short, realism is not coherently expressible.

I

Consider the following remarks by Wittgenstein:

One man is a convinced realist, another a convinced idealist and teaches his children accordingly. In such an important matter as the existence or non-existence of the external world they don't want to teach their children anything wrong . . .

But the idealist will teach his children the word 'chair' after all, for of course he wants to teach them to do this and that, e.g. to fetch the chair. Then there will be the difference between what the idealist-educated children say and the realist ones. Won't the difference only be one of battle cry?

$$(Z,^3\ 413\text{--}14)$$

Rightly or wrongly, Wittgenstein is accusing realism and non-realism of being idle talk; talk which takes us away from the directions in which we should be looking if we want to clarify the grammar of our beliefs concerning chairs. Similarly, the accusation against theological realism is that it is idle talk. If this accusation is a just one, realism has never been integral to faith. This does not mean that we must embrace non-realism. Penelhum and Trigg are wrong in thinking that I have done so in my work. Theological non-realism is as empty as theological realism. Both terms are battle cries in a confused philosophical and theological debate, which is not to deny that these slogans may cause all sorts of trouble for believers and unbelievers alike.

Why have Penelhum and Trigg failed to appreciate the radical character of Wittgenstein's critique? A large part of the answer lies in their neglect of the grammatical issues involved in 'believing'. They take themselves to be reflecting, philosophically, a straightforward relation between belief and its object. Similarly, theological realism takes itself to be the expression of a truism: we cannot believe in God unless we believe there is a God to believe in. If that were denied, it seems belief would be robbed of its object. Aren't we all realists? What we need to realise is that, as yet, *no* grammatical work has been done to elucidate the relations between belief and its object.

Instead of elucidating these relations, theological realism often indulges in philosophy by italics. We are told that we would not worship unless we believed that God *exists*. We are told that we cannot talk to God unless he is *there* to talk to. We are told that, for the believer, God's existence is a *fact*. And so on. But nothing is achieved by italicising these words. The task of clarifying their grammar when they are used remains. Realists speak of the relation between belief and its object as though the character of that relation can be taken for granted. But is the relation between belief and its object the same no matter what the character of what is believed? Realism prevents us from answering this question by ignoring the very circumstances which would enable us to answer it – the circumstances in which 'really believing' has its sense.

The realist accuses the non-realist of conflating 'believing' with the fruits of believing. The fruits of believing, the role belief plays in human life, are said to be the consequences of believing. What, then, is 'believing'? According to Trigg, it is a mental state, as a result of which certain consequences follow. There are, of course, occasions where an assertion gives us information about the state of mind of the asserter. For example, 'He's coming! I can't believe it!' (*RPP*,[4] Vol. I, 485). But if I say, 'I believe it will rain', I am not referring to my state of mind. 'I believe it will rain' can be replaced by 'It'll rain'. Wittgenstein writes:

> What does it mean to say that 'I believe P' says roughly the same as 'P'? We react in roughly the same way when anyone says the first and when he says the second; if I said the first, and someone didn't understand the words 'I believe', I should repeat the sentence in the second form and so on. As I'd also explain the words 'I wish you'd go away' by means of the words 'Go away'.
>
> (*RPP*, Vol. I, 477)

'I believe' is not a report or description of a mental state. It is doing something, making an assertion. But, according to Trigg and Penelhum, the essence of 'believing' cannot be found in action, in doing anything, since, according to them, action is itself based on something called 'belief'. But, once again, what does this conception of belief amount to? Is it not entirely vacuous? Wittgenstein imagines someone saying, '"If I look outside, I see that it's raining; if I look within myself, I see that I believe it." And what is one supposed to do with this information?' (*RPP*, Vol. I, 815). Would it make sense to wonder what the odds are that actions will in fact follow as a consequence of my mental state of believing? (See *RPP*, Vol. I, 823.) Wittgenstein is challenging this whole way of thinking:

> How does such an expression as 'I believe . . . ' ever come to be used? Did a phenomenon, that of belief, suddenly get noticed? Did we observe ourselves and discover this phenomenon in that

way? Did we observe ourselves and other men and so discover the phenomenon of belief?

(RPP, Vol. I, 62–4)

Compare these remarks with the following:

> Someone says: 'Man hopes.'
> How should this phenomenon of natural history be described? – One might observe a child and wait until one day he manifests hope: and then one could say 'Today he hoped for the first time.' But surely that sounds queer! Although it would be quite natural to say 'Today he said "I hope" for the first time.' And why queer? One does not say that a suckling hopes that . . . but one does say it of a grown-up. – Well, bit by bit daily life becomes such that there is a place for hope in it.
>
> <div align="right">(<i>RPP</i>, Vol. II, 15. Cf. <i>Z</i>, 469)</div>

But the realist divorces 'believing' and 'hoping' from the situations in human life in which they have their sense. On the realist's view, our actions are based on the trustworthiness of our beliefs. This means, as Wittgenstein says, 'I should have to be able to say: "I believe that it's raining, and my belief is trustworthy, so I trust it." As if my belief were some kind of sense-impression. Do you say, e.g., "I believe it, and as I am reliable, it will presumably be so"? That would be like saying: "I believe it – therefore I believe it"' (*RPP*, Vol. I, 482–3).

One way of referring to the criticisms Wittgenstein makes of realism is to say that the realist wishes to speak of the relation of belief to its object, without specifying the method of projection which specifies what the relation comes to. As a result, what Penelhum and Trigg mean by the relation of belief to its object remains completely obscure. Wittgenstein asks:

> How do you know that you believe that your brother is in America? . . . Suppose we say that the thought is some sort of process in his mind, or his saying something, etc. – then I could say: 'All right, you call this a thought of your brother in America, well, what is the connection between this and your brother in America? Why is it that you don't doubt that it is a thought of your brother in America?'
>
> <div align="right">(<i>LRB</i>,[5] p. 66)</div>

If we simply say that the thought pictures the fact, this obscures the fact that it is only within a method of projection that the distinction between successful and unsuccessful picturing has any application. For example, where photographs are concerned, 'having a likeness' is obviously a central feature of the method of projection by which we speak of photographs and their subjects. Wittgenstein comments, 'If I give up the business of being like [as a criterion], I get into an awful mess, because anything may be his portrait, given a certain method of projection . . . ' (*LRB*, pp. 66–7). But Trigg robs us of any reference to a method of projection when he says, 'It is a great mistake to confuse the meaning of a concept with the occasions on which it is learnt' (p. 20). Wittgenstein describes the realist's dilemma as follows:

> The first idea [you have] is that you are looking at your own thought, and are absolutely sure that it is a thought that so and so. You are looking at some mental phenomenon, and you say to yourself 'obviously this is a thought of my brother being in America.' It seems to be a super-picture. It seems, with thought, there is no doubt whatever. With a picture, it still depends on the method of projection, whereas here it seems you get rid of the projecting relation, and are absolutely certain that this is thought of that.
>
> (*LRB*, p. 66)

This is exactly how it seems when Trigg says, 'The fact that our commitments can never be "free-floating" but are always directed means that there must be a propositional element lurking behind every commitment' (p. 42). The sense of the proposition seems to be given independently of any method of projection. What Trigg is left with is a free-floating conception of a proposition. Lewy suggested that the connection between belief and its object is given via a convention. He said, 'The word designates.' Wittgenstein replies, 'You must explain "designates" by examples. We have learnt a rule, a practice, etc.' (*LRB*, p. 67).

Trigg's attempts to separate our beliefs and concepts from our practices are doomed to failure. To illustrate the possibility of such separation he says, 'There is no contradiction in supposing that none of the things by means of which we were taught "red" are red any more (because they have all been repainted some other colour)' (p. 21). Trigg operates with a simple picture of words as labels we attach to objects. Of course, a labelling procedure is itself a method of projection. The attaching of the label to an object is not simply given independently of the procedure. Our beliefs about colours also have their sense within practices and situations with which we are familiar. Trigg's suggestion, on the other hand, is wholly unfamiliar. He suggests that his opponents are committed to saying that if some object is believed to be red, that object cannot change its colour! Of course, they are committed to no such view. They know, like Trigg, what it means to talk of changing colours, fading colours, renewing colours, etc., etc. But such talk has its sense within our practices. Trigg, like the rest of us, from an early age, saw things being painted over, sometimes with a different colour, sometimes with the same one. He saw colours fade in the sun. He came to appreciate the marvellous changes of colour in the natural world which the seasons bring. Our beliefs about colours are not confined to any *one* of these situations, but Trigg's reaction is to sever 'believing' from them all! But unless we agreed in our colour reactions, we would not know what it means to entertain beliefs about colours changing, fading or being renewed. But our reactions are what we do. They are not the consequences of our beliefs. Without agreement in reactions there would be nothing to have beliefs about.

Wittgenstein's critique of realism, then, is not confined to theological realism. If it were, the suggestion might be that religious beliefs, unlike beliefs of other kinds, are rooted in our practices and our commitments. Sometimes, it is easy to give this impression in emphasising differences between religious beliefs and other kinds of beliefs. For example, in *The Concept of Prayer*, I said:

> To say 'This is the true God' is to believe in Him and worship Him. I can say 'This theory is true, but I couldn't care less about it' and there is nothing odd in what I say. On the other hand, if I say 'This is the true God, but I couldn't care less' it is difficult to know what this could mean. Belief in the true God is not like belief in a true theory.[6]

Without denying grammatical differences between religious beliefs and theoretical beliefs, my remarks in this instance create the impression that whereas belief in God is internally related to practice and commitment, belief in a theory is not. But why take indifference to a theory as the paradigm of believing it? Similarly, when Trigg says, 'No philosopher worries about the difference a belief that there are elephants in Africa could make to a person' (p. 36), his words, like mine, do not get to the root of the issue concerning the relation of belief to its object.

The theological realist argues, as Trigg does: 'It must be recognised that there are two distinct parts in religious commitment, the acceptance of certain propositions as true, and, as a result, a religious response, expressed in both worship and action' (p. 42). The realist argues that the same distinction can be made with respect to all our beliefs. On the one hand we believe certain things are true, and on the other hand we commit ourselves and act accordingly. But what is involved in believing something to be true? The realist can give no intelligible answer to this question. His failure is due to his exclusion of the method of projection within which the relation of belief to its object has its sense. So when the theological realist seeks to divorce the meaning of believing from our actions and practices, he effects a divorce between belief and practice which would render *any* kind of believing unintelligible.

We cannot, as the realist supposes, give the same kind of account of belief in every context. To say that the relation between belief and its object varies is to say that methods of projection vary. Wittgenstein gives us numerous examples to illustrate this. Here are some of them:

> What are the criteria that we believe something? Take a particular theory of Eddington's about the end of the world; in 10 years, the world will shrink, or expand, or something. He might be said to *believe* this. How does he do this? Well, he says that he believes it, he has arrived at it in a certain way, is rather pleased that he has reached this knowledge, and so on. But what could be called actions in accordance with his belief? Does he begin to make preparations? I suppose not – Compare believing something in physics and the case where someone shouts 'Fire!' My saying 'I believe' will have different properties and different consequences, or perhaps none.
>
> (*LFM*,[7] p. 136)

Again:

> Ask yourself: What does it mean to *believe* Goldbach's theorem? What does this belief consist in? In a feeling of certainty as we state, hear, or think of the theorem? (That would not interest us.) And what are the characteristics of this feeling? Why, I don't even know how far the feeling may be caused by the proposition itself.
>
> Am I to say that belief is a particular colouring of our thoughts? Where does this idea come from? Well, there is a tone of belief, as of doubt.

I should like to ask: how does the belief connect with this proposition? Let us look and see what are the consequences of this belief, where it takes us. 'It makes me search for a proof of the proposition.' – Very well; and now let us look and see what your searching really consists in. Then we shall know what belief in the proposition amounts to.

(*PI*,[8] Vol. I, 578)

But now, contrast these examples with the following:

A man would fight for his life not to be dragged into the fire. No induction. Terror. That is, as it were, part of the substance of the belief.

(*LRB*, p. 55)

The differences in the character of these beliefs is shown by the practices of which they are a part. The practices cannot be cut off from the beliefs in the way suggested by the realist's account of 'believing'. What would 'believing' be after such a divorce? Consider the following example:

One would like to say: 'Everything speaks for, and nothing against the earth's having existed long before . . . ' Yet might I not believe the contrary after all? But the question is: What would the practical effects of this belief be? – Perhaps someone says: 'That's not the point. A belief is what it is whether it has any practical effects or not.' One thinks: It is the same adjustment of the human mind anyway.

(*OC*,[9] 89)

But it is to practice, what a man does, that one would look to determine whether he believes something or not. What kind of example would one have to think of to imagine a severe dislocation between a man's words and his beliefs? Consider the following:

Imagine an observer who, as it were automatically, says what he is observing. Of course he hears himself talk, but, so to speak, he takes no notice of that. He sees that the enemy is approaching and reports it, describes it, but like a machine. What would that be like? Well, he does not act according to his observation. Of him, one might say that he speaks what he sees, but that he does not *believe* it. It does not, so to speak, get inside him.

(*RPP*, Vol. I, 813)

Notice that Wittgenstein does not object to saying that the belief does not get inside this man. He might also have said that the man had not made the words he spoke his own. But it is what surrounds the words, or rather, in this case, the absence of expected surroundings, which leads to his characterisation of the words. Again, it is the absence of certain surroundings which leads to our refraining from attributing certain beliefs to animals. For example, 'A dog believes his master is at the door. But can he also believe his master will come the day after tomorrow? – And *what* can he not do here? – How do I do it? – How am I supposed to answer this' (*PI*, p. 174). As we have seen, the answer is found by looking at what we do in connection with such expectations. These activities do not play any part in a dog's life. That being so, we cannot attribute beliefs to the dog which have their sense within such activities.

In all these examples, it can be seen that what the relation between belief and its object amounts to can only be seen within the method of projection within which the belief has its sense. The reason why I have dwelt on so many non-religious examples is that the theological realist speaks as though, in relation to religion, philosophers of religion, influenced by Wittgenstein, have introduced a way of discussing what believing amounts to which departs from the ordinary meaning of believing. It has been said that Wittgensteinian philosophers had a motive for doing this, namely their desire to protect religious beliefs from the stringent tests to which beliefs are subject in other spheres. As we have seen, these tests vary. To see what our beliefs come to, we must turn to the very contexts which the realists want to rule out of consideration, namely the actions and practices we engage in. We cannot appreciate the relation between belief and its object while ignoring the appropriate method of projection. Methods of projection vary. In bringing out differences between them, we can also bring out the grammatical differences between various beliefs. This is the philosopher's task where religious belief is concerned, not because it is a distinctive kind of belief, true though that is, but because this is the philosopher's task in endeavouring to understand what is involved in *any* kind of believing.

II

Let us suppose that someone says that 'I believe in God' pictures the object of belief, or refers to it. How is the 'picturing' or 'referring' to be understood? As we have seen, this involves exploring the method of projection involved. The method of projection cannot be taken for granted. We have yet to explore the relation between 'I believe in God' and the object of the belief. The relation can be explored by asking how we would set about deciding whether two people believe in the same God. Rush Rhees has shown how *not* to answer this question:

> If one lays emphasis . . . on the fact that 'God' is a substantive, and especially if one goes on . . . to say that it is a proper name, then the natural thing will be to assume that meaning the same by 'God' is something like meaning the same by 'the sun' or meaning the same by 'Churchill'. You might even want to use some such phrase as 'stands for' the same. But nothing of that sort will do here. Questions about 'meaning the same' in connexion with the names of physical objects are connected with the kind of criteria to which we may appeal in saying that this is the same object – 'that is the same planet as I saw in the south west last night', 'that is the same car that was standing here this morning'. Supposing someone said 'the word "God" stands for a different object now.' What could that mean? I know what it means to say that 'the Queen' stands for a different person now, and I know what it means to say that St Mary's Church is not the St Mary's Church that was here in So-and-So's day. I know the sort of thing that might be said if I were to question either of these statements. But *nothing* of that sort could be said in connexion with any question about the meaning of 'God'. It is not by having someone point and say 'That's God'. Now this is not a trivial or inessential matter. It hangs together in very important ways with what I call the grammar of the word 'God'. And it is one reason why I do not think it is helpful just to say that the word is substantive.[10]

Another way of making the same point is to say that 'I believe in God' does not picture its object as a photograph does. In the later relation, the criterion of likeness is central. For example, Wittgenstein says, 'I could show Moore the picture of a tropical plant. There is a technique of comparison between picture and plant' (*LRB*, p. 63). Believing that a particular picture is in fact a picture of the plant has its sense from the technique in which likenesses and comparisons play a central role. But such techniques have nothing to do with belief in God even when religious pictures are involved. Wittgenstein gives the following example: 'Take "God created man". Pictures of Michelangelo showing the creation of the world. In general, there is nothing which explains the meanings of words as well as a picture, and I take it that Michelangelo was as good as anyone can be and did his best, and here is the picture of the Deity creating Adam' (*LRB*, p. 63). Wittgenstein is saying, ironically, that if we did think this was a photograph or the representation of a likeness, we could trust Michelangelo to have made a good job of it! But, of course, we do not treat it in this way. 'If we ever saw this, we certainly wouldn't think this the Deity. The picture has to be used in an entirely different way if we are to call the man in that queer blanket "God", and so on. You could imagine that religion was taught by means of these pictures' (*LRB*, p. 63). To say that God is in the picture, is not to say that it is a picture of God. To believe in the truth of such a picture is to adopt what it says as one's norm of truth. To say God is in the picture is a confession of faith.

The realist will not wait on the language of religion. Even when some of its central features are pointed out to him, he draws the wrong conclusions from them. Wittgenstein provides the reminder: 'The word "God" is amongst the earliest learnt – pictures and cat- echisms, etc. But not the same consequences as with pictures of aunts. I wasn't shown [that which the picture pictured]' (*LRB*, p. 59). The realist takes this to mean that we *could* have been shown that which the picture pictures, but, as it happens, we were not. It is as if one said, 'We *could* have had a picture of God creating Adam (after all, it must have looked like something) but Michelangelo's picture does not represent it.' Perhaps the realist will say that because God is transcendent, it is hardly surprising that this should be so. Wittgenstein imagines someone saying: 'Of course, we can only express ourselves by means of these pictures . . . I can't show you the real thing, only the picture', and he responds, 'The absurdity is, I've never taught him the technique of using this picture' (*LRB*, p. 63).

The realist does not appreciate that when Wittgenstein says we were not shown that which the picture pictured, he is not referring to an omission which ought to be rectified. He is not referring to an omission at all. Rather, he is remarking on the *kind* of picture he is talking about, namely one which does not have its sense in a method of projection in which the important criterion is the likeness of the picture to what it pictures. If the latter relation is what we are looking for, Wittgenstein's point is that there is nothing for the picture to be compared or likened to – that is part of the grammar of the picture.

What, then, is involved in believing the picture? Wittgenstein replies: 'Here believing obviously plays much more this role: suppose we said that a certain picture might play the role of constantly admonishing me, or I always think of it. Here, an enormous difference would be between those people for whom the picture is constantly in the foreground, and the others who just didn't use it at all' (*LRB*, p. 56). But this is precisely what Trigg denies. He argues: 'The important thing about talk of God is that it is about God. The place it holds in the life of an individual must be a secondary consideration' (pp. 74–5). But, as we have seen, on this view we are unable to give a coherent account of what believing in God amounts to. Further, no way could be found of determining whether two people are worshipping the same God, since, here, too, what we would refer to is what belief comes to in the believer's life, to what spiritual matters amount to for him.

Why are realists so reluctant to embrace these conclusions? They fear that the fruits of belief are emphasised in such a way as to neglect, or even ignore, the object of the belief, namely God. Some non-realist accounts of religious belief have fuelled these fears. The most well-known of these is R.B. Braithwaite's notorious suggestion that it is unnecessary for believers to assent to the truth of religious beliefs.[11] Braithwaite characterises these religious beliefs as stories, the essential function of which is to give psychological aid to moral endeavour. It is conceivable that this endeavour should be aided by stories and beliefs other than religious ones. Little wonder, then, that this leads the realist to conclude that, on this view, religious belief could be dispensed with altogether. What is essential is the efficacy of moral endeavour. The non-realist gives a reductionist account of religious belief. Religious concepts are explained away in non-religious terms. This is the root of the realist's fears.

According to Penelhum, my views, too, give rise to similar misgivings. He refers to my remark in *Death and Immortality*:

> . . . that eternal life for the believer is participation in the life of God, and that this has to do with dying to the self, seeing that all things are a gift from God, that nothing is ours by right or necessity . . . In learning by contemplation, attention, renunciation, what forgiving, thanking, loving, etc. mean in these contexts, the believer is participating in the reality of God; *this is what we mean by God's reality*.[12]

Penelhum argues that I am advancing a view of religious beliefs 'as expressions of certain preferred religious attitudes', a view which, he argues, 'eliminates suggestion of supernatural facts' (p. 180). But this is certainly not my view. On the contrary, in *Religion Without Explanation*,[13] in an explicit criticism of Braithwaite, I emphasised the internal relations between religious belief and the endeavour it informs. Penelhum and other realists fear that belief in God is being reduced to ways of talking about forgiveness, thankfulness and love. What I was saying, however, is that, in these contexts, we cannot understand what forgiveness, thankfulness and love amount to without recognising that these are *religious* conceptions. We are talking of God's forgiveness, God's love, thankfulness to, and love of God.

Ironically, it is Penelhum who divorces belief in God from these matters. For him, belief in God is one thing, the fruits of belief are its consequences. On this view there is no internal relation between belief and its consequences. This much is clear from Penelhum's treatment of the following example:

> While faith should issue in serenity and spiritual liberation, it in no way follows from this that serenity and liberation can only come from faith, or that everyone who seeks or achieves those conditions must *have* faith. I do not wish to enquire here what alternative courses might produce some of the affective elements in faith, but possible candidates are alternative sets of belief (such as those of Freudianism and Marxism), brainwashing, music, and drugs. To call spiritual liberatedness faith is to identify faith with one of its fruits or manifestations.
>
> (p. 180)

For Penelhum, then, the *same* serenity can be a consequence of quite different beliefs.

Penelhum does not ask himself how we would decide whether a certain disposition is of God, or whether it is a case of bad faith explicable in Freudian or Marxist terms, a case of drug-induced behaviour, the result of brainwashing, or a case or non-religious absorption in music. How would Penelhum obey Paul's injunction to test the spirits to see whether they are of God? Of course, when not philosophising, Penelhum, like the rest of us, would consider the character of the disposition. He would consider the place and surroundings of the disposition in the person's life. But, philosophically, it is this very context that his realism declares an irrelevance. As we have seen, the essence of belief is said to be presupposed by such dispositions. Believing is thought of as a mental state. I have already discussed the confusions which come from such a philo-sophical dichotomy.

Yet, what if one gives a closer examination to the notion of a mental state? Wittgenstein comments: 'Is "I believe . . . " a descrip-tion of my mental state? – Well, what *is* such a description? "I am sad", for example, "I am in a good mood", perhaps "I am in pain"' (*RPP*, p. 470). Clearly, if we go on to speak of what is involved in sadness, good and bad moods, we will be led, once again, to those contexts of action and practice which realism ignores. Ascribing mental states, like ascribing beliefs, does not happen *in vacuo*. It, too, has its sense within human practices. Without this mediation of sense, the notion of a mental state becomes as metaphysically iso-lated as the realist's conception of believing.

What if we do take proper account of the place believing in God has in human life? Then we find the possibility of speaking of Penelhum's example of serenity in a way far beyond the reaches of realism. For example, if a believer is in a state of serenity, someone may say of him that he is possessed by the spirit of God. God, it is said, is in the serenity. It might well be part of what Brother Law-rence called 'the practice of the presence of God'. It is hard for Penelhum and Trigg to take these claims seriously, because, for them, anything called an affective state or attitude is merely a conse-quence of a belief said to be logically independent of it. But, we ask again: what *is* the belief? Do not religious believers speak of God at work in men's thoughts and deeds, at work in what Penelhum and Trigg call the fruits of belief? But if the essence of belief is not to be found in its so-called fruits, how can God be said to be present in them? *In this way, realism cannot take seriously the central religious conviction that God is at work in people's lives. The reductionism which the realist finds in non-realism is all too prevalent in the realist's account of believing in God.*

Trigg believes that Wittgenstein, too, gives an account of religious belief in terms of attitudes from which the essence of believing is missing. On this view, religious beliefs are simply one way of ex-pressing attitudes which can also be expressed in other ways. But Wittgenstein holds no such view. He asks us to consider the follow-ing example: 'Suppose someone, before going to China, when he might never see me again, said to me: "We might see one another after death" – would I necessarily say that I don't understand him? I might say [want to say] simply, "Yes, I *understand* him entirely."' At this point, Lewy suggests that Wittgenstein's reaction is a way of expressing a certain attitude. This is precisely the way Trigg wants to describe what Wittgenstein is doing. But Wittgenstein rejects this account of what he is saying: 'I would say "No, it isn't the same as saying 'I'm very fond of you'" – and it may not be the same as saying something else. It says what it says. Why should you be able to substitute anything else?' (*LRB*, pp. 70–1). Wittgenstein is insisting on the irreducibility of religious pictures. He is not giving a reductionist account of them. With some pictures matters are different: 'Of certain pictures we say that they might just as well be replaced by another – e.g. we could, under certain circumstances, have one projection of an ellipse drawn instead of another. [He may say]: "I would have been prepared to use another picture, it would have had the same effect . . . "' But in other cases, religious cases included, he says, 'The whole *weight* may be in the picture' (*LRB*, pp. 71–2). For example, belief in the Last Judgment is not the expression of an attitude concerning morality which, as it happens, is expressed on this occasion in this way. On the contrary, belief in the Last Judgment makes morality something different from what it would be otherwise.[14]

Wittgenstein's remarks show how different he is from those non-realists, such as the late Bishop of Woolwich, who argue that religious beliefs are simply the outward forms of attitudes which can survive their demise. The forms of the religious beliefs may change, but, it is claimed, the attitude which the successive beliefs express remains the same. Wittgenstein, on the other hand, is insisting that the whole weight may be in the picture. In that case, the loss of the picture may constitute the loss of what is essential in a belief. When a picture is lost, a truth may be lost which cannot be replaced. This is a far cry from the view of Wittgenstein as a non-realist who sees religious beliefs as expressive attitudes which have no necessary relation to the object of the belief. It is in the use of the picture that the relation of belief to its object is to be understood. It is this use, this method of projection, which the realist ignores. What Wittgenstein is trying to do is not to get the realist to embrace non-realism. Rather, he is trying to get him to look in a certain direction, to our actions and practices, where religious belief has its sense. For example, Wittgenstein says:

Religion teaches us that the soul can exist when the body has disintegrated. Now do I understand this teaching? – Of course I understand it – I can imagine plenty of things in connexion with it.

And haven't pictures of these things been painted? And why should such a picture be only an imperfect rendering of the spoken doctrine?

Why should it not do the *same* service as the words? And it is the service which is the point.

(*PI*, 178)

III

For the realist, as we have seen, belief in God is presupposed by the religious life which is seen as the fruits of the belief. The belief is said to be cognitive, and the religious life is said to be its expressive consequences. The challenge to realism is to give an account of its conception of belief. It must be remembered that the realist is claiming to show what *the essence* of believing in God is. The religious life, it is suggested, desirable though it may be, is secondary by comparison.

In one attempt to show that it makes sense to speak of believing in God without reference to any affective state or attitude in the believer, realists refer to the belief that devils are supposed to have. Clearly, the devils do not worship. So here, it seems, we have a case of belief without the fruits of belief. In relation to God, however, affective states and attitudes range from love and worship, to hate and rebellion. In the case of the devils, although the affective state present is not that of worship, an affective state is clearly present nevertheless. As Penelhum has to admit, the devils believe and *tremble*. This is not the kind of example the realist is looking for.

Let us remind ourselves, again, of the realist's claim. He is arguing that belief must not be equated with its fruits. Believing in God, on his view, is logically independent of any role it plays in the religious life. My criticism has been that this is tantamount to trying to give an account of the relation of belief to its object, without reference to *any* method of projection. It may be argued, however, that this conclusion is premature.[15] What the realist is urging, it may be said, is not that the essence of religious belief can be understood without reference to a method of projection, but that the method of projection involved does not feature the characteristic commitments of the religious life. As we have seen, this is too generous to the philosophical implications of realism, but let us suppose the objection stands. What then? The essence of religious belief may then be compared to those *minimal* beliefs which can be found in every walk of life. Notice, however, that 'I believe in God', in its essence, is said, by the realist, to be presupposed by what believing in God amounts to *in the religious life*. Thus, the *essence* of believing in God would, on this view, be a *minimal* belief. Let us examine the implications of this suggestion.

If we forge too close a link between belief and commitment, it is argued, we shall find ourselves denying a host of ordinary beliefs. Consider, for example, 'I believe that "elm" is the name of a tree'. It certainly does not follow from this that I can pick out an elm. To say that 'I believe in God' involves some affective state or attitude, is like arguing that 'I believe "elm" is the name of a tree' involves the ability to pick out an elm. Is this so? The aim of the argument is to show that just as we should not deny that someone believes that 'elm' is the name of a tree just because he cannot pick out an elm, so we should not deny that the indifferent and the apathetic believe in God when they say they believe in Him simply because their belief involves no affective state or attitude of a religious kind. In short, you can have belief without commitment.

In replying to this argument, the first thing to remember is that, in relation to each example of belief, there is an appropriate method of projection which gives it its sense. 'I believe "elm" is the name of a tree' is not a watered-down version of 'I believe this is an elm'. It need involve little more than believing what one has been told about trees. It must be remembered, however, that this involves one's acquaintance with trees and conventions of naming. The grammar of talk about trees and naming operates as a background to the belief, minimal though it is. The person would have to be able to pick out trees. One has not dispensed with a method of projection. One cannot do that with *any* kind of belief. This is true of a belief which is even more minimal. Suppose someone says, 'I believe there are trees' when he is entirely unacquainted with trees. He is looking forward to seeing his first tree, or his first picture of a tree. Here, what his belief amounts to has its sense within the context of his acquaintance with physical objects, with descriptions of physical objects, and with acquiring knowledge of new physical objects. Someone may say, 'I believe there's something called "trees", but I don't know what it is'. This is simply a confession that there is something the person believes he can find out about, but its grammar, as yet, is unspecified. As a result, what believing in it would amount to is, as yet, also unspecified.

When we try to apply these examples to religious belief, we see how differences emerge. If someone says, 'I believe in God', we still have to ask what the belief amounts to in his life. I knew a person who became upset if someone called him an atheist, or when he heard that someone else was an atheist. But what did *that* amount to? Nothing more, in this case, than a kind of feeling of respectability which was shocked from time to time in the way described. This is hardly the essence of 'believing' which the realist seeks for, one said to be presupposed by religious commitment. What if someone says 'I believe in God but, as yet, I am completely unacquainted with him'? I suppose that could be construed as meaning that I believe there is something in religion which is there to become acquainted with. Once again, however, in this case, the grammar of the 'something' in question and what becoming acquainted with it would involve is, as yet, entirely unspecified. Again, this cannot be the essence of belief the realist is searching for. Of course, in the case of trees, someone may believe they exist and be entirely indifferent to the facts. But that does not mean that the sense of the belief is unmediated in a method of projection. On the contrary, the belief has its sense in our talk about physical objects, a familiar feature of which is our indifference to the existence of many of them. But if we want to treat 'I believe in God, but I couldn't care less' in *this* way, that presupposes treating 'God' as a substantive and saying that one is indifferent to the existence of the 'something' it 'stands for'. We have already seen, however, that this is to import an alien grammar into our language concerning God. To make *this* assertion of God's existence the essence of believing, the realist would have to show otherwise: he would have to show that that grammar is appropriate.

When we turn from the futile search for this minimal sense of belief back to the paradigm of religious belief which has its home in religious life, we see that to say 'I believe in God' is to make a confession. Believing is called a virtue, and failing to believe a sin. Believing is something capable of growth, and this growth is said to be the increasing presence of God in one's life. Yet, this is the paradigm realists ignore. The realist would like to say that, whether believing plays any significant role in a person's life or not, he can simply believe that there is a God. But this 'simply believing' has, as yet, been given no application. One recalls Wittgenstein's response we have already quoted: 'But the question is: What would the practical effects of this belief be? – Perhaps someone says: "That's not the point. A belief is what it is whether it has any practical effects or not." One thinks: It is the same adjustment of the human mind anyway' (*OC*, p. 89). For Trigg, to emphasise 'the practical effects' implies that 'beliefs are not really beliefs at all. They are the frills on a commitment to a certain way of life, instead of the justification for it' (p. 36). What we have seen is that by ignoring the role of belief in human life, realism is left either with its conception of belief as a mental state, a philosophical chimera, or with a minimal conception of belief which provides, not the essence of believing the realist seeks, but, at best, deviations, distortions and approximations, when compared with what really believing in God involves.

The realist offers a further consideration in favour of denying that we find what is involved in believing in God by looking to the role the belief plays in people's lives. Trigg seems to think that emphasising this role entails denying that God existed before men. Trigg says:

> The existence of God is in no way dependent on our individual or collective thoughts of Him. This is an indispensable part of the concept of the Christian God. Part at least of the notion of God as Creator must involve the belief that God existed when men did not. It is obvious, too, that the very idea of God being limited by being dependent on anything or anybody must be incoherent.
>
> (p. 89)

But where does Trigg have to turn to find out what is meant by calling God our Creator, or to find out what is meant by saying that God existed before men? To that very context of Christian thought and practice which he seems to think does not allow us, by appealing to it, to say these things. But Trigg must not take for granted the grammar of believing in God as a Creator, or the sense of saying that God existed before man. That grammar has to be explored.

It is part of our talk about mountains that we say that they existed before men. It is not part of our talk about banking to say that it existed before men. Banking is a human institution created by men. Within religion, things are said about God of a time which precedes man's existence. That does not mean that God existed before men in the sense in which mountains, rainbows or rivers did. These are all empirical phenomena and my beliefs concerning their prior existence allow me to ask questions about what they looked like, how long they had existed, whether some of these empirical phenomena have ceased to exist, and so on. Nothing of this sort makes any sense where God's reality is concerned. That being the case, these examples cannot throw any light on the religious beliefs. What kind of language do we hear in these beliefs? Here is an example: 'The earth was without form, and void; and darkness was upon the face of the deep . . . the Spirit of God moved upon the face of the waters.' That is not like saying that any kind of object moved on the face of the waters. We know that from the way we might speak *now* of a place being filled with God's presence, or of God being found in the deep. Ask yourself what might lead you to speak in this way, or what disagreement about this way of talking might amount to. What is it to curse God's presence in all things, and why is it that if we spit in his face we can't miss? If these religious utterances can be said with meaning, why not the words in Genesis? True, those words, referring to the time they do, have an added dimension, as do Simone Weil's words when, drawing a contrast with perceived beauty, she said, 'The forest is at its most beautiful when there is no one looking at it.' It is important to note, however, one further major difference in the religious example of God being before man. The 'before' involved, unlike the case of mountains, rivers, etc., is not a temporal 'before'. We are told: 'Before the mountains were brought forth, or even thou hadst formed the earth and the world, from everlasting to everlasting, thou art God.' All things have their meaning in God, for the believer. That is why God is not a maker, but a creator. The sense of these religious beliefs is not given independently of the method of projection in which they have their natural home. Realism distorts that natural setting.

One concluding point. Philosophers who are realists think of themselves as the defenders of the real. The final irony is that they, like some of their non-realist opponents, can give no account of the assurance often found in real belief. Realists are foundationalists, for whom beliefs never yield certainty. Belief is a second best to knowledge. But it has always been an embarrassment to foundationalists that their analyses obviously fail to capture the primary language of faith.[16] They cannot capture the conviction involved in a confession of faith. Penelhum and Trigg, along with other foundationalists, turn the conviction into mere probability. Wittgenstein illustrates the ludicrous result:

Suppose someone were a believer and said: 'I believe in a Last Judgment,' and I said: 'Well, I'm not so sure. Possibly.' You would say that there is an enormous gulf between us. If he said 'There is a German aeroplane overhead,' and I said 'Possibly, I'm not so sure,' you'd say we were fairly near.

(LRB, p. 53)

Wittgenstein points out that if their ideal conditions were realised, so that foundationalists wouldn't be dependent on probabilities any longer, what comes to pass wouldn't be what is expressed in the religious belief.

> Suppose, for instance, we know people who foresaw the future; make forecasts for years and years ahead; and they described some sort of Judgment Day. Queerly enough, even if there were such a thing, and even if it were more convincing than I have described, belief in this happening wouldn't be at all a religious belief. Suppose that I would have to forego all pleasures because of such a forecast. If I do so and so, someone will put me in fires in a thousand years, etc. I wouldn't budge. The best scientific evidence is just nothing.

(LRB, p. 56)

Penelhum and Trigg play with probabilities. Penelhum admits that the lack of the epistemic certainty he seeks affects the character of religious believing:

> But it is quite clear, I think, that if one lacks certainty, even if one considers the beliefs one has to have a good measure of probability, this lack cannot fail to have the result of making trust less *unreserved*, and making the faith to a marked degree a matter of acting-as-if, that is, a matter of resolution.

(p. 179)

Trigg speaks in the same way, and makes similar admissions. He says:

> . . . a faith does not imply certainty. It is much more a determination to remain committed in spite of apparent difficulties . . . There is no contradiction in my facing up to the possibility that my beliefs may be mistaken, while in the meantime holding firmly to my faith. I can be totally committed and at the same time admit that I might be wrong. I am however basing my life on the assumption that I am not.

(p. 55)

Contrast with this Wittgenstein's remarks:

> Also, there is this extraordinary use of the word 'believe'. One talks of believing and at the same time one doesn't use 'believe' as one does ordinarily. You might say (in the normal use): 'You only believe – oh well . . . ' Here it is used entirely differently: on the other hand it is not used as we generally use the word 'know'.
>
> (*LRB*, pp. 59–60)

Here is one central expression of religious belief: 'He that loveth not knoweth not God: for God is love . . . No man hath seen God at any time. If we love one another, God dwelleth in us, and his love is perfected in us. Hereby know we that we dwell in him, and he in us, because he hath given us of his Spirit.' In Penelhum's and Trigg's hands, this testimony becomes merely the consequence of belief, not to be confused with the essence of belief. That essence of belief, in turn, is said to be devoid of certainty, being a matter of acting as if there were a God, or acting on the assumption that one is not mistaken about this. What has happened to the God who is said to dwell in men and in whom they are said to dwell? It is the realist who severs belief from its object. Such severance is unavoidable, since realism ignores the method of projection in which the relation between religious belief and its object has its sense.[17]

Notes

1. Terence Penelhum, *God and Skepticism* (The Netherlands: Reidel, 1983), p. 161.
2. Roger Trigg, *Reason and Commitment* (Cambridge University Press, 1973), p. 75. All quotations from Penelhum and Trigg are from these two works cited.
3. Wittgenstein, *Zettel* (Oxford: Blackwell, 1967).
4. Wittgenstein, *Remarks on the Philosophy of Psychology*, Vol. I, (Oxford: Blackwell, 1980) p. 485.
5. Wittgenstein, *Lectures and Conversations on Aesthetics, Psychology and Religious Belief* (Oxford: Blackwell, 1966).
6. D.Z. Phillips, *The Concept of Prayer* (Oxford: Blackwell, 1981), pp. 142–50.
7. Wittgenstein, *Lectures on the Foundations of Mathematics* (New York: Ithaca, 1976), p. 136.
8. Wittgenstein, *Philosophical Investigations* (Oxford: Blackwell, 1953), I: 578.

9.   Wittgenstein, *On Certainty* (Oxford, Blackwell, 1979), p. 89.
10.   Rush Rhees, 'Religion and Language', in *Without Answers* (London: Routledge, 1969), pp. 127–8.
11.   R.B. Braithwaite, 'An Empiricist's View of the Nature of Religious Belief', in B. Mitchell (ed.), *The Philosophy of Religion* (Oxford University Press, 1971).
12.   D.Z. Phillips, *Death and Immortality* (London: Macmillan, 1970), pp. 54–5.
13.   See D.Z. Phillips, *Religion Without Explanation* (Oxford: Blackwell, 1982), pp. 140–5.
14.   Cf. Peter Winch, 'Wittgenstein: Picture and Representation', in *Trying To Make Sense* (Oxford: Blackwell, 1987). I have benefited a great deal from this paper and from discussing its wider implications for the philosophy of religion with Peter Winch.
15.   The consideration of this argument was necessitated by probing questions put to me by my colleague H.O. Mounce.
16.   See D.Z. Phillips, *Faith After Foundationalism* (London: Routledge, 1988), Chapter One.
17.   I am grateful to Timothy Tessin for proofreading my contributions to this volume.

Saying is Believing

ALFRED LOUCH

What is a realist? Professor Hick has obligingly listed the familiar protagonists bearing the realist label or its opposite: the realist as opposed to the phenomenalist or idealist, for example, or to the nominalist. He readily admits that, when he calls himself and his allies 'realists', and Professor Phillips and his friends non-realists, he does not suppose himself to be taking a position different from theirs on what is perceived or whether concepts are real. *Amici curiae* filed by Berkeley, Price or Austin and by Plato or Roscellinus would be of little help in defining the controversy he takes to exist between himself, as realist, and various non-realist foes.

It is useful to know where not to start. But alas knowing that some signposts are misleading is not at all the same as knowing which among the remaining arrows point in the right direction. My remarks are therefore attempts to see what exactly is at issue, if anything. The labour is worth it if one assumes that where there's smoke, there's fire.

Perhaps Professor Hick can guide us a step further. God is an object, he says, or more politely, the concept of God is referential. Phillips, as well as others of the non-realist camp, he tells us, do not share this view. But Hick's quarrel with Phillips is not really about referentiality, but whether Phillips can say he believes in God unless he admits that God is an entity. Atheists of course deny that God is an entity. But no one can deny this and assume the mantle of faith. Non-realists say they believe, but they don't. They're mistaken, or worse dishonest.

When can we say a person doesn't really believe even though he says he believes? The accused in a murder case protests 'I really did believe the mushrooms were edible.' Can the jury be expected to buy that? After all, the accused was a world authority in the field of mycology; could such a person believe that *amanita phalloides* were edible? If so, why didn't he have some himself then?

Your child says, 'There's a bogeyman in the corner of my room.' You say, 'Nonsense, there's nothing to be afraid of.' But the child persists. There's nothing there, you say, dispelling the shadows with your lantern, meaning – maybe – 'You see, you don't *really* believe

. . . ' Believing the mycologist guilty, you won't allow that he believes. Wanting to get to bed yourself, you dismiss the child's
fancies.

Does this bear on the topic of this volume? Have we gathered
together to probe the authenticity of our convictions? If so, we want
to know whether our beliefs are sincerely held, not whether they
entail accepted chunks of reality. You may ask, how could anyone in
the twentieth-century believe that God would turn the hurricane
away from Pat Robertson's church and allow it to devastate New
York instead. This is not a doubt as to whether, for Robertson, God
is an entity.

So what can it mean to say belief must have an object – or,
contrariwise, to assert that beliefs are free floating, detached from
referential moorings? My stories do not support either claim, but
point rather to the naturalness of either response depending on the
context and the conversation.

Generally it's rude to say, 'You don't *really* believe.' 'I believe
there's beer in the fridge,' I say, 'Help yourself.' You don't find any.
But you don't say to me, you didn't really believe after all. Still, if I
believe there's beer in the fridge I must know what a bottle of beer
looks like. If I said 'I believe there's beer there,' but couldn't pick a
Worthington out of a line-up including a hawk and a handsaw,
you'd rightly and indignantly say, 'You don't know what you're
talking about.' Does that win the day against Phillips? Well, some
beliefs are certainly about things.

But then: 'I believe God's in His Heaven, all's right with the
world,' and someone says, 'Pick God out of the line-up.' 'Well,' you
say, 'it's none of the above.' (Was God in wind, the earthquake, the
fire?) You don't mean, do you, that 'I believe in God' is like 'I believe
there's beer in the fridge'? But perhaps that is what Hick means.
Certainly Phillips denies it, but not because he denies, grandiosely,
that beliefs are referential, but because he says, sensibly, it all
depends.

But below the confusing talk about objects and reference one
senses a deeper aim. Hick wants to say Phillips can't get away with
claiming to believe in God. 'You can't fool us Phillips', I hear Hick
saying, 'when you talk about God moving upon the face of the
waters. You don't believe in God, you only believe in your feelings
aroused by the view of Swansea Bay from your study window.'
Phillips asks: well then, what must I do to be believed that I believe?
You must admit 'God exists' is a proposition, Hick says, and accept
the responsibility for proving it.

What a shocking thing. I would have thought it impious for believers to treat God's existence as a hypothesis. But it is also odd to think beliefs in general are hypotheses, though a hypothesis is undoubtedly something that can be believed. An anthropologist hears his informant say: there's a dragon in the forest.[1] The informant, Filate, says: go kill it please, indicating thereby his faith in the white man's superior firepower. The anthropologist temporises: we white men may have superior firepower, but we're not so good at tracking dragons. Ah, we say, reading his confessions, *that* Sperber – he doesn't believe in the dragon. And he doesn't believe Filate believes either.

Filate, he thinks, is putting him on, teasing him a bit, knowing how serious these nosy anthropologists are. (See how they take everything down in their notebooks, or record it on their infernal tapes?)

Well of course there's no dragon, so you try to size up the informant, thinking that the claimed belief in the dragon might be a ploy. I am absolutely sure (the child says, hand over breast) I did not so much as put my hand in the cookie jar. One element in your scepticism of belief affirmations is, no doubt, your conviction that no dragon exists or that cookies do not disappear without someone taking them. (Realism?) But you don't challenge the belief unless you also suspect motives. It is then not conceptually difficult to accept that someone believes X in the absence of X, or in the possibility (for you) of imagining X. 'Crazy old Queen,' Alice could have said, 'she really does manage to believe six contradictions before breakfast,' just as the more modestly deranged believe the earth is flat, or that we ought to get the TV crews ready to cover the Second Coming.

Filate does *look* frightened as he gazes at the forest. Indeed, the sense of danger gets to Sperber as well – for isn't the dragon in the forest, however we picture it, or whether or not we can picture it, the expression of our dread, just as the view of Swansea Bay is expressed by 'the spirit of God moves upon the waters'. 'Ah, look at this beatific smile,' you say, looking at Phillips. There are objects to be seen – the darkness of the forest, the glimpse of the leopard. But Filate need no have a view as to whether the dragon is green or red, scaly or slimy, bipedal or quadrupedal. He really had no idea of a beast answering to a particular material description at all. Nor would it be quite right to say his belief is his fear, for he, like all vulnerable human creatures, has many fears. There is something special about this fear, not a free-floating anxiety of a sort familiar to psychoanalysts, but a fear, and a belief, directed toward and evoked by the forest, the darkness at the horizon of the world. The dragon is not an object like the crocodile, a leopard or python. But the believer moves by means of such vivid presences to a conception of those empty places beyond (tendentious adverb), though connected with, a world of comfortable (and uncomfortable) bodies. The forest is there, a palpable limit to understanding but an equally palpable source of fear. The sea is there too, suggesting a no less awesome if more benign account of the limits of experience. Kants' emotions, as he stands in awe of the starry heavens, should be accepted as offered: does anyone have a more referentially transparent conception of their belief in God's existence?

Realists, I think, do not like poetry. They are not content to accept a conception of religious belief which, so to speak, attaches laterally to the essential furniture of the world. They want a vertical reference of propositions about God to the thing itself – oblique ties to the material world and to human practices won't do. We're all realists, they say, when it comes to the beer in the fridge or the microbes in the milk. So proper religious convictions must have the same form. Is God then a spatio-temporal being? If non-realists protest this absurdity by offering a counter-theory, they appear to argue that convictions and the world are unrelated, as if we could believe in dragons in the forest without an experience of the forest.

But Phillips doesn't mean to offer a *theory* of belief. He wants to show that realists, who claim that religious beliefs are like other beliefs, affirm something incoherent, that all beliefs are alike in some significant way, by, for example, standing in some particular relation to objects. Notorious difficulties in stating a coherent and viable theory of reference are simply ignored. 'Beliefs have objects' thus becomes comfortably vacuous.

And anyway, 'God exists' is not, for the realist, like 'there's beer in the fridge' at all. For otherwise a smart alec like Nikita Kruschev could shame them into atheism by reporting that his astronauts didn't find God, just as we had to say there's no beer in the fridge after all. You don't believe in God at all, the realists say, if you can admit he may *not* be there. Perhaps this is only a way of expressing the depth of their conviction. But no, that won't do. For then Phillips could be allowed his affirmation of faith by speaking of the spirit of God moving upon the waters. Realists seem to be serious in saying that it is inconceivable that what they believe does not exist. Is this a new version of the ontological argument? I can't really believe in

God unless God's real. I believe in God therefore God is real. But then, is God an object, an entity, or is that concept necessarily contingent? I can be most profoundly convinced that beer is in the fridge, yet the fridge is empty.

If believing God exists entails the existence of God, it no longer makes sense to say that the belief has an object. But besides, imagine Jesus saying: Ah, Thomas, if I showed you that the reality of God follows logically from believing him, would you then believe? Thinking this way about religious belief has clearly gone off the rails.

Have we missed something still? Perhaps realists mean only that we should be required to test our faith, by fire or by verifying procedures. Realism is, as it were, *how* you put your faith on the line. By contrast, Wittgensteinian talk (Phillips's talk) about language games is a cheap way of claiming the right to religious belief: all you have to do is show how your prayers, hymns, chants and sacrifices hang together, requiring no authentication outside of chapel. Non-realist worshippers merely say, in Phillips's engaging image, 'Welcome, come and see for yourself.' They invite the passer-by heading for the pub or the football match to share their practice.

I smell Calvinism in the realist's repudiation of this approach. Faith does not cost enough this way. Phillips, they say, we simply won't let you say you believe in God. You aren't serious, you're trying to have the rewards without paying for them. Your way makes it too easy to say 'I believe'.

But how should it be harder? In times of persecution it would be harder of course. There are those – we know their type – who express their beliefs ostentatiously within the community of believers, but on the street burn incense to the emperor. Does such a person *really* believe? It depends, doesn't it, on how much you trust your fellow communicants, and how forgiving you are prepared to be. But anyway that test is no longer available. What Hick offers in its place is a dominant conception of what it is to know and what is worthy of being believed – the sort of thing physicists do, and how they do it. So if I say I believe in God, and Hick asks me to put it on the line, I don't take an oath or risk my life in affirming my faith. Instead I subject my beliefs to the conditions of the prevailing epistemology. Somehow 'God exists' is like 'the proton exists', 'like' in the sense that evidence ought to be sought, and should be forthcoming.

Two thoughts about this. It would grossly misinterpret Wittgenstein to suppose that he sought to justify religious faith by seal-

ing it off as a different language game from the prevailing epistemology. He asked, I believe, about the role played by faith among those
who subscribe to standards of scientific rationality. This is an anthropological, not a theological question. I cannot see that he had a
secret theological agenda.

The other point. An observer of the dialogue embodied in this
volume perhaps thinking along these lines was bewildered as to
what the participants really believed. He understood, you see, the
power of liturgy and icons, the movement of prayer or prostration.
But talking about 'God exists' as a proposition, for which evidence
or proof might be forthcoming, struck him as an odd exercise for the
faithful. What you fail to see, I said, is that discussion like this *is* their
religious practice. For how, in affirming their faith, can they juggle
their baggage of protestant abstractions and their commitment to the
up-to-date worlds of laboratory and market? Some worship through
song or prayer, others through argument.

Note

1.   The story about to be told is borrowed from Dan Sperber, 'Apparently
      Irrational Beliefs', in Martin Hollis and Steven Lukes (eds), *Rationality
      and Relativism* (Cambridge, Mass.: MIT Press, 1982), pp. 149–80.

Believing – And Having True Beliefs

JOHN HICK

Mr Phillips has written powerfully and eloquently against the idea that belief is a mental state unconnected with our actions and dispositions to act. On the contrary, he says, to hold a belief is in large part to behave in a certain way, or to be in a dispositional state to behave in that way, or range of ways. And I for one entirely agree with this. I think that belief is largely dispositional. And so to believe in the reality of a loving God who is the ultimate lord of the universe is not only to *think* that God is real but also to live on that basis, worshipping God, trusting in God even amidst life's hardships and tragedies, seeing other human beings as God's children, experiencing one's life as being lived in the presence of God, expecting the ultimate fulfilment of God's loving purposes. To believe in God and yet live as though there is no God is not genuinely to believe in God. All this seems to me to be entirely true and very important.

But Mr Phillips has the astonishing idea that religious realism is the denial of this! He thinks that religious realism is the view that there need be no connection between believing that God exists and the manifestation of that belief in people's lives. But there is absolutely no reason why a religious realist should not regard believing as largely dispositional. There is no reason why a religious realist should hold that belief is a mental state unrelated to our actions, emotions and practical dispositions. Religious realist and non-realist are equally free to adopt a dispositional account of belief.

But we need to distinguish between what it is to have a certain belief, and what it is for that belief to be *true*. Mr Phillips seems to assume that for a religious belief to be true is for it to be believed, so that for God to exist consists in human beings believing in God and behaving appropriately. At this point a religious realist does differ, profoundly, with Mr Phillips. Religious realism is the view that the existence or non-existence of God is a fact independent of whether you or I or anyone else believes that God exists. If God exists, God is not simply an idea or ideal in our minds, but an ontological reality, the ultimate creative power of the universe.

115

And the reason why so much of Mr Phillips's discussion is not relevant to this issue is that it is a different issue from the one that he discusses, namely whether authentically religious belief in God involves commitment and affects a person's whole life.

Changing Our Beliefs: A Response to D.Z. Phillips

DON CUPITT

Suppose that a serviceman unexpectedly fails to return from the war. At first his wife imagines that he is merely delayed and will soon appear. Nor is this belief without some confirmation, for his last letters are still arriving, and a comrade telephones with a message from him promising a speedy return. At this stage her friends do not doubt that her belief that he is alive is a straightforwardly factual belief that may be vindicated. Its empirical status is still being sustained by plausible arguments and scraps of evidence.

But he does not come. Months, and then years, roll by. The scraps of tangible evidence have long ceased to come in, and the reasons for hoping that he may yet be alive have grown weaker and weaker. But his wife – or widow – refuses to give up hope. She remains a realist about her own faith, because to her it seems that her belief that her husband is still alive is as much a factual conviction as ever it was. Because she has been morally *constant*, she thinks she can claim to be *logically* constant. But, alas, moral constancy cannot secure logical constancy in this way – as is only too obvious to her friends. Perhaps twenty or thirty years have gone by; at any rate, a time eventually comes when they are forced to conclude that her commitment is expressive rather than factual (and perhaps none the less admirable for that). Her faith expresses her virtues and intentions; it keeps her spirits up and gives her a reason for living. It is autonomous; indeed, it has *perforce* become autonomous, because it is no longer sustained by external arguments and scraps of evidence in the way it was when it began. But it works; it makes sense to her, and it makes sense of her life. Nothing will persuade her to give it up.

However, there is in this situation a slight embarrassment. The woman is a realist, but her friends take a non-realist view of her faith. The gap makes her friends feel bad about having to humour one whom they sincerely admire. They themselves are sometimes a little unsure whether she is a faithful Penelope, or has become slightly crazed. But a philosopher friend named Dewi comes to their rescue by explaining that indeed she really *does* believe that her husband is still alive, that the belief makes excellent sense in terms of the part it plays in her life, and that because it *presently* unifies her life around certain virtues and little daily practices it stands on its own feet. Harking back to the distant time when her belief had a more factual status is unnecessary, as well as unkind. Indeed, it might well be argued that as all empirical support has dropped away her faith has become purer, more disinterested and morally more beautiful. Completely non-factual faith is truly supernatural faith.

Along these lines he who thinks that it is not a philosopher's job to *change* things, may seek to remove the slight discomfort caused by the gap between the woman's view of her own faith and her friends' view of it. His aim is therapeutic. But, we may ask, is he doing her a good turn, or not? Perhaps she has another friend who says to her, 'Sooner or later you must remake your life. Do not imagine that to do so would be disloyal to him. You still bear his name, and he remains in your heart . . . '

6

Religious Beliefs, Their Point and Their Reference

JOHN H. WHITTAKER

Most beliefs have a point. This is a commonplace observation about beliefs, but it hides much that is philosophically problematic, and it is surprising that philosophers have left this aspect of believing largely unattended. The point of a belief consists of its *implications*, not implications about the truth or falsity of other propositions which follow from it but implications about what believing in it amounts to. The point of a belief is what one adheres to when one *abides* by a belief, or what one follows when one accepts its truth. To take a familiar example, one abides by the belief that nature is uniform by treating natural phenomena as instances of lawlike regularities. Conforming one's expectations to this pattern of explanation is what believing in the truth of the principle amounts to. Similarly, we abide by the belief in the unconscious by explaining human behaviour in terms of motives of which the agents themselves are unaware. The belief suggests this novel form of explanation, and we follow this pattern in keeping to its point. No doubt these examples are oversimplified. There may be more than one aspect to a belief's point, and a belief might have to be considered in relation to other beliefs before its point becomes clear. But at least the examples show us that there are beliefs that we do not understand unless we realise that their affirmation entails a corresponding reorganisation in our thinking. If one lacks this understanding, we say that he or she has failed to grasp the point of a belief.

Religious beliefs are prime examples of pointed beliefs – and this feature of their logic should not be passed over lightly. When the implications of this idea are fully spelled out, the philosophical controversy over realism and non-realism in religion tends to disappear. Because religious beliefs are logically inseparable from their points, a belief cannot be properly understood unless its point is grasped. And until a belief is properly understood, its 'reference' cannot be made out and the conditions for its truth cannot be specified in any but a formal way. One can say that the referents of the belief must be 'real' if the belief is to be true, but without understanding the point of the belief at issue, one cannot say what this 'reality' entails. Just as the human will must be 'real' if we are to believe that human's have a will, there must be a real God if we are to believe that there is a God. But this says *nothing ontologically* about what the will is, nor does it say anything about what God is. The necessity of the will's 'real existence' and of God's 'real existence' is a purely formal point which might be made of any truth claim (*p* is true only if *p* is really the case). The realism/non-realism issue conflates this formal point with ontological claims about the nature of God's reality.

That is the point which I want to make in this essay. But since confusion runs high on this matter, we need to be careful about the way in which the argument is put.

The notion of a belief's point, for example, is ambiguous. In one sense of the word 'point', an assertion might be used for a purpose which is quite independent of its meaning. I might say, 'it's cold in here,' and the point of my saying this might be to get someone else to close the door to the room. Whether or not the assertion is put to this use has nothing to do with its meaning. One might understand the meaning of the assertion without realising that he was being asked to close the door. So in this sense of the word 'point', one need not understand the point of a belief to understand its meaning. But there is another sense of the word 'point' which concerns a belief's *logical* analysis. The illustrations which I just gave are good examples. To suppose that a person might have hidden motives for behaviour is largely what it *means* to believe in the human unconscious, so that a person who professed belief in the unconscious but did not abide by this aspect of the belief's sense would be missing the point. In such cases, the meaning of the belief is internally related to its point, and one must see the point of a belief in order to understand its meaning. Everything that I have to say about beliefs and their points presumes this logical connection. The determination of a belief's point is a determination of its sense.

I suspect that all beliefs must have a point of this kind, but it will do for our purposes to stress that *regulative* beliefs have points of this sort. To accept a 'regulative' belief one must not only assent to its truth but must also bring one's thinking and practice into conform-ity with the regulative ideal which it represents. At least one must understand what it would mean to do so and intend to conform to the belief's regulative force. Thus, if one agrees with the movie actress Shirley Maclaine that nothing happens by chance, one must know how to conform to the intent of this belief as a governing ideal. Presumably, every event whatsoever must be explicable in principle, although I suspect that the actual point of this belief is more modest than this. The belief may cover only *coincidental* events, and its point may be that such accidents are not really accidental, i.e. that they have an explanatory ground in our subconscious life and that we are responsible for their occurrence. In any case, one needs to understand the force of this belief, or the 'regulation' which it intends in our thinking, before one can see the point of affirming it.

Such regulative beliefs might also be described – in fact, might better be described – as 'principles'.[1] The basic principles in any area of discourse establish the form which explanation is to take in the relevant field of concern. The claim that all behaviour represents an attempt to reduce anxiety is obviously a principle in this sense, since it tells us what is to count as a psychological explanation of our action. But so too is the behaviourist's claim that a human being has no soul, since this belongs to the behaviourist's programme of denying mentalistic explanations of human behaviour. These two principles put different strictures on what counts as a proper explanation in psychology.

Generally speaking, such principles differ from hypotheses in that they determine both the form that explanation is to assume and the way that evidence is construed in substantiating that form. Thus, there is a difference in the justification of principles and hypotheses. To justify a principle one needs to show that the form of explanation which it underwrites is appropriate to the world, i.e. that it leads to genuine understanding. To justify a hypothesis one simply has to assemble a sufficient amount of the relevant evidence, assuming that the question of what counts as evidence is not at issue. The justification of hypotheses, therefore, is relatively straightforward: their truth or falsity depends on evidence. But the justification of principles is more complex, since evidence cannot be used to substantiate the principles which define them without begging the question.[2]

For the most part, religious beliefs are principles. Not only is the possible justification of religious claims as obscure as the justification of principles, but the role that these beliefs play is comparable to the regulative role of principles. The adoption of religious beliefs determines the way in which the phenomena of life are regarded, so that the 'evidence' that illustrates a religious doctrine's truth is construed in accordance with it before being presented. Take the belief that everyone is a child of God, for example. This belief teaches us to look upon other people from a higher vantage point, beyond the perspectives we ordinarily invoke when we judge them. Thus, believers are never to say that a certain wicked person is beyond the reach of concern, no matter how bad he might be. The perspective that we use in assigning guilt is to be supplement by a higher view which remains open to love, forgiveness, mercy, etc. To believe that we are the children of God is to be prepared to elevate one's vantage point in this way. Yet to defend this belief on evidential grounds, one can only point to people and invite others to construe them in the same way. We cannot first discover that someone deserves forgiveness regardless of his sins and then present this as an independent discovery that bears out the belief. Discovering that one deserves forgiveness and believing that we are all children of God come to the same thing. One discovers such a thing *in adopting the belief*.

Assessing the worth of oneself and others from this higher vantage point is part of what it means to believe in God. It is part of the *point* of belief. Consequently, if one were to ask what *sort* of judgment followed from the adoption of the religious principles we've been discussing, the answer would be in part: *assessments of worth*. That is the particular kind of regard which is enjoined by belief. The believer who faithfully adheres to the belief in God does not allow judgments about another's worth or one's own worth to come to closure in condemnations. Nor does one allow one's own judgments about the purpose of life to end in nihilistic denunciations. Instead, the believer holds on to a sense of life's value even in the face of its unrelieved sufferings and unabated evils. At least this is what a Judaeo-Christian believer does. In maintaining the existence of a divine being, a faithful person maintains the unshakable conviction that his own miserable and sinful life, and that of his neighbour, might nonetheless be hallowed.

If this point is inseparable from the meaning of such teachings, then I see no alternative to describing these beliefs as *evaluative* or *teleological* principles. I see no alternative, in other words, to saying that the *reference* of the belief in God is teleological. Just as moral beliefs about goodness refer to the good, teleological principles of ultimate worth refer to ultimate value, the source of meaning for believers. The belief in God seems to refer to an entity, but teleological judgments of purpose are separable from this metaphysical assumption just as moral judgments are separable from the notion of a divine lawgiver. God, in other words, does not refer to an entity whose existence or non-existence is prior to the evaluative implications which are ordinarily supposed to follow from it. The belief in Gods is teleological through and through, meaning that there is no distinction between the object to which 'God' refers and the teleological implications which the existence of this 'object' has. The claim that God exists is a teleological principle governing a whole range of assessments which believers are to make about their lives, and the referent of this principle must be described *in the same language in which its point is described*. If it has an evaluative point, then its referent must belong to the field of evaluative 'objects'. If this point is teleological, its content cannot be descriptive.

The view of theistic language which I am suggesting may seem reminiscent of the account of religious language offered by R.B. Braithwaite,[3] but it is actually quite different. Braithwaite treats Christian doctrines as if they were stories designed to motivate moral commitments by vivifying the intention of these commitments. To the extent that these 'stories' might be used for other purposes, e.g. entertainment, the point that they bear in reinforcing the moral commitments of believers is *separable* from their sense. The point that they have in reinforcing moral commitments is *not* the kind of sense that regulative beliefs have in *shaping* the judgments which follow from them. Thus, according to Braithwaite, there is no essential connection between religious beliefs and the evaluative regard that they entail. This relation is accidental, contrary to the view that I am presenting.

The kind of evaluation involved in religion, moreover, is strictly *moral* according to Braithwaite, whereas this evaluation is *teleological* on my view. The greatest difference between my own view and that of Braithwaite, however, is the fact that my account recognises the possibility that religious beliefs might be true. I share his belief that religious claims are generally not true of empirical states of affairs, or of anything comparable to empirical facts, such as invisible facts in a value-free supernatural realm. But since I believe in the possibility that empirically inadjudicable principles might be true,[4] I differ sharply with him about the truth-bearing status of religious claims. If religious principles prove to be capacitating, so that their adoption increases understanding of purposive issues, then we have no reason to deny their truth – and they do not have to be empirically verifiable to be capacitating in this respect. This means that religious principles might be true *in the role of teleological judgments,* a role which their points indicate that they play.

Since the *kind* of reference that a belief must have to be true is the issue, however, our attention needs to be concentrated more sharply on this issue. So far I have argued in this way: if one cannot understand a belief except by understanding its point, and if the point of a belief is logically inseparable from its meaning, then one cannot understand what it would mean for the belief to be true unless one understands its point. If the point of a belief is not descriptive but teleological, then the 'facts' which its truth requires must also be teleological. In short, religious claims which *look* like supernatural descriptions *function* like teleological principles, and they must be treated accordingly.

Consider Wittgenstein's way of expressing the matter. 'Grammar', he says, 'tells us what kind of object anything is' – and then he goes on to add the parenthetical remark 'God as grammar.'[5] The implication of this is that one cannot understand the kind of object that people use a term like 'God' to refer to without understanding the use which governs this term's meaning. The referent of a term must be described in a way that reflects the grammar of the term's use. If this term is used to make teleological assessments, then the 'object' to which God refers must be described teleologically.

Now one might object to this analysis by saying that God is a substantive being whose nature it is to sustain the purpose of all things, so that establishing the existence of this being simultaneously establishes a ground of purpose. Those who maintain this objection pack evaluative properties of sense into an object-referent and then present the existence of this God-object as a descriptive question of fact. Grammar, in their view, tells us only what *properties an entity (referent) must have,* after which the question of this referent's existence becomes a separate issue, whose decision might involve matters entirely divorced from evaluation. The existence of *that* sort of God is not a *teleological* question but a *metaphysical* issue. Teleological implications will follow from the existence of this God, assuming that this can be metaphysically established; but the question of God's existence on this view is an independent question of fact. If there is a God, then there is a source of purpose and we are entitled to trust in life's meaning. But *is* there an entity referred to by the word 'God'? Metaphysical realists hold this question to be distinct from the question of life's ultimate purpose. That, again, is where I think that they are mistaken.

D.Z. Phillips also resists this metaphysical formulation of the issue. If one presents the question of God's existence as a religious issue by locating it in its proper life-context, then he has no complaint. To this extent Phillips is a realist who believes that God must exist, that he must be 'real', possess externality, etc. This point needs to be emphasised because he is commonly misunderstood of this issue. Yet if one supposes that the existence of God is a *metaphysical* question to be decided on *metaphysical grounds* prior to the evaluations which grow out of one's own experience, then he disagrees. To that extent he is a non-realist, meaning not that he believes in the unreality of God but that he objects to realism *as a metaphysical thesis*.

Here it might be said that the issue of whether or not one describes the question of God's existence as a metaphysical issue is a purely verbal dispute. But it is not. The way one presents this question matters because the way in which one approaches the justification of religious claims depends on it. Metaphysical realists propose justifications which go beyond the reasons which ordinary believers have for their beliefs, whereas anti-realists, if we are to call them that, do not. Anti-realists believe that framing religious questions metaphysically *changes* them. They lose their point because the *essential* connection between their content and their evaluative role is served.

This anti-metaphysical stance can be clearly recognised in Phillips's discussion. He argues that the existence of God cannot be decided independently of those conditions which give talk of God its sense. Yet that is exactly what metaphysicians try to do to decide the question of God's existence independently of the human activities in which the term 'God' is employed. Apart from such employments of the term, we have no 'method of projection' for understanding its object. We don't know the kind of discourse that we are dealing with, and so we don't know the kind of thing that we are talking about. For there is no univocal, overarching manner in which all questions of existence (e.g. of numbers, values, mental states, electrons, social forces, etc.) are to be settled, just a there is no referring relation which is common to terms and their 'objects' in all so-called language-game. Metaphysicians assume that there must be an intelligible manner of couching generic questions about the existence of these objects *prior* to any particular linguistic activity. This assumption is implicit in metaphysical attempts to discover the existence of 'real' objects, and it explains why Phillips repeatedly challenges philosophers to explain what the existence of God means independently of *religious* assertions about his being.

If one asks why metaphysicians should believe that questions of existence and reference are logically prior to the diverse grammatical settings in which these issues are couched, one answer is that we are misled by analogies in the superficial grammar of our language. We use terms like 'brick' to refer to visible physical objects, mistakenly supposing that all other references we make must be variations on this paradigmatic usage. Thus, we tend to think that the object which we refer to by using the term 'God' must be an entity which resembles a physical entity except for being incorporeal, empirically undetectable, eternal, omnipresent, and so on. Such qualifications leave no sense in the idea that God bears a resemblance to a physical object, yet the thought that God must refer to an entity of some kind remains as a vague holdover from the paradigmatic use of physical-object terms.

I have no quarrel with Wittgenstein or with Phillips on any of these points; but unlike them, I use the (admittedly somewhat awkward) notion of a belief's teleological force to prevent us from assuming that we know all about the referents of religious claims without first understanding the distinctive role that these beliefs play in our thinking. The intent of this term 'teleological' is to shift the burden of justification away from purely metaphysical concerns toward those concerns that are relevant to judgments of purpose. Instead of casting the question of God's existence as a non-evaluative question about a metaphysically 'real' object, I think that the issue should be drawn in ways that involve the believer in deliberations of worth. This suggests that the 'object' that the word 'God' ordinarily refers to must be evaluatively construed, as if it were an object like the object of the word 'good'.

Metaphysical realism in religion, in other words, is comparable to Platonic realism in morality. Just as Platonists believe that 'good' must refer to an abstract object, metaphysical realists believe that 'God' must refer to an incorporeal object. Yet just as moral discourse does not collapse without a Platonic interpretation of moral referents, religious discourse need not collapse without a metaphysical accounts of its reference. Moral thinking continues unaffected by disputes over Platonism, and religious discourse can proceed in the same way without being altered by objections to metaphysical realism.

Nevertheless, several sources of resistance must be overcome if we are to treat religious claims as teleological assessments. Inasmuch as teleological claims resemble moral judgments in supervening descriptive states of affairs (facts), we tend to believe that facts must have a certain priority over values. There have to be facts to evaluate, in other words, before there can be any moral or teleological judgments made about them. It is easy to confuse this priority of facts with the necessary priority of God's existence as a factual matter. Yet the only facts which are needed here are worldly facts, not supernatural facts about transcendent beings. The claim that God exists is not comparable to a matter of fact but to the moral claims that supervene these facts, and so it is actually wiser to treat *super*naturalism as a form of supervenience. None of this says anything about the particular *kind of object* that God must be, since that depends on the particular *kind of supervenience involved*.

If supervenient judgments followed from matters of fact, then there might be some reason for thinking that the existence of a metaphysical entity is required to give life's ultimate purpose its ground. Yet teleological assessments cannot be derived from non-evaluative descriptions, just as an 'ought' cannot be derived from an 'is'. When we are dealing with people, however, this issue becomes clouded. Since people ordinarily have reasons for their actions, the fact that an act was performed by a person usually means that the act was performed for a purpose. The act has a purpose because a human gave it a purpose, and this conferred purpose represents the act's reason for being. If it could be established that God exists *as a personal being of some kind*, then we might assume that he acts for a purpose and that his acts have a purpose because he gave them a purpose. And we might further assume that human life only has a purpose because he designed us with a purpose in view. None of these claims about purpose, however, follow from the contention that a personal God exists. Such a God might act without any purpose at all, just as people do. Or the purpose of God's acts might be one thing, and the purpose which people have for their lives might be another. Such a God might not even exist, but people might still have a purpose, they might still be capable of being fulfilled, etc. The assumption that purpose only arises as the result of God's *will* is an anthropomorphism mistakenly extended to the metaphysical picture of God. It leads us to believe that we only have to decide the existence of a God who wills and the most important questions about life's purpose will be settled. This strategy of stepping back from teleological questions in order to deal with supernatural contentions as factual matters injects only confusion into the proper defence of faith.

Even if we admit that certain religious teachings have evaluative or teleological import, however, aren't we driven by the logic of these claims to acknowledge the existence of a being whose existence or non-existence *might* be considered independently of these concerns. Consider Christianity's claim that human beings are saved by grace, for example. This is a teleological claim since the grace which people receive figures into their self-assessment, allowing them to count themselves worthy despite their various sins. But can there be grace without a giver? Can there be forgiveness that does not come from someone? Presumably, the answer to such rhetorical questions is 'no', and so the realist assumes that there must be a God who grants people this grace.

The argument here takes its direction from the superficial grammar of Christian discourse, not from what Wittgenstein called its 'depth grammar'. Superficially, thanking requires an object, so much so that when someone feels fortunate over a turn of events, he may thank his 'lucky stars'. Here the lucky stars may simply fill in a place required by surface grammar – one has to thank something, so one might as well make it lucky stars. Similarly, one talks of a giver in talking of grace because the concept of grace has a grammar very close to that of 'gift', and where there are gifts our language leads us to believe there are givers. Underneath this grammar, however, a deeper grammar governs the use of this term. Believers use it to mark the fact that they are not forgiving themselves or imposing the idea of forgiveness on their experience. Forgiveness is not an *achievement* which is to be brought about by one's own acts, it is something which can be only attained passively through a kind of resignation or letting be. Once one has acknowledged this, the pressure to suppose that someone has *given* us the right to forgiveness disappears.

Perhaps a simpler analogy will help to explain. Since people generally cannot go to sleep by *doing* things to make themselves fall asleep, they might suppose that they must relax and wait for sleep to be given to them by the god of the night. They might even thank the god of the night for the gift of sleep, but this would not mean that sleep was literally a gift. Similarly, we know that we cannot always *do anything* to bring forgiveness on ourselves, and so if we are to feel forgiven we must stop *trying* to forgive ourselves and let the feeling of forgiveness overtake our repentance. To encourage that we speak of forgiveness as a gift because this makes it easier for us to *understand* the way in which forgiveness comes. But we do not need to think that it comes to us literally from a giver, just as we need not suppose that sleep comes to us as a literal gift.

Even if the depth grammar of religious concepts *did* necessitate the idea of a personal being, the existence of such a being would be teleologically projected, i.e. it would follow from the kind of evaluative claims that believers make. Trying to establish the existence of such a being from a non-evaluative perspective would be *religiously* pointless. This effort might lead to a 'God of the philosophers', but there would be no connection between this God and the 'God of religion'.

In short, the 'truths' of faith are generally teleological assessments which can only be distorted by being represented as non-evaluative metaphysical issues. These truths cannot be analysed as if they were descriptions which correspond to factual states of affairs. For we are given no bridge which will take us from such questions of fact to the point of religious assertions, which is to enable ultimate judgments of purpose. I regret that the term 'teleological' is not as clear as I would like it to be, and I am painfully aware that I have been generalising without qualification about religious language. These improvements will have to await other essays. Here I've tried only to explain that metaphysical realism in religion is neither necessary nor desirable, that it distorts the justification of religious claims by portraying them as descriptions, and that it is superfluous to the point of a working, practical faith.

Notes

1. For a detailed discussion of the logic of principles, see John H. Whittaker, *Matters of Faith and Matters of Principle: Religious Truth Claims and Their Logic* (San Antonio, Tex.: Trinity University Press, 1981), especially Chapter 2.
2. Ibid., Chapters 2, 5.
3. R.B. Braithwaite, *An Empiricist's View of the Nature of Religious Belief* (Cambridge University Press, 1955).
4. Whittaker, op. cit., Chapter 5.
5. Ludwig Wittgenstein, *Philosophical Investigations* (New York: Macmillan, 1953), paragraph number 373.

Belief in God: Metaphysics and Values

JOHN HICK

In this volume, two kinds of non-realism are developed. One, offered by Don Cupitt, openly accepts its own negative and atheistic implications. The other, offered by D.Z. Phillips, seeks to conceal these implications by professing to be neither realistic nor non-realist but to occupy a third position. This third position is often hinted at but was never actually produced. Mr Whittaker pursues this latter strategy. He suggests that when we realise that religious beliefs have a practical 'point' which shows in our attitudes, behaviours, emotions, etc., and that to abide by them is to proceed in one's life in a distinctive kind of way, then 'the philosophical controversy over realism and non-realism tends to disappear' (p. 119).

This seems to me not to be the case. Whether interpreted realistically or non-realistically, religious beliefs have a practical point and are abided by in one's life as a whole. To show – even though this hardly needs showing – the 'pointed' character of religious belief in contrast, for example, to mathematical beliefs, is not relevant to the realist/non-realist debate; but to be irrelevant is not thereby to avoid the choice which the realist/non-realist issue presents.

However, Mr Whittaker seeks to avoid this choice by exploiting the ambiguity of 'teleological'. The term is crucial in his paper, and he apologises in his last paragraph that 'the term "teleological" is not as clear as I should like it to be' (p. 129). But I suggest that its unclarity has in fact been necessary to its role in his argument.

Telos can mean either (a) a future end or fulfilment, or (b) a final or supreme value. In a realist interpretation of theistic language, it means both; in a non-realist interpretation, it means only the latter.

Using 'teleological' in sense (a), to say that religious beliefs are teleological is to say that they are grounded in a teleological, or end-directed, conception of the universe and of human life. From this point of view, our life receives its true meaning from the fact that it is part of God's creative process, leading to the final fulfilment symbolised in Christianity as the Kingdom of God. This teleological conception is one version of the realist use of religious language. On

130

this view, to affirm the reality of God is, *inter alia*, to affirm that the universe of which we are a part has a certain definite character or structure in virtue of which ultimate trust, acceptance, gratitude are appropriate. Because we believe by faith in God's reality we have faith that life's tragedies are not final, that evil will not finally be triumphant, that through life's baffling mixture of light and darkness a good purpose is gradually being fulfilled. This realist understanding of teleology thus has a powerful religious 'point', in that to accept this theistic conception of the universe is to live in a certain way, to feel about life in a certain way, and to have certain ultimate expectations which colour one's present experience. Thus sense (a) of 'teleology' includes within it sense (b).

But Mr Whittaker proposes to jettison sense (a) but retain sense (b). In this sense, 'teleological' means 'evaluative'. Thus, for Mr Whittaker, religious beliefs are 'principles' guiding our actions (p. 122), 'assessments of worth' (p. 123) which are 'evaluative' (p. 123). They are 'not descriptive but teleological' (p. 124) – i.e. teleological, not as referring to the development of the universe through time, but as expressing an evaluative attitude to life independently of the ontological character of the universe. It seems that, for him, in religious language one is expressing one's valuation of human life in terms which, if understood realistically, would involve reference to a transcendent divine reality on which the structure of the universe depends – though Mr Whittaker does not want the language to be understood in this realist way.

Thus the basic feature of Mr Whittaker's approach is its assumption of a disjunction between the ontological or metaphysical affirmation of God, and the value-laden character of belief in God. He assumes that theistic belief has to be one or the other but not both: one must *either* believe in an ontologically existent God, belief in whom, however, makes no difference to human life, *or* in the range of differences which belief in an ontologically real God makes, without, however, there being an ontologically real God. Thus he repeatedly rejects 'the question of God's existence as an obscure, non-evaluative, question about a metaphysically "real" object' (p. 126). But why should a metaphysically real God be thought of as a 'non-evaluative . . . object'? In the central Christian tradition God is thought of as the ultimate reality, existing independently of human beliefs and disbeliefs, who is responsible for the teleological character of the universe, and as holy, loving and just, so that it is impossible to know God without one's whole life being thereby affected.

To the extent to which someone genuinely believes in God, that person lives in trust, obedience and answering love. It is thus impossible, as Mr Whittaker also emphasises, to know what is meant by God without knowing something of the difference that God's existence makes for our lives.

And so Mr Whittaker is, in my view, right in stressing that one cannot believe in God without this affecting one's whole life, but wrong in failing to see that the theistic belief which properly affects one's whole life is belief in a God who exists independently of human belief and whose goodness and ultimate sovereignty give final meaning to our lives.

Part Four
Religious Realism

7

A Critique of Don Cupitt's Christian Buddhism

BRIAN HEBBLETHWAITE

Numerous references in his recent writings indicate the sense of kinship which Theravada Buddhism has for Don Cupitt. It is not only in the Buddha's hostility to metaphysics that Cupitt finds a kindred anti-realism. In *Life Lines* Cupitt remarks that realism has 'an itch of egoism about it whereas the non-realist easily learns a Buddhist lightness and good-humour'.[1] This alleged link between realism and egoism is to be contrasted with the Buddhist 'no-self' doctrine, compared by Cupitt to the deconstructed, decentred, hyper-relativism of those forms of 'post-modern' philosophy which he embraces as cognate with his own view of religion. Moreover, the sequence of images, myths, constructed 'life-worlds', between which we have to choose, is like an album of photographs, and 'there is something very Buddhist about a photograph', says Cupitt.[2] The comparison between early Buddhism and post-modern French philosophy is pursued further in *The Long-Legged Fly*,[3] where Cupitt takes the Buddhist quest for the cessation of desire to be a matter of rooting out erroneous conceptions of the self and of combating possessive individualism.

There are limits to Cupitt's enthusiasm for early Buddhism, however. He does not find in Buddhism the ideal of disinterested love, which is Christianity's contribution and which still inspires even an anti-realist Christian faith. Again in *Life Lines*, Cupitt says: 'Just to will the death of God is atheism, and just to recognise and accept the Void is Buddhism; but to accept that for Love's sake, one must die in union with the god is Christianity.'[4] So, while Cupitt shares the Buddha's hostility to metaphysics, admires the way he prefigures post-modern deconstructionism, agrees with his negation of the self, and applauds his lightness of touch, Cupitt prefers and commends the Christian ideal of selfless love.

I do not intend to try to assess the plausibility of Cupitt's understanding of early Buddhism, though it is far from clear that the
Theravada is in fact as anti-metaphysical as Cupitt suggests. Furthermore, a case could be made for thinking in much more positive
terms of Buddhist disinterested compassion, so that the difference
between Christianity and Buddhism, ethically speaking – the difference, that is, between love and compassion – might not be so great,
and, consequently, Cupitt's preference for Christianity might seem
somewhat arbitrary. But I should like to draw attention to another
reference to Buddhism in the work of another critic of objective
theism, Alistair Kee. In his contribution to the Macquarrie Festschrift,
Being and Truth,[5] Kee remarks upon the resonances between Karl
Jasper's philosophical faith – the insistence on non-objectifiable transcendence – and Buddhism. Now there are subtle differences between an existentialist insistence on non-objectifiability in talk of
transcendence and Cupitt's explicit rejection of theological realism.
It would be possible to read the Buddha and Jaspers and the mystics
to whom Kee also refers as exemplifying not so much a rejection of
metaphysics as a recognition of the unsayable – of the way in which
any attempt to state the truths of ultimate reality inevitably falsifies
what is beyond human conceptualisation. I suspect that such a view
is vulnerable to Cupitt's bluff assertion that the emperor has no
clothes. Fear of falsification through objectification can all too easily
lead to a complete rejection of realism, not only in respect of God or
the transcendent, but also in respect of science, anthropology and
culture. The question whether Kee's position can, at the end of the
day, be differentiated from Cupitt's is a question which reflection on
the latter's extreme anti-realism presses upon us. The same is true of
the question whether D.Z. Phillips's insistence on the autonomy of
God-talk in the context of religious forms of life can in the end be
differentiated from Cupitt's anti-realism.

Little more will be said about Buddhism as such here. It is Cupitt's
anti-realism that I wish to discuss. For over the years Cupitt has
developed a way of understanding the ethical ideals and spiritual
disciplines of Christianity as not only possible for one who categori-
cally rejects belief in an objective God and in life after death, but as
requiring such a rejection. But Cupitt's purely humanist, expressivist
and voluntarist understanding of Christianity is not simply a matter
of being a non-realist in religion. It is bound up with – and necessarily so, as I shall argue – a much wider anti-realism, with a
Heideggerian reading of the history of philosophy as culminating in

the death of metaphysics with an allegedly Wittgensteinian reduction of ontology to linguistically constructed 'objects' and 'life-worlds', and with a post-modernist Derridaean deconstruction of all essences, including the human self and its inherited cultures and life-ways. The novelty of Cupitt's position is the way in which, from the ashes of all this destructive criticism, there emerges, Phoenix-like, the Christian ideal of disinterested love, as something inspiring and demanding, a creative project that stands out amongst the innumerable other possibilities in the post-modern supermarket as eminently worthy of choice and commitment. Moreover, commitment to this ideal can, for Cupitt, still be expressed and enacted in the traditional language and liturgies of the Church.

In the main part of this paper, I propose to subject Cupitt's anti-realist position to criticism, first for its religious inadequacy, then for its intellectual inadequacy, and, thirdly, for its ethical inadequacy.

I begin with its religious inadequacy, since one of our difficulties is that Cupitt is liable to *sound* much more religious than his critics. To turn from Cupitt's passionate advocacy of an anti-realist faith to the meticulous work, say, of Plantinga or Swinburne may seem to be a matter of turning from the living heart of religion to a dry-as-dust intellectual world of abstraction. On a superficial view, we might seem to be renouncing Jerusalem in favour of Athens. And it might seem more than just churlish in the Christian critic to speak disparagingly of the evidently powerful faith and spirituality that inform Cupitt's writings. However, it is surely incumbent upon religious people to reflect not only on the sense of their religious position – its inner sense and the sense it makes of everything else – but also on what it is that constitutes its religious plausibility and power. We cannot take it on trust that the plausibility and power of Christian spirituality remain the same when the language and liturgies of the church are re-interpreted without reference to an objective God or life after death.

For the heart of the Judaeo-Christian tradition has been a matter of discovery and experience, in communal as in individual life, of a *relation* between believers and an all-surpassing personal and spiritual resource that creates, enables and sustains their faith and spirituality. In order to test the adequacy of Cupitt's reconstruction, we have to ask what sense he makes of Christian talk of *grace*. For him, this seems only a matter of the sheer gratuitousness of the faith possibility. Like wonder at the beauty of the earth, religious faith amazes us and becomes an inspiring possibility for us. But Cupitt can hardly speak of amazing grace. He can only speak of amazing faith as a gratuitous possibility in our lives.

Much could be said of the difference, phenomenologically speaking, between traditional Christianity's understanding of faith in relational terms as expressive of a relation of dependence of believers on their God, and Cupitt's one-dimensional, non-relational, understanding of the community of faith. But phenomenological arguments alone will not suffice. Cupitt is well aware that his understanding of Christianity is different from that of the majority of his co-religionists throughout history. He thinks that Christianity's self-understanding must change radically, and he has a theory based on his reading of the history of philosophy of why it must change. In pointing out the difference between Cupitt's non-realist reconstruction of Christian faith and the traditional faith of the Church, we are not, therefore, simply making a phenomenological point. We are questioning, rather, the religious adequacy of a view which abandons these key features of Christianity.

The first question that arises is whether such a view could ever hope to sustain a Church. It might I suppose, inspire a few heroic individuals, but surely it could never have created the Christian movement or have maintained it as a world religion, fostering the simple faith of millions as well as the sanctity of such as St Francis or Mother Teresa today, and succouring at all times the broken and the outcast. Even at the most humdrum level, I do not see how one could expect to have a congregation of existentialists or anti-realists.

This may seem just a sociological point. It is an empirical fact that it was faith in God that created the Christian movement, and it is an empirical fact that Christianity is sustained by faith in God. But it is more than that. The sociological fact is secondary to and dependent on the soteriological fact that an anti-realist faith cannot save us from sins. This remark need not be taken in any narrow pietistic sense. The point is rather that it is a quintessentially Christian insight that God alone can effect the necessary transformations of human life.

It is easy to reply that ideologies as such can change individuals and effect major social transformation. Marxism is a case in point. The phenomenology of conversion to Marxism is strikingly similar to that of religious conversion, and Marxist ideology has transformed many societies radically. But this assimilation abstracts from the realities of religious experience. Conviction of and commitment to the inevitable historical triumph of socialism is one thing. Christian experience of grace quite another. The former is a deliberately secular, this-worldly reading of the dynamics of human history. The latter is inextricably bound up with its reference beyond history to a transcendent spiritual power. Once admitted to be a purely human construct, the Christian vision loses its power, except for a small elite. Actually, even Marxism needs to be sustained by conviction of historical inevitability. Once that is demythologised, Marxism too tends to lose much of its power. So in fact the assimilation goes the other way.

The case of Buddhism might seem more appropriate at this point than that of Marxism. For early Buddhism is the classical example of a *religion* that exerted striking spiritual power and sustained the faith of millions, without appeal to God, grace or an enabling spirit. But the actual history of Theravada Buddhism should give the anti-realist some pause. A case can be made for thinking that its virtual demise in India and its development into Mahayana Buddhism in the Far East reveal a degree of religious inadequacy in the original austere ethic and spiritual discipline. It is hardly coincidental that what replaced Buddhism in India was a renewed devotional theism (and, in part, a renewed metaphysical theism) and what developed in the Far East was precisely a religion of grace.

Another religious inadequacy in Cupitt's anti-realist faith may be discerned if we consider the exigencies of worship. In Christian worship the infinite source and goal of the whole creative process becomes the explicit focus of the creature's adoration, gratitude and praise. Worship, as Peter Geach has pointed out,[6] is an intentional verb, and much has been said about what constitutes the proper object of worship. The dangers of idolatry, of absolutising the finite, and getting caught in what Paul Tillich categorises as the demonic,[7] reinforce the sense that only the transcendent, infinite love of God can be appropriately worshipped and adored. In a non-realist faith all this goes. Worship loses its intentionality.

Some attention must now be given to Cupitt's charge that a religion of dependence on an allegedly transcendent power is bound to be immature. This basically Freudian objection – at the root of so much protest atheism – suffers from immense implausibility when confronted with the facts of the religious life. It is difficult to know whether it has become a purely a priori theory imposed upon the facts whatever they are, or whether it is just a wild generalisation induced from a small range of experienced cases of indubitable religious immaturity. But something is surely wrong with a theory that prevents its holder from distinguishing, even empirically, be-

tween mature and immature religious believers. The *theoretical* dis-
advantages of the view that all dependence relations entail immaturity are equally great. One ceases to be able to explore with any
sensitivity the kind of theological anthropology which sees in our
creaturely status a defining attribute of what it is to be a human
being. Of course, much depends on the way in which this relation of
dependence is understood. It can be affirmed slavishly, blindly or
immaturely. But a religion of grace, worship and discipleship is not
necessarily experienced in those inadequate ways. Rather, the mature Christian learns the meaning of true freedom through embrac-
ing the will of the God who is love.

The religious inadequacies of the anti-realist view can be summed
up in the charge that it fails to do justice to religious experience. This
means that there is an argument from religious experience to the
reality of God. The widespread occurrence of a religious sense of
encounter with a spiritual reality behind and at the heart of things –
ranging, as it does, from a sense of absolute dependence, through
numinous experience of various kinds, to a sense of standing in a
gracious personal relation to the God and Father of our Lord Jesus
Christ – constitutes a prima facie case for theological realism.

I wish to make three points about the appeal to religious experience, two positive and one negative. The positive points are these: in
the first place, it is worth nothing that the argument from experience
is an *argument*. So already before leaving the topic of the religious
inadequacies of an anti-realist faith, we are involved in its intellectual inadequacies. Then secondly, it is important to remember that
the more specifically rational considerations to which we are about
to turn are to be held in conjunction with the appeal to experience. It
is the same ultimate reality to which both reason and religious
experience appeal. There is no need to drive a wedge between the
God of the Bible and the God of the philosophers. The philosophers
are only exploring the rational aspect of that to which the religious
sense gives prima facie plausibility.

The negative point about appeals to religious experience is that
they are unlikely to convince by themselves – unless of course one
has oneself enjoyed what strikes one as an absolutely self-
authenticating experience of God. That contingency apart, one has to
admit that a general appeal to the prevalence of alleged experiences
of the holy or of grace is vulnerable to alternative explanations, if
unsupported by rational argument or appeal to revelation, prefer-
ably both. One sees this in Hick's unwillingness to support his case

beyond appeal to experience.[8] Hick is more vulnerable to counter-argument than he would have been had he given more weight to the rational arguments. Hick's further reluctance to support his case by appeal to special revelation – in the interests of a global religious ecumenism – renders his position increasingly vulnerable to Cupitt's charge that his religious object has become so vague as to be indistinguishable from no object at all. For this reason, Cupitt claims that Hick is now on the side of the anti-realists – against the latter's intention, no doubt.

With these preliminaries in mind, I turn to the intellectual inadequacies of Cupitt's anti-realist faith. Cupitt's position is now so extreme – his anti-realism extending not only to religion and ethics but to science, our whole life-world, indeed everything – that it is not too easy to get a purchase-hold for criticism. Moreover his anti-realism is buttressed by a reading of the whole history of philosophy as requiring this development. In due course, this reading will have to be challenged, but we may begin, more straightforwardly, with the remark that any thoroughgoing anti-realist position is bound at some stage to contradict itself. For it can contain no account of that which constructs its life-worlds, its cultures, its ideals and its religions. In order to escape this impasse Cupitt speaks in *Life Lines* of 'the productive life-energy' manifesting itself in a variety of representations including the Christian ideal, which somehow, gratuitously, supervene upon the deconstruction of all essences, including the human self and will. But what on earth is this shadowy Schopenhauerian metaphysical principle doing in Cupitt's anti-metaphysical world-view? He says that there is simply nothing to be said about it except that it manifests itself in various representations. Indeed in his glossary to *Life Lines*, he says that he uses it only as a heuristic device for generating interpretations.[9] But these remarks cannot obscure that fact that even the most thoroughgoing anti-metaphysics has to fall back on an ultimate metaphysical principle – in this case a totally unexplained and arbitrary one. For the basic question of metaphysics – how are we to account for our world's capacity to produce personal beings such as ourselves? – this question will not go away.

This question does not have to be directed at such an obscure starting-point as the 'productive life-energy'. Anti-realism can be attacked from a more straightforward starting-point, namely its great implausibility where the given world of relatively stable natural kinds is concerned. It is a striking fact that when belief in an objective God is rejected, even the simplest truths are liable to be rejected too. The classical admission of this is Nietzsche's famous aphorism that after the death of God truth is fiction. But the very implausibility of this attack on even the simplest truths can itself become the basis for a defence of theism. For commonsense truths, tested and refined by scientific enquiry, resist deconstruction with such compelling power that they themselves become the starting-point for an argument from truth to God. For if, without God, the most obvious truths disintegrate, then the fact that they do not disintegrate – the fact that we exist in a world whose stable, indeed rational, nature is discoverable – is suggestive of the reality of God to account for the existence, stability and rationality of things.

The fact that Cupitt's anti-realism in religion requires this wider, general anti-realism about everything constitutes a powerful argument against it. For it is not very difficult to defend philosophical realism in matters of common sense and natural science, as Michael Devitt has shown with admirable clarity in his book, *Realism and Truth*.[10] Admittedly, such a defence entails the rejection of a long tradition in Western epistemology, which interposed a private world of images or ideas between our knowing minds and the realities of which we are aware in the course of our interaction with persons and things. We have to question, indeed reject, the Kantian 'turn to the subject', which formalised this cutting off of the human mind from the world of real objects. The implausibility of this approach is again shown up by the extremism of Kant's view. Kant treats not only the basic categories of thought, but also space and time as our own modes of processing the data of sense. Things as they are in themselves disappear behind a screen of our making. Kant was not, of course, as extreme as Cupitt. Kant thought that all human beings necessarily go on to process the data the same way in terms of the same universal conceptual scheme. Modern conceptual relativism, embraced by Cupitt, has broken this unitary system up, and speaks of different culturally conditioned conceptual schemes, processing the data in different ways. Against this whole constructivist trend we need to argue that the data of sense and the concepts of the understanding, far from constituting a barrier or a screen preventing knowledge of reality, are much more plausibly to be construed as the means of direct access to the real, which products of evolution such as ourselves have best developed precisely in order to enable accurate awareness of the world of things and persons with which we have to do.

There is a problem, however, with this highly plausible defence of realism. It finds difficulty in accounting for the fact that the physical universe has evolved persons. There is a tendency to try to reduce mind to matter and give a physicalist account of mind. Here, for once, we may agree with Cupitt in rejecting such materialism, which does not begin to do justice to the experienced character of mind and value. But having agreed with Devitt against Cupitt about the objectivity of things, we are not going to follow Cupitt in trying to solve the problem by denying objectivity as such. Much more plausible is to move in the opposite direction and take quite seriously the objectivity of mind and value. The very fact that the universe has the capacity to produce minds becomes the premise for a design argument for the existence of God. For, while scientific explanations can plausibly be given for most changes and developments within the given system of matter or energy, operating in accordance with certain fundamental constants and laws, no explanation whatsoever is provided or could be provided by natural science for the existence of this matter or energy, with its extraordinary capacities. How are we to account for its ability to produce, through cosmic and biological evolution, rational, personal beings, such as ourselves, beings endowed with freedom, openness to the future, self-transcendence, the capacity to appreciate the values of beauty, goodness and truth, and moreover to recognise the *claim* of the moral law. All these features cumulatively reinforce the case for thinking that only a transcendent, creative intention, itself of surpassing value, can explain the existence and nature of the universe and what it has produced.

It may certainly be surmised that the vague intimations of a mind and heart of love behind the whole cosmos, which both reason and experience yield, will only be clarified and systematically developed into a coherent and plausible world view, if divine revelation takes place. Only a little of the nature and intention of the Creator can be read off the existence and nature of a person-producing universe. But reason and experience lead us to expect revelation, and if God has acted to make himself known to his personal creatures then the possibility of a much more comprehensive and systematic theology arises – a theology whose intellectual scope and religious power are bound to enhance greatly the intellectual plausibility of realist faith.

Cupitt summarises the difficulties of what he calls designer realism in a short passage which bears examination:

Its difficulties are well known. They include the logical problems of the design argument itself, the facts of evil in the world, its naively mythical anthropomorphism, and the puzzle about what the kind of disembodied person it envisages could possibly be. Most disabling of all is its curiously weightless quality; it often seems to differ little in practice from a mere expression of innocent cosmic optimism.[11]

These controversial points are thrown out without any serious supporting arguments. Once again Cupitt's extremism is revealed in its inability to make discriminations between good and bad arguments in theodicy or between a serious Christian hope for the future of God's world and a facile optimism. In fact the logical problems of design arguments can be and are being explored and resolved in contemporary philosophy of religion with a rigour far exceeding Cupitt's impressionistic generalisations. The problem of evil too has received searching and penetrating treatment in modern theodicy from writers such as Farrer, Hick, Plantinga and Swinburne, and the weaknesses in arguments of anti-theodicists from Hume to Mackie have been pointed out. The charge of anthropomorphism against the classical concept of God as Creator does scant justice to the Christian theological tradition which has always tried to safeguard divine transcendence and reckon with the inevitable limitations in human thought about the 'incomprehensible' deity. In fact, it is the critics of objective theism who can be observed to be thinking anthropomorphically, indeed in caricatures, of what they have rejected. Certainly the notion of infinite, incorporeal spirit is not easy to think, still less to 'envisage'. But the idea that because we ourselves are embodied persons, personality is essentially corporeal is nothing but positivist prejudice. Finally, the attribution of a curiously weightless quality to designer realism ignores the way in which the recognition of design behind the world process belongs to the whole tradition of Christian belief in God. There is nothing weightless about the Christian doctrine of creation and its discernment of purpose and meaning in the universe.

The intellectual inadequacy of Cupitt's position may be summarised as its total failure to account for the existence and nature of the world – and in particular for the world's finely tuned capacity to evolve rational persons, who find themselves inexorably claimed by the moral law and drawn out of themselves by the lure of beauty and love. It fails to account for humanity's religious sense the world over. And it fails utterly to account for objectivity and truth.

I turn to the ethical inadequacy of Cupitt's anti-realist faith. This may be pinpointed by reference to the Prometheanism of the view that humanity has it in itself to create or invent value. Keith Ward has acknowledged the ethically proper, indeed essential, senses in which men and women are morally autonomous beings.[12] They are free and responsible, and must acknowledge and interiorise for themselves the claims of the moral law. But Cupitt has pushed the notion of ethical autonomy to quite untenable extremes. Only if men and women create their own realms of value are they autonomous moral beings in his sense. But this position, like all forms of anti-realism, self-destructs. It undermines the very nature of value which of its essence lays a claim upon the mind and heart of the moral agent. It is indeed up to us to decide whether we will acknowledge and respond to the needs of the neighbour in distress, but in no way do we ourselves create that obligation. Respect for human rights is not an optional stance. Such a view reduces morality, as it does religion, to a purely human product – an item on the supermarket shelf.

Cupitt alleges that the religious voluntarist, in affirming the Christian ideal against the background of a Nietzschean void, is not like the atheist existentialist, overcoming nothingness by an act of Promethean self-affirmation.[13] On the contrary, the self too is dissolved. Christianity is rather a matter of the 'productive life-energy's' inexplicable resurgence. Love appears out of nothing purely gratuitously. I have already commented on Cupitt's wilful obscurantism in introducing the notion of the 'productive life-energy'. He forbids us to take this as a veiled reference to the creative Spirit of God. But, in that case, there is no alternative to treating the affirmation of Christian love as a purely human phenomenon or possibility. It may not be an act of individual will; it is a purely human creation all the same. But the point of the Prometheus legend, like that of all powerful myths, is not restricted to the portrayal of an individual's rebellion and taking to himself the prerogatives of God. On the contrary, the figure of Prometheus symbolises *humankind*'s arrogation of divine prerogatives. Cupitt's purely human Christianity is just an open to the charge of Prometheanism as is atheistic existentialism.

This is the point at which the tables must be turned on Cupitt's remark that 'realism always has an itch of egoism about it'. On the contrary, the ethical significance of theological realism lies in the way in which it sees our own true good as consisting precisely in being drawn out of ourselves, away from our fantasies and self-projections, into relation with the Love that made us. In face of that reality, our illusions fall away and our self-assertion is overcome. This theological realism is the very reverse of egoism. Christian self-noughting, Christian altruism, is no aimless, arbitrary deconstruction of the self. It is a redirection, a refocusing of the self and the community on a power, a Spirit, a love, not ourselves, that makes for righteousness – to fill out Matthew Arnold's famous phrase with the theological content that it still requires for intelligibility.

Christian ethics teaches us that men and women, whether as individuals or as a community, do not have it in themselves either to invent *or to realise* the good. A further ethical inadequacy of Cupitt's position, therefore, lies in its failure to do justice to people's need for resources from beyond, if they are to be enabled to change and to live altruistically. This is, of course, the ethical aspect of man's need for grace.

The ethical insecurity of Cupitt's view is manifested in his location of all values on the surface of things, a range of merely human possibilities to be embraced at will. Worse than this, the affirmation of complete relativity – and hence the 'affirmation of everything'[14] leads quite explicitly to an Eastern dissolution of all objective distinctions whatsoever. But if that is seriously meant, then the distinction between good and evil disappears as well, and we are left with 'an endless blissful flux of experience', whose amoral consequences were most powerfully brought out in R.C. Zaehner's final book, *Our Savage God*.[15] I do not attribute such an overt transcendence of good and evil to Cupitt himself. He still commends the virtue of disinterested love. But without metaphysical depth or objective support in the nature of things this virtue remains fragile and insecure.

To sum up the ethical inadequacies of Cupitt's position: it is implausibly Promethean in treating man as the inventor of right and wrong, and at the same time it is wilfully blind to man's need for resources of transformation and sanctification from beyond. It is also in danger of total collapse, if ethical distinctions themselves are part only of the surface of things, to be dissolved and transcended in the flux of experience.

Having surveyed the religious, intellectual and ethical inadequacies of Cupitt's 'Christian Buddhism', we may conclude this paper with some reflections on the different ways in which the history of philosophy can be read. It is, of course, possible to trace the collapse of metaphysical realism through Hume and Kant to Schopenhauer and Nietzsche, and then to interpret twentieth-century philosophy, particularly in the light of Wittgenstein and Heidegger, as drawing the consequences of this collapse and offering instead a range of purely human options, among them an anti-realist, expressivist version of Christianity. It is clear that, for Cupitt, there is no alternative. But in fact there are many different ways of reading the history of philosophy, and many different possibilities for a recovery of metaphysics today. For the steps in Cupitt's story may have included some major false steps, which have led philosophers further and further into error, until the implausibility of the consequences forces us to re-examine the whole story from way back in the sequence. Kant's transcendental idealism may serve as an example. As argued above, its constructivist, relativist consequences have now led to such extreme forms of anti-realism that common sense and working science alike rebel, and force us to reconstruct a more objective conception of the universe in which we find ourselves. The trouble began much earlier than Kant. It is widely recognised today how damaging was Descartes' peculiarly solipsistic project of enquiry or Locke's assumption that 'ideas' were the immediate objects of experience. None of these great philosophers were atheists; but, for all that, much of the story traced by Cupitt concerns their increasingly atheistic successors' determination to draw out the full consequences of a consistent atheism. Bishop Berkeley foresaw that this would be so, and tried to stem the tide by dispensing with matter altogether and requiring God to account for the order of our ideal world. Entirely different reasons for postulating God have been advanced in the present paper. I have claimed that theism guarantees reality, objectivity and truth, in both the material and the spiritual spheres. What strikes one as extraordinary in Cupitt's position is the way in which he unquestioningly embraces atheist philosophy and translates the heart of Christianity into a completely atheistic form. But the Christian philosopher really has no business to be holding on to the coat-tails of atheism, as it has expressed itself since Nietzsche in ever more bizarre and self-destructive philosophical forms. As Alvin Plantinga has argued, Christian philosophy has its own agenda and has a right to its own perspectives.[16] From its own theistic standpoint it must question the presuppositions and shibboleths of post-Enlightenment thought. It must attack the implausible subjectivist epistemology characteristic of that philosophy and it must attack the reductionist scientism which accompanied it. At the same time, Christian philosophy must expose the manifest contradiction between these two pervasive aspects of post-Enlightenment philosophy. For either the turn to the subject renders modern science incomprehensible or else modern science renders the human subject incomprehensible. The task of Christian philosophy is to show that only theism makes sense of both. With such rational support we can then take seriously again the claims of divine revelation and the testimony of religious experience to the reality of God.[17]

Notes

1. D. Cupitt, *Life Lines* (London: SCM Press, 1986), p. 123.
2. Ibid., p. 192.
3. D. Cupitt, *The Long-Legged Fly* (London: SCM Press, 1987).
4. Ibid., p. 130.
5. A. Kee and W.T. Long (eds), *Being and Truth*, Essays in Honour of John Macquarrie (London: SCM Press, 1986), pp. 62–84.
6. See P.T. Geach, *God and the Soul* (London: Routledge & Kegan Paul, 1969), p. 108.
7. See P. Tillich, *Systematic Theology*, Vol. 3 (London: James Nisbet, 1964), p. 108–13.
8. See M. Goulder and J. Hick, *Why Believe in God?* (London: SCM Press, 1983).
9. Cupitt, *Life Lines*, op. cit., pp. 221ff.
10. M. Devitt, *Realism and Truth* (Oxford: Blackwell, 1984).
11. Cupitt, *Life Lines*, op. cit., p. 69.
12. K. Ward, *Holding Fast to God* (London: SPCK 1982).
13. Cupitt, *Life Lines*, op. cit., p. 130.
14. Cupitt, *Life Lines*, op. cit., p. 188.
15. R.C. Zaehner, *Our Savage God* (London: Collins, 1974).
16. A. Plantinga, 'Advice to Christian Philosophers', *Faith and Philosophy*, Vol. 1, No. 3, 1984, pp. 253–71.
17. I have endeavoured to make out the case against Don Cupitt's views and for objective theism in B. Hebblethwaite, *The Ocean of Truth* (Cambridge University Press, 1988).

A Response to Brian Hebblethwaite

DON CUPITT

As always, Brian Hebblethwaite's paper is vigorous and enjoyable, but where has he been these past thirty years? Even back in the 1950s, when I began to study the philosophy of science, my teacher Norwood Russell Hanson was already maintaining that 'all observations are theory dependent'. Sense-experiences and scientific activities do not take place in some privileged region outside culture and history: on the contrary, sense-experience *itself* has a history, and the history of science is an integral part of general cultural history.

Slowly, during the past thirty years, many of us have been digesting the implications of all this. It seems that the traditional Anglo-Saxon first-facts-and-then-interpretations realist epistemology has to be given up. Interpretation reaches all the way down – and so we have turned with fresh interest to the study of German idealism from Kant to Nietzsche, and then to post-structuralism. Being better grounded in history and the social sciences, the Continental tradition got there some years before we did, recognising that there is no starting-point anywhere which is not already an interpretation and that there can be no final interpretation which silences everyone and terminates enquiry. A new 'de-centred' kind of metaphysics appears, which sees our communicative life as both retrospectively and prospectively rootless and endless. We recognised that this was happening when in the 1970s we coined the term 'foundationalism' to signify the ways of thinking that had suddenly become encapsulated and were rapidly receding into the past. We see now that we are always *in medias res*, in secondariness. The philosopher can no longer pretend to be a shaman of Reason who has journeyed to a higher world and has learned extra-historical Truths. Our whole life is lived within a *contingent* cultural-linguistic totality that slowly shifts over the course of time, and that has no outside.

All this has been happening in philosophy – not to mention the wider world – during the past generation. The possibilities it leaves for Christian thought are explored in my books. I find it hard to understand why Brian Hebblethwaite should wish the Christian

Church to cut herself off from what is happening, and to die from the top. That will be the result, if she must remain forever locked into the mentality of dogmatic realism that passed away at the end of the eighteenth-century. Hebblethwaite seems reluctant to face an obvious fact about the late twentieth-century world, namely that the more realistic your idea of God nowadays, the more utterly anti-Christian your morality. (Anyone who doubts this may care to check out the realist God's attitude to AIDS.)

I don't accept all of Brian Hebblethwaite's criticisms of my books. D.Z. Phillips and I find it hard to be both more religious and less religious than the opposition. My account of Christian ethics has now appeared. (It is linguistic: through language we define things, assign to them their values, and so determine the way they get treated. Christian ethics begins as a work of revaluation by creative redescription.) But otherwise I am certainly disposed to accept many of Hebblethwaite's criticisms. I am indeed a nomad, and by Brian Hebblethwaite's standards my books are indeed 'extreme' – just *because* they are a Christian writer's response to our present spiritual condition.

8

Realism, Non-Realism and Atheism: Why Believe in an Objectively Real God?

JOSEPH RUNZO

The transcendent God has for many become an unavailable God. As Jean-Paul Sartre proclaims in his play *The Devil and the Good Lord*:

> I supplicated, I demanded a sign, I sent messages to Heaven, no reply. Heaven ignored my very name. Each minute I wondered what I could *be* in the eyes of God. Now I know the answer: nothing. God does not see me, God does not hear me, God does not know me . . . I am going to tell you a colossal joke: God doesn't exist.[1]

Still, however seemingly irrelevant or absurd the idea of God may be to the modern, scientific and humanistic mind, it is anything but irrelevant or absurd to Jewish or Christian or Muslim or Ramanujan faith in God. For on these world-views the idea of God is inextirpable; it is not an expendable idea at the periphery of a larger system, but foundational to the very world-view itself of the monotheist. Yet even though the idea of God is foundational for theists, *what* God is has been called into question. Is God the *ex nihilo* creator of the universe, transcending the natural order in the aseity of Godself, or is this really talk about a no-God? Has not the *immanent* God of the formative periods of the Judaeo–Christian–Islamic traditions been transmogrified into the utterly *transcendent* God of the philosophers of the Middle Ages, and then into the *noumenal* God of the revolutionary Kantian perspective, until now . . .

> We shall eventually be no more able to convince men of the existence of a God *'out there'* whom they must call in to order their

lives than persuade them to take seriously the gods of Olympus
. . . this whole way of thinking can be the greatest obstacle to an
intelligent faith . . . If Christianity is to survive, let alone to recap-
ture 'secular' man, there is no time to lose in detaching it from this
scheme of thought . . . [2]

In the twentieth-century, while the life of intense monotheistic
commitment has long stood in the mainstream of history, scientific
naturalism or humanism has established itself as a viable alternative
for the thoughtful person in our modern scientific culture. This has
driven the very conception of the nature of theism itself to an acute,
historical turning point. For theists the question has become whether
to retain a realist conception of God, or jettison theological talk
altogether, or turn from the old realist conception of God to a non-
realist view, more honest to ourselves and to God.

I shall defend theological realism. First I will present and assess a
number of salient reasons, both philosophical and theological, *for*
holding a non-realist view of God. I will then consider the relative
strength of the challenge of atheism to both theological realism and
theological non-realism. I will conclude by offering a modified realist account of theism which is intended both to respond to the
challenge of atheism and to account for the most trenchant grounds
for holding a non-realist view of God.

I

The theological realist/non-realist debate rests on certain shared
presuppositions. (I will be explicitly addressing the realist/non-
realist religious debate as it applies to talk about *God*, but many of
the considerations I raise apply to non-theistic views as well.) Often
in debates about God the question of God's existence has been seen
as the fundamental question to settle. But suppose there were an
argument which proved the existence of an external, self-subsistent
God. Or, suppose there were an argument which proved that it is
impossible that an external, self-subsistent God exists. In the former
case, theological realism would become incontrovertible; in the latter case, non-realism would be the theist's only rational alternative,
assuming that talk about God is not, in and of itself, meaningless.[3]
Thus the very debate between theological realists and non-realists
inherently presupposes that no convincing argument proves, and no

convincing argument disproves, the existence of an external, self-subsistent God.

For despite, for example, an extraordinary tradition of attempted proofs of God's existence, either (a) it seems highly unlikely that a convincing proof or disproof of God's existence can be constructed, or (b) that not only have no arguments been successful, but for *religious* reasons no proof or disproof of God's existence *could* be successful. To take the first position, (a), Hume marshals a potent set of considerations in the *Dialogue Concerning Natural Religion* against the likelihood that any *a posteriori* argument from nature to God's existence, and particularly any teleological argument, could be successful. As Hume notes, *for all we can know* on the basis of empirical evidence:

> . . . were this world ever so perfect a production, it must still remain uncertain whether all the excellences of the work can justly be ascribed to the workman . . . Many worlds might have been botched and bungled, throughout an eternity, ere this system was struck out . . .[4]

And Kant offers an even wider-ranging rejection of the traditional ontological, cosmological and teleological arguments for God's existence in the *Critique of Pure Reason*.[5]

But even if considerations like those advanced by Hume and Kant against specific arguments for God's existence fail, Kant provides a fundamental reason why all such arguments will ultimately fail.[6] By distinguishing between phenomena and noumena, Kant is able to draw the epistemological conclusion that we could never *know* the existence or nature of God *qua noumenal*: 'Through concepts alone, it is quite impossible to advance to the discovery of new objects and supernatural beings; and it is useless to appeal to experience, which in all cases yields only appearances.'[7] For, 'even if God were to make an immediate appearance, I would still need rational theology as a presupposition. For how am I to be certain that it is God himself who has appeared to me, or only another powerful being?'[8]

The alternative reaction, (b), to arguments for and against God's existence, namely their rejection on *religious* grounds, is exemplified by Kierkegaard. For instance in the *Concluding Unscientific Postscript* he argues that the most valuable feature of religiosity is infinite passion and that one cannot have infinite passion unless the object of one's passion is highly improbable. A contemporary proponent of the notion that the desire to appeal to evidence or arguments for God's existence inhibits true religion is Don Cupitt, whose work we will return to below.

III

Against an implicit background consensus, then, about the failure of both theistic and atheistic proofs, two rather different types of issues separate realists and non-realists: philosophical points of dispute, and theological (or religious) points of disagreement. I do not think these philosophical and religious concerns, singly or collectively, irrefutably support either realism or non-realism. Nor, more generally, do I think that this is a dispute in which one side must be wholly right and the other wholly wrong. Though I will be defending realism, as we shall see the impetus for non-realism is based on considered, thoughtful reasons, both philosophical and religious, which at the least should make the realist reassess his or her position. Moreover, as we shall also see, the realist/non-realist debate is quickly obviated by dogmatic declamation on either side.

In that spirit, let us look at several philosophical considerations which argue in support of a non-realist rather than a realist view of God. One of the most important derives from the post-Kantian view that if God is noumenal, then *no* historical evidence could ever provide adequate support for belief in the existence and acts of God. Kant himself distinguishes between 'internal' and 'external' revelation.[9] He endorses internal revelation, which is 'God's revelation to us through our own reason' – i.e. natural theology (or what Kant calls transcendental plus natural theology). But he argues against external revelation – that is, religious experience and supernatural revelation – as grounds for warranted belief about God.[10] On Kant's epistemology all experience is structured by the mind of the perceiver. This is why regarding religious experience Kant argues that 'even if God were to make an immediate appearance, I would still need rational theology as a presupposition.' We could never know directly from our experiences that what appears to us (phenomenally) to be the case *vis-à-vis God*, is the case. Since all of our experiences are conceptualised, what we perceive may be just how *we* perceive things, and not how things are in themselves. Hence, neither direct external religious experience (which would later become an historical event) nor historical enquiry about past religious experiences, could ever provide sufficient grounds for *knowing* the existence, acts or nature of God.

In this century, this Kantian position has been conjoined with the conclusions of historical-critical Biblical criticism that the Biblical texts do not provide neutral information, but rather variant *theological* perspectives on the historical events they refer to, events which are often long removed from the actual writing of the books themselves. This has led theologians like Tillich to conclude that:

> . . . faith does not include historical knowledge about the way in which [significant religious events] took place . . . faith cannot be shaken by historical research even if its results are critical of the traditions in which the event is recorded.[11]

For the non-realist, these concessions about historical evidence can become a potent argument *against* realism. In order to circumvent the problem that historical evidence provides insufficient warrant for belief in a mind-independent, self-subsistent God, Kant appeals to pure reason, Kierkegaard turns to an infinitely passionate leap of faith,[12] and Tillich appeals to religious experience[13] while other Neo-Reformed theologians have appealed to the kerygma. The counter to such attempts is that humans will still be isolated on the phenomenal side of the phenomenal/noumenal divide, whether the human attempt to bridge this divide involves pure reason, a leap of faith, an appeal to religious experience, or a turn to the kerygma.[14] For just as historical enquiry is itself inextricably embedded in and thus limited by both the socio-historical context of the enquirer, and the historical context of the record of the event, so too our reason, our commitments, our experience, and even one's understanding of the central proclamations of the world's great religious traditions, are all delimited by the perspective and structured by the socio-historically conditioned mind of the human agent. So continued adherence to belief in a mind-independent divine reality becomes unsupportable. I will attempt to take account of this powerful objection to theological realism when I present an alternative, modified realist position below.

A second way in which the transcendence of a putatively self-subsistent God is thought to negate any possibility that a realist notion of God is meaningful is the idea that language itself must fail to successfully denote or even refer to such a being.[15] In this vein, Gordon Kaufman has argued that:

... if God is ... not to be identified with any of the realities of our experience in the world – then God is absolutely unique, one who cannot be grasped or understood through any of our ordinary concepts or images ... all of our concepts and images ... will never be applicable literally.[16]

Were Kaufman right about this entailment, then this failure of language would seriously undermine a realist conception of God. And indeed, in his recent book, *Theology for a Nuclear Age*, Kaufman lends support to a non-realist view by suggesting that:

The proper criterion for our talk about God ... is not the postulation of some being or reality beyond the world but rather concern with the relativising and humanising activity going on within the world ... God should today be conceived in terms of the complex of physical, biological and historico-cultural conditions which have made human existence possible, which continue to sustain it, and which may draw it out to a fuller humanity and humaneness.[17]

However, I think that Kaufman is mistaken about this purported failure of language.

The problem underlying the question of literal predication of God *qua* noumenal is not unique to monotheism. Since, as Kaufman agrees, all experience is radically conceptualised, the question is not whether *religious* experiences can provide literal knowledge of God in Godself, but whether *any* experiences can in general provide knowledge of the noumenal. There are three conditions which must be met for this to be possible: (a) one must possess the requisite conceptual resources (whatever they are) to have concepts which *are* applicable to the noumenal; (b) one (subsequently) must actually form ideas which could be literally true of the noumenal; and (c) there must be an appropriate connection between one's ideas and the noumenal, so that one's intended truth-claims actually refer to the noumenal.

Now, it is true that even if what we believe is true about God *qua phenomenal* turns out to be true also of God *qua noumenal*, we could never *know* that that was so. We cannot *know* that we possess the requisite conceptual resources to apply to God in Godself, or *know* that we have formed ideas which could be true of God *qua* noumenal, or *know* that our ideas do really properly refer to the noumenal God. But just because we cannot know these things to be true *vis-à-vis* the noumenal God, this surely does not entail that they are not the case. I don't see how it could be shown that it is *impossible* that our concepts or beliefs do in fact correctly refer to the noumenal. Quite the contrary, as the theological realist must hold and I shall argue below, it is precisely a matter of reasonable *faith* that one's religious experiences and theological concepts *do* provide the basis for proper reference and proper talk about God in Godself.

IV

Turning to a third argument, one of the most important and interesting philosophical arguments against theological realism has been developed by D.Z. Phillips. On the basis of a Wittgensteinian language-games analysis of the religious discourse, Phillips provides two considerations which conjointly argue for non-realism: (a) Phillips suggests that religious language-games do not involve truth-claims about a self-subsistent God, and (b) in conjunction with this non-cognitivist approach, he treats religious language-games as inherently exclusionary.

For the most part, Phillips proposes a non-cognitivist view of religious discourse. (Phillips's view is considerably more subtle and complex, but I would like to focus on this one aspect of his work.) In general on a non-cognitivist view, religious statements are regarded as exhortations to lead a certain sort of life, or as prescriptions on how to lead one's life, or as expressing certain kinds of sentiments or attitudes, such as encouragement to lead a moral life. Religious statements, then, are *not* to be understood as expressing truth-claims about the nature or acts of God.

In developing a non-cognitivist view of theological statements, Phillips argues that 'knowledge of God is not theoretical knowledge: it is not a matter of coming to know more *about* anything.'[18] Drawing a sharp distinction between the truth-claims of ordinary cognitivist language-games and contrasting religious language-games, Phillips offers this comparison:

> ... if someone used the pictures of ... plants as proof of the reality of the plants someone might say, with justification, 'I shan't be convinced if you can only show me these pictures. I shall only be convinced when I see the plants'. If, on the other hand, having heard of people praising the Creator of heaven and earth, glorify-

ing the Father of us all, feeling answerable to the One who sees all, someone were to say, 'But these are only religious perspectives, show me what they refer to', this would be a misunderstanding of the grammar of such perspectives. The pictures of the plants refer to their objects, namely, the plants. The religious pictures give one a language in which it is possible to think about human life in a certain way.

And he concludes that:

When these thoughts are found in worship, the praising and the glorifying does not refer to some object called God. Rather, the expression of such praise and glory is what we call the worship of God.[19]

Hence Phillips suggests that 'forms of life . . . do not point beyond themselves to a mystery which they disclose.'[20]

I have argued against this non-cognitivist aspect of Phillips's position elsewhere.[21] In response, Phillips has stated that his fundamental claim is 'that to understand what a religious truth-claim amounts to, attention has to be paid to the grammar of the language in which it is made . . . [and] that it is only within the form of life that we grasp what talk of mystery in this context amounts to.'[22] I think Phillips is right that any mode of comprehension can only be fully understood from the perspective of the form of life or the world-view of that mode of conception. His own work has been instrumental in making us more acutely aware of this *vis-à-vis* religion. Yet I suggest that this does not entail in turn that religious language-games, or forms of life, or world-views (whatever terms this point is cast in) cannot, additionally, be making reference to and denote external, religious entities or states of affairs. Likewise, it seems to me that it need not follow, as Phillips suggests, that disputes about God between believers and non-believers cannot be over matters of fact.

Phillips argues that 'to say that religious pictures must refer to some object . . . that they must describe matters of fact . . . distorts the character of religious belief.'[23] To think of religious faith as purely a matter of belief, or even to treat the cognitive and affective aspects of the religious life as separable, is indeed a grave mistake. This is to impoverish religion, to fail to see that it is based on *ultimate* concern, involving the integration of the whole person. Phillips has helped us see this. Yet religious faith is a dispositional state of the person involving a totality of conative and affective states *as well as* cognitive states of belief (in the narrower, epistemic sense). So to say that religious 'pictures' *do* refer to some object, or *do* describe matters of fact is not to deny that their significance is found in the role they have in people's lives. While we must avoid an intellectualist distortion of faith, theological cognitivism *in and of itself* need not result in a pernicious intellectualist distortion.

Turning to a second point, Phillips's non-cognitivist analysis leads to the even more fundamental view that religious language-games are exclusionary. First, if there is no reference to external, religious facts, then each religious language-game will be exclusionary precisely in so far as it thereby cannot be compared with other language-games, religious or non-religious, *vis-à-vis* external facts or states of affairs. Second, Phillips has defended the general epistemological view that language-games (or world-views) are by nature self-contained. Hence he holds that 'the criteria of truth and falsity in religion are to be found within a religious tradition,' and that 'Religious language is not an interpretation of how things are, but determines how things are for the believer.'[24] If language-games or world-views are incommensurate in the sense that the criteria for truth and reality are completely internal, then it follows that *whatever* ontology is held within one world-view cannot be compared to the ontology held within any other world-view. And this would clearly undermine the notion that there is a self-subsistent reality, God, whose existence is independent of individual world-views. But I do not think that this strong view of the incommensurability of language-games or world-views is tenable.

As Phillips has deftly argued, different world-views are often thoroughly incompatible. Yet while incompatible, they cannot be utterly incommensurate. It is self-stultifying to suppose that one can only understand a language-game or world-view if one actually employs or holds that language-game or world-view. For instance, any judgment about the value or truth of *religion* presupposes the applicability of other world-views than the speaker's own to that judgment. Otherwise one is expressing a mere opinion, which will have no public credence. Phillips himself regards certain religious beliefs as superstitious, e.g. the idea that 'prayer is a way of getting things done which competes with other ways of getting things done,' or taking the notion of the Last Judgment literally.[25] In both cases, Phillips intends to contrast superstitious religious beliefs with

veridical or proper religious beliefs. But if this is going to be convincing to those who are not already inclined to accept these conclusions,
shared standards about what could count as a genuine religious
belief must be presupposed.

This implies that some of the conceptual resources of incompatible world-views must overlap and be mutually applicable to the
issues in question. This of course does not in any way settle the issue
of whether theological discourse is about an entity which is 'out
there'. But just to the extent that language-games or world-views are
shared social structures, involving shared standards and public criteria of success, they will (indeed they must) be able to refer to the
same external states of affairs, and theological realism will become a
cogent and supportable view.

V

In addition to philosophical reasons supporting theological non-
realism, there are several potent religious reasons for holding a non-
realist as opposed to a realist position. I will address three. One can
either offer descriptive or prescriptive religious reasons against realism. Phillips proposes the descriptive thesis that if religious language is properly understood, it is actually non-cognitive and to that
extent non-realist. But the principle theological objections to realism
are prescriptive.

One longstanding objection to theological realism is the charge
that it is inherently religiously defective because God is viewed as so
transcendent that the notion of the divine personal attributes becomes contentless, and God becomes an unavailable no-God. The
realist has several possible replies here. One is to emphasise the
immanence of God along with God's transcendence. Another is to
suggest a means of meaningfully speaking about God. These have
traditionally centred on the notion of analogical predication; more
recently they have centred on the use of models and metaphors. And
still another is to take the primary texts, symbols, images and creedal
statements, and demythologise them. That is, take these traditional
elements of religion and eliminate a too literalistic division between
humankind 'down here' and a God 'out there', emphasising instead
the central message of a God who confronts humans in their very
lives now. But whatever path of theological construction is followed

in this regard, it will be a matter of the details of dogmatic theology whether or not the God so described is both transcendent *and* immanent.

I don't see that it is, in itself, logically or conceptually impossible that God could be both transcendent and immanent. Were this true, then of course the standard Christian traditions of such notions as the Incarnation and the Holy Spirit will turn out to be logically hopelessly confused. The lesson is that a realist theology *will* be postulating a transcendently unavailable God unless God is understood as a personal being who is infinitely attractive and with whom humans can interact in devotion, in love, in moral sensitivity and in joy.

A second, theological objection to realism, which cannot be mitigated by the particular form which dogmatic theology takes, is the trenchant suggestion that theological realism can literally inhibit or even distort the life of faith. This is part of the impetus behind Phillips's analysis of religious discourse. As already noted, he objects for example to the notion that 'prayer is a way of getting things done which competes with other ways of getting things done.' The underlying problem here is that significant religious attitudes are trivialised. Or, to take another example, just as prayer is sometimes treated as a 'magical' way of producing what is in one's own best interest, non-realists frequently regard belief in life after death as having the same irreligious, superstitious quality. For by believing in life after death, one is susceptible to treating religion as important primarily because of a future 'pay-off', and consequently there is an inclination to be less serious about the meaning and morality of one's present life.

One of the most provocative explications of the idea that theological realism actually inhibits the religious life has been developed by Don Cupitt: 'There cannot and must not be any religious interest in any extra-religious existence of God; such a thing would be a frivolous distraction.'[26] To support this non-realist conclusion, Cupitt argues that while traditional, orthodox, theological realism is heteronomous, 'modern people increasingly demand autonomy.' In his aptly named book, *Taking Leave of God*, Cupitt offers two central and mutually reinforcing reasons against theological realism. First, he offers the historical point that a thoroughly heteronomous religion is no longer possible within our contemporary socio-historical context:

It is not merely that people would sharply resent any serious attempt to reimpose it, but rather that it is impossible to reimpose it. Having attained autonomous consciousness, I cannot knowingly revert to a condition in which a bit of my consciousness is hived off and becomes the awesome, inscrutable will of God that directs my course through life. In the age of autonomous morality and consciousness you can only have heteronomous religion as a kind of affectation.[27]

Second, Cupitt argues that 'it is a contradiction to suppose that my highest spiritual freedom could be determined for me from without, and by the act of another.'[28]

In view of these two observations, Cupitt concludes that traditional theological realism can only lead to pessimism, since it engenders a sense of one's own worthlessness, and to scepticism since religion is viewed as only a means to some other end, and not itself intrinsically valuable. Therefore, Cupitt sets out to show how we can give up theological realism and yet retain true religiosity by (a) fully internalising all religious ideas, doctrines, themes and so on, and (b) autonomously adopting religious principles as intrinsically valuable. To do this he calls for a 'New Covenant' which enables religion to reach its highest development by allowing for an inner transformation of human nature which comes from within, as it cannot come from some external, objective authority.

Since he thinks that there is no way to show (indeed he thinks it is doubtful) that there is a supernatural 'Creator-Mind', objective theism does not matter – 'What matters is spirituality':

God is a unifying symbol that eloquently personifies and represents to us everything that spirituality requires of us. The requirement is the will of God, the divine attributes represent to us various aspects of the spiritual life, and God's nature as spirit represents the goal we are to attain . . . God is the religious concern, reified.[29]

And, reminiscent of Gordon Kaufman's notion that 'God should today be conceived in terms of the complex of physical, biological and historico-cultural conditions which . . . draw [human existence] out to a fuller humanity and humaneness,' Cupitt suggests that when we say that God is spirit, we should understand spirit as 'the capacity to exceed one's natural capacities, the power of self-knowledge and self-transcendence'.[30]

In sum, much like Phillips's view that religious language is 'not about matters of fact', Cupitt concludes that 'religious language is not descriptive or metaphysical but intensely practical.'[31] However, while Phillips offers a primarily descriptive analysis of religious language, i.e. if properly understood, it should be understood in non-realist terms, Cupitt expressly recognises that traditional theological language has been realist and offers a non-realist view on prescriptive grounds. In either case, any theological realism which hopes to be religiously significant and intellectually attractive must take account of this concern for enhanced spirituality which Cupitt and other non-realists have brought more keenly to our religious sensitivities.

A third religious reason supporting theological non-realism is connected to this concern for the way in which a distorted dependence on a self-subsistent, transcendent God can inhibit the religious life. The notion that we can know that there is a transcendent God (in Kant's words, 'the most perfect being') can lead to religious presumptuousness. This is the problem of absolutism – the idea that there is one and only one Truth and that much of the project of religion is to help provide access to that Truth. One obvious advantage of the sort of non-realist view which Cupitt develops is that it obviates the presumption of an exclusive insight, or appeal, to a higher authority. If the theological realist hopes to offer an attractive and reputable view within the modern recognition of historicity, of the inescapable enculturation of our own views, and of the radical changes in human world-views across history, the realist must avoid the fatal siren call of the old absolutism. ·

VI

Theological non-realism, then, has developed from a number of important philosophical and religious concerns. How can we best take these concerns into account and resolve the debate between the realists and non-realists? Direct realist responses to non-realism quickly lead to an impasse. For not unlike the famous debate between Father Copleston and Bertrand Russell over whether there might be proof of God's existence, the fundamental point of dispute between realists and non-realists is over the question of sufficient reason. The non-realist offers a vision of the religious life which emphasises spirituality and offers an account of the meaning of religious discourse without reference to a God who possesses aseity. The realist most fundamentally argues that the spiritual life makes sense and religious discourse is meaningful if it involves ontological reference to an external, self-subsistent God. In effect, realists hold that unless such a God exists, there is little if any point to religion; non-realists, on the other hand, hold that the true significance of the religious life can be found apart from any such metaphysical conceptions. This is like Copleston's suggestion that the existence of the universe needs 'a total explanation, to which nothing further can be added,' to which Russell responds, 'Then I can only say that you're looking for something which can't be got . . . I should say that the universe is just there, and that's all.'[32]

The question which Russell raises against Copleston points to the appropriate context for understanding the realist/non-realist debate. As Kant realised, religion will be a matter of superstition and the product of each individual's baser self-interests unless it is assessed on the grounds of its appeal to *any* rational person. Thus, the impasse between the theological realist and non-realist can be broken if we treat the debate not as restricted to these two groups but as occurring within the larger community of rational persons. For the atheist (as well as the agnostic) is a participant in this debate, and the question is not just what kind of religious conception one will have – realist or non-realist – but even more fundamentally, whether it is rational for a person to have *any* religious commitment in our scientific, pluralistic and secular age.

For instance, Cupitt's characterisation of the essence of religious spirituality sounds much like the view from which Feuerbach argues that religion is seriously misguided:

> . . . it is our task to show that the antithesis of divine and human is altogether illusory . . . The divine being is nothing else than the human being, or, rather, the human nature purified, freed from the limits of the individual man, made objective – *i.e.* contemplated and revered as another, a distinct being. All the attributes of the divine nature are, therefore, attributes of the human nature.[33]

And Freud's characterisation of religion as an illusion in so far as it is belief where wish-fulfilment is a prominent factor applies equally to realist and non-realist conceptions of religious belief. Feuerbach sees religion (by projecting an idealised personal being) as alienating humans from themselves; Freud perceives religion as overtly restrictive and a detriment to progress where 'scientific work is the only road which can lead us to a knowledge of reality outside ourselves.'[34]

Perhaps Antony Flew has best summed up the problem facing both realists and non-realists when he argues for the presumption of atheism, i.e. the notion that 'inquiry must start from a position of negative atheism [that is, non-theism], and that the burden of proof lies on the theist proposition.'[35] This is a serious challenge to realist and non-realist alike. For the question is why *in any sense* believe in God; why *in any manner* pursue the religious life? Or, put in Jamesian terms, what is the 'cash value' of religion, what is the 'particular go of it'?[36] Is talk of God, and sin, and grace, and salvation, just a noise signifying nothing? Is religion no more than a debilitating illusion, as Feuerbach and Freud suggest? Hence, rather than the realist responding to the non-realist that without ontological reference to a self-subsistent God, religious faith is foundationless, and the non-realist denying this notion of sufficient reason, the issue for both is: 'Why talk about God at all?' And the question is, which view – that of the realist or the non-realist – offers the best response to this challenge?

VII

Basically then, the realist/non-realist debate is a debate about the choice of world-views – which world-view should guide one's actions and understanding.[37] *First*, there is the choice between religious versus non-religious world-views, and then, if the latter is adopted, there is a choice between theological realist and non-realist world-views. Standard meta-criteria for deciding between alternative hypotheses or systems are the principle of parsimony, the coherence and comprehensiveness of each system, and the significance of the questions answered.

Parsimony clearly favours both atheism and non-realism over realism. However, the principle of parsimony is a secondary criterion. *Ceteris paribus*, if a system answers a greater number and variety of significant questions, or if it offers a more coherent and comprehensive explanation than another system, it will be chosen over that other system even if the latter is more parsimonious. So the choice which the presumption of atheism forces to the surface in the realist/non-realist dispute is the choice between which kind of religious world-view is the more coherent and comprehensive, and which answers the more significant questions.

To take the latter point first, by and large theological realists and non-realists are trying to answer the same sorts of questions about human destiny, the significance of the divine, the importance of the moral life, and so on. Moreover, where realists and non-realists disagree about either which questions need to be answered or the hierarchy of significance of the questions to be answered, they are likely to reach an impasse. For instance, the realist wants to know if God possesses aseity and whether there is life after death. The non-realist thinks that the first is either an unanswerable or misguided question and that the latter preoccupation seriously inhibits genuine religion. Therefore, we must turn to other criteria than the number and significance of the questions each view answers.

This indicates that the most important meta-criterion for deciding between realist and non-realist theological world-views would seem to be the question of coherence and comprehensiveness of the explanation offered. Here again it appears that we find an impasse. From their own points of view, realists and non-realists will each think that their own system is coherent and sufficiently comprehensive. But in fact now we have reached the crux of the debate. For the presumption of atheism challenges precisely such claims to coherence and comprehensiveness, realist and non-realist alike. I think it can be shown that theological realism provides the more coherent and comprehensive explanation of the nature and destiny of humankind, and thus the better explanation for engaging in the religious life.

VIII

Theological realism has at least three interrelated advantages over non-realism. The first has to do with the reality of God.

Given a Kantian perspective, God in Godself, the noumenal God, is not directly accessible to human perception or understanding. But if a realist follows out Kant's metaphysics, then God appears to us *qua* phenomenal. Though there is only one real, noumenal God 'behind', so to speak, phenomenal divine reality, this does *not* mean that God of whom theology speaks is somehow unreal or less real than the noumenal. If the God we confront, the God of history, is God *qua* phenomenal, it does not follow that this God is just a product of our needs or imagination, or is a mere metaphysical shadow. Noumenal reality and phenomenal reality are two different categories of reality, and the terms denote two different senses of 'reality'. There is nothing less real about war and human kindness, tomatoes and tornadoes, because *they* are part of phenomenal reality and not noumenal reality. Likewise the God of history, the God one confronts, is no less real for not being in the category of the noumenal. Like wars and tomatoes and human kindness, the God of history, the God a monotheist confronts, *is* part of reality – for what could be *more* real than that which we do experience? To try to escape the reality of our experience for something putatively 'purer' is to fall prey to the worst element of a degenerate Platonism. For this is to turn away from the only means we *do* have for understanding the divine and our humanity in relation to the divine.

Moreover, this conception of the ontological status of God as a causally efficacious entity in our phenomenal world enables the theological realist to meet the possible problems of subjectivism or conceptual isolation to which non-realists' views are susceptible. The appropriate sort of considerations which should be used in adhering to a monotheistic world-view would be whether one thinks that the meaning of life, or the significance of morality, or the presence of goodness in the universe, can best be explained in theistic terms and are best accounted for in the religious life. Whereas the non-realist can only point to either inner-subjective or inter-subjective valuations of the moral life and spirituality as criteria for the acceptability of the religious life, the realist posits an external state of affairs, namely the existence and acts of the God of history, the God one confronts, which provides the ultimate check on the justification for theistic faith and a religious way of life. These external states of affairs will provide objective, trans-schema criteria for the epistemic justification of theistic faith.

True, such tests for objectivity will only be applicable among the community of persons whose world-views share relevant overlapping conceptual resources. But that is how considerations of objectivity function in any area of human endeavour. In the sciences, for example, checks against proceeding 'unscientifically' only have a place within scientific world-views. The chemist does not consider whether his or her procedures would be acceptable to an alchemist or aborigine. All one needs for a strong check on the objectivity of a theist's beliefs, just as all one needs in the sciences, is a sufficiently overlapping set of world-views which share the relevant concepts and the intent to make reference to some mutually accepted external state of affairs.

This leads to a second advantage of theological realism. Since theological realism inherently emphasises the importance of the cognitive content of religious belief, the realist position supports the central role which reason has in the religious life. On the Kantian (and Wittgensteinian) view that all experience is radically conceptualised, one will quite literally not be able to have any experience of the divine without the relevant conceptual resources. For *all* experiencing is experiencing-as. And what we experience is determined, in part, by the conceptual resources, the world-view, which we bring to experience. Thus *what* is revealed in God's self-revelation and *what* is experienced about God will be inextricably structured by the world-view of the human percipient. So to say that a person is a theist is in part to say that they have a particular world-view, for it is their world-view which enables them to experience the world *as* under the providence of God, or to experience the world *as* an environment for theocentric soul-making, etc. Consequently, without the conceptual resources to understand and experience God, and without the necessary 'cognitive map' of the world which our world-views provide for praxis, it is not possible to engage in explicitly theistic life. Some theology, however elementary, is a necessary condition for the religious life. And as theological realism strongly emphasises, cognition is not a secondary element in that life, but is foundational to any genuinely religious life.

This brings us to a third, and perhaps most important, advantage of theological realism over non-realism. Non-realism runs the danger of reducing the religious life to the morally good life.[38] For instance, Cupitt argues that:

> The main interest of religion is in the conquest of evil by the transformation of the self. We seek to escape from a self that is mean, narrow, darkened, acquisitive . . . and we seek to become autonomous, free, creative, universally-loving and disinterested spirit that has gained release from bondage to sin and death.[39]

This same vision and encouragement of the morally transformed self can be evoked as effectively, it seems to me, without any reference to religion. Bertrand Russell, utterly rejecting any notion of the value of religion, expresses one of the most moving appeals to 'abandon the struggle for private happiness, to expel all eagerness of temporary desire, to burn with passion for eternal things . . . this is the free man's worship':

> One by one, as they march, our comrades vanish from our sight, seized by the silent orders of omnipotent death. Very brief is the time in which we can help them, in which their happiness or misery is decided. Be it ours to shed sunshine on their path, to lighten their sorrows by the balm of sympathy, to give them the pure joy of a never-tiring affection, to strengthen failing courage, to instill faith in hours of despair.[40]

Here again, we are faced with the presumption of atheism. *Surely* many atheists and agnostics have led self-sacrificing lives that command our admiration. Why suppose we need recourse to religion in the quest to become better persons? The realist has an answer which is unavailable for the non-realist. *If there is* a God who is independent of our own human needs and desires, independent of our ultimate limitations and finite perspectives, then it makes an enormous difference whether one tries to come to understand that God and tries to so conform one's life to the divine spirit that one comes to love the things God loves, *because God loves them*. Furthermore, this is not, as Cupitt suggests, to abdicate our moral autonomy, for one must *willingly* decide for oneself to love the things God loves. The non-realist enjoins us to be better persons by transcending our current self-centred selves; the realist enjoins us to be better persons by responding to a transcendent eternal Thou. Through freedom and will, a human being can transcend his or her present place in the natural order but will remain in the natural order. If there is a self-subsistent God, transcendence not just within but beyond the natural order becomes possible.

IX

This is not to argue that only theological realism could be correct, but that it provides a stronger response to the presumption of atheism, a better explanation of and motivation for the religious life, than non-realism does. However, we have seen that there are good reasons supporting a non-realist view. How then might theological realism be modified to take account of the inherent strengths represented by the attraction of non-realism? I will suggest three such features of a modified theological realism.

One strength of non-realism is its outgrowth from the recognition of human historicity. As Karl Barth so vividly puts it:

> . . . we must be prepared for men to take up new positions, new points of view; we must expect new dogmas; we must not be surprised if new motor power is attached to the old carriage of this world, for surely these new things appear every day![41]

I suggest a modified realist position which takes account of this by acknowledging that as each monotheistic community attempts to speak about God in Godself, they will foremost and most directly be speaking about god as *they* experience God, God *qua* phenomenal. And, putting this observation together with the recognition of the historicity of human thought, its relativity to culture and time, we must conclude that there is no one correct trans-historical or cross-cultural understanding of God. For all of our understandings are enculturated. All of our understandings are relative to our own world-views.

Second, I suggest a modified theological realism which avoids the absolutism of Kant's view that *God* is noumenal and that all that theology and religious experience provide is a phenomenal perspective on the noumenal God. If the God of history does not have the ontological status of an existent entity with causal properties in the phenomenal world, then what theology would be most directly referring to would be merely a human idea of the noumenal. This means that we would be unable to speak directly about *God* – we would only be able to speak about something about which we can know that we do not know its true character. Contrariwise, what can be more real than the things we do experience and confront, whether they be the mundane objects of everyday life, other persons – or the God of history? On this modified realist account, the phenomenal God is a real God.

Third, another strength of non-realism is the appropriate humbleness which it brings to our religious attitudes. By denying the possibility that we need only come to know the will of a creator-God who is 'out there' in order to know The Truth and the proper way to salvation, we are made acutely aware of our own failings and our own moral and spiritual responsibility. But this same acute awareness of our responsibility for the views which we come to hold and the actions which we undertake is brought out by the modified realist recognition of the relativity of our views to time and place.

For this recognition forces us to see the presumptuous homocentrism of supposing that we can have direct access, whether by theological conception or religious experience, to God in Godself.

X

However, that very strength seems to raise a serious problem for a modified theological realism. Are we not left on 'this side of the abyss' from God in Godself, even if the God of history, the phenomenal God we confront, is a real God, causally efficacious in our world? Have we not come full circle to the original problem that the postulated *God in Godself* remains an unreachable and therefore unavailable God?

There are four ways to think about God. We can think about God only as God in Godself. But this seems to lead to the notion of an utterly transcendent, unavailable God. We can take the non-realist path, and thereby avoid the problem of divine transcendence. But as we have seen, this raises an even more serious difficulty: why be religious at all, why go beyond humanism? We can claim that God is a real, self-existent being in our experience, but deny altogether that there is a noumenal God. Such a phenomenalist approach also avoids the problem of divine transcendence, but at the cost of giving up the idea that God could exist in Godself, apart from our minds. The fourth alternative is to postulate that beyond the God we confront, there is a self-subsistent noumenal God.

At least two mutually reinforcing considerations argue for the notion of a noumenal God. Regarding the very idea of the noumenal, it seems to me that there could be no argument, except the crassest verificationism, which shows that there could not be things-in-themselves. How could we *know* this to be the case? Second, it is precisely the existence of things-in-themselves 'behind' the phenomenal world which would explain why there is a shared sense of the bruteness of the world and shared limitations at the core of our experiences. It would explain why different perceivers under similar conditions cannot perceive just anything, no matter what their socio-historical world-view, why the world seems to press itself upon us whatever our own concepts and past experiences.

Yet the postulation of the noumenal itself raises the question of our relationship to the noumenal God. John Hick argues for an *inductive* link to the Real, the noumenal God, via the cross-cultural and trans-historical quantity and consistency of the religious experiences of humankind.[42] In focusing on religious experience, I think Hick points us in the right direction. I am not as confident as Hick that the apparently conflicting truth-claims among the world's great religions do not considerably weaken the strength of this inductive inference. But I think that he has identified the crucially important idea of a 'basic religious conviction' – that in different ways the religious experiences of humankind are a *response* to a divine noumenal reality. Commensurate with this, I want to emphasise an aspect of this relation between humankind and the noumenal God: a crucial link between humans and God in Godself is *faith*.

Although we cannot know that what we experience and understand religiously does tell us about the character of the noumenal God, it is a matter of *faith* that one's theological conceptions, however elemental, and one's religious experiences, however mundane, do provide the basis for properly referring to, and therefore speaking about, God in Godself. Given the dichotomy between the noumenal God and the God of history, faith in God implicitly involves the trust that one does possess concepts and beliefs which are not only applicable to 'The' God of one's own history, but also to God in Godself, and thus that God in Godself is somehow manifest in one's own experience of the God one confronts in history.

As Tillich has so accurately pointed out, faith inherently involves doubt.[43] The risk of faith, we can now see, has two aspects: it is the risk that our theological conceptions do not in fact refer to an existent *phenomenal* God, and it is the risk that our human beliefs fail to correctly refer to the *noumenal* God. But the commitment of faith includes the trust that they do both. Tillich defines revelation as 'the experience in which an ultimate concern *grasps* the human mind.'[44] And Karl Barth suggests that: 'Religion brings us to the place where we must wait, in order that God may *confront* us.'[45] Revelation is not a matter of the conveyance of true propositions about God; rather, revelation is the *self*-manifestation of God. And thus, justified belief in God has two essential foundations: reason and *faith* – where faith is the human response to God's self-manifestation.

Faith involves the ultimate commitment that one has indeed confronted God in Godself, a divine reality that is independent of our human minds. And it is the experience and life of faith which bridges the abyss that separates us from an otherwise unavailable God.[46]

Notes

1. Jean-Paul Sartre, *The Devil and the Good Lord*, trans. Kitty Black, Act III, scene x.
2. John A.T. Robinson, *Honest to God* (Philadelphia: Westminster Press, 1963), p. 43. (Italics mine.)
3. I will assume here that talk about God, whether realist or non-realist, is at least semantically meaningful. In particular, it seems to me that the attempts to formulate verificationist principles, which would succeed in showing that realist theological language is meaningless, have clearly failed. For a classic presentation of verificationism against theism see A.J. Ayer, *Language, Truth, and Logic* (New York: Dover, 1952), Introduction, pp. 5–16, and pp. 115–17. A clear and concise response is offered by George I. Mavrodes in 'God and Verification', *Canadian Journal of Theology*, Vol. 10 (1964), reprinted in Malcolm L. Diamond and Thomas V. Litzenburg, Jr. (eds), *The Logic of God: Theology and Verification* (Indianapolis, Ind.: Bobbs-Merrill, 1975), p. 223. See also Alvin Plantinga, *God and Other Minds: A Study of the Rational Justification of Belief in God* (Ithaca, NY: Cornell University Press, 1967), pp. 156–68. John Hick takes a different tack, accepting the verificationist challenge and arguing that the existence of God is a potentially verifiable fact. See Hick, 'Theology and Verification', *Theology Today*, Vol. 17 (1960), reprinted in Basil Mitchell (ed.), *The Philosophy of Religion* (Oxford University Press, Oxford Readings in Philosophy, 1971), pp. 53–71.
4. David Hume, in Nelson Pike (ed.), *Dialogues Concerning Natural Religion* (New York: Bobbs-Merrill, 1970), Part V (pp. 48 and 51). Cf. Part II (p. 32).
5. Immanuel Kant, *Critique of Pure Reason*, trans. Norman Kemp Smith (London: Macmillan, repr. 1973), pp. 500–24.
6. Note that Kant's moral argument is not intended as a proof of God's existence but as support for the conviction that God exists: 'I must not even say, "*It is* morally certain that there is a God, etc.", but "*I am* morally certain, etc."' Ibid., p. 857.
7. Ibid., p. 530.
8. Immanuel Kant, in Allen W. Wood and Gertrude M. Clark (eds), *Lectures on Philosophical Theology* (Ithaca and London: Cornell University Press: 1978), p. 161.
9. Ibid., p. 160.
10. See Kant, *Lectures*, op. cit., p. 30, and *Critique*, op. cit., pp. 525–31.
11. Paul Tillich, *Dynamics of Faith* (New York: Harper & Row, 1958), p. 89.
12. Kierkegaard thinks that 'the greatest attainable certainty with respect to anything historical is merely an *approximation*' and that any belief which is based upon an approximation is, by that very fact, 'essentially incommensurable with an infinite personal interest in an eternal happiness', which is precisely what faith requires. (Soren Kierkegaard, *Philosophical Fragments*, trans. David F. Swenson, 2nd ed., trans. rev. by Howard V. Hong (Princeton, NJ: Princeton University Press, 1962), p. 25 and p. 26).

13. Tillich, op. cit., p. 61. Though Tillich denies that the Ultimate Concern is 'a being', I take it that Tillich holds a realist view of the divine reality.
14. On the failure of appeals to the kerygma to solve this problem see my 'Relativism and Absolutism in Bultmann's Demythologizing Hermeneutic', *The Scottish Journal of Theology*, Vol. 32, No. 5 (1979), pp. 401–19.
15. I attempt to show that reference to the noumenal God is possible in *Reason, Relativism and God* (London: Macmillan, 1986, and New York: St. Martin's Press, 1986), pp. 242–53.
16. Gordon Kaufman, *The Theological Imagination* (Philadelphiha: Westminster Press, 1981), p. 268 and p. 72.
17. Gordon D. Kaufman, *Theology for a Nuclear Age* (Philadelphia: Westminster Press, 1985; Manchester: Manchester University Press, 1985), pp. 37 and 42. Despite the non-realist tone of these remarks, Kaufman has indicated in conversation that he does not mean to deny that there is a noumenal God, but is, rather, agnostic about what we could *know* about God *qua* noumenal. I think that in the passage cited, and in similar passages, he has not been clear about when he is talking about God *as we* perceive and understand God versus God in Godself. It is, I take it, meant to be talk about the phenomenal world when Kaufman says: 'The divine activity . . . must . . . apparently be conceived now as inseparable from, and as working in and through, the activity of the human spirit itself, as it creatively produces the cultures which make human life human' (p. 40).
18. D.Z. Phillips, *The Concept of Prayer* (New York: Schocken Books, 1966), p. 60. See also *Faith and Philosophical Enquiry* (New York: Schocken Books, 1971), p. 29.
19. D.Z. Phillips, *Religion Without Explanation* (Oxford: Blackwell, 1976), pp. 148–149.
20. D.Z. Phillips, 'Religion and Epistemology: Some Contemporary Confusions', in *Faith and Philosophical Enquiry*, op. cit., p. 138.
21. See 'Religion, Relativism, and Conceptual Schemas', in *The Heythrop Journal*, Vol. 24, No. 1 (1983), and *Reason, Relativism and God*, op. cit., pp. 176–86.
22. D.Z. Phillips, review of *Reason, Relativism and God* in *The Times Literary Supplement*, 14 November, 1986, p. 1289.
23. Phillips, *Faith and Philosophical Enquiry*, op. cit., p. 1, and *Religion Without Explanation*, op. cit., p. 150.
24. Phillips, 'Philosophy, Theology, and the Reality of God', op. cit., p. 12, and 'Religion and Epistemology', in *Faith and Philosophical Enquiry*, op. cit., p. 132.
25. Phillips, 'Religious Beliefs and Language-Games', p. 103, and 'Belief and Loss of Belief', p. 116, repr. in *Faith and Philosophical Enquiry*, op. cit.
26. Don Cupitt, *Taking Leave of God* (New York: Crossroad, 1981), p. 9.
27. Ibid., p. xi.
28. Ibid., p. 96.
29. Ibid., p. 9.

30. Ibid., p. 88.
31. Ibid., p. 164.
32. Bertrand Russell and F.C. Copleston, 'A Debate on the Existence of God', repr. in John Hick (ed.), *The Existence of God* (New York: Macmillan, 1964), pp. 173 and 175.
33. Ludwig Feuerbach, *The Essence of Christianity*, trans. George Eliot (New York: Harper & Row, Harper Torchbooks, 1957), pp. 13–14.
34. Sigmund Freud, *The Failure of an Illusion* (Garden City, NY: Doubleday, rev. 1964), p. 50.
35. Antony Flew, *The Presumption of Atheism and Other Philosophical Essays on God, Freedom, and Immortality* (London: Elek, 1976), p. 18.
36. See William James, 'Pragmatism's Conception of Truth', in *Pragmatism and the Meaning of Truth* (Cambridge, Mass.: Harvard University Press, 1975).
37. When I speak here of 'choosing' a world-view I do not mean that we choose a world-view, among alternatives, *in toto* – that would be impossible. Rather, we can alter our world-views, retaining portions of our old world-view but making sufficient, fundamental changes such that we would say that we now hold a new, different world-view.
38. This is not to say that a theological realist might not run the same risk. Kant, in identifying genuine religion as 'the recognition of all duties as divine commands', falls into just this problem. See Kant, *Religion Within the Limits of Reason Alone*, trans. Theodore M. Green and Hoyt H. Hudson (New York: Harper & Row, Harper Torchbooks, 1960), p. 142.
39. Cupitt, op. cit., p. 164.
40. Bertrand Russell, 'A Free Man's Worship', in *The Meaning of Life*, p. 61.
41. Karl Barth, *The Epistle to the Romans* (Oxford University Press, 6th edn, repr. 1972), p. 435.
42. John Hick, *The Problems of Religious Pluralism* (New York: St. Martin's Press, 1985), p. 37. See also Hick, *God Has Many Names* (Philadelphia: Westminster Press, 1982).
43. See Paul Tillich, *Dynamics of Faith* (New York: Harper & Row, 1957), p. 20.
44. Ibid., p. 78. Italics mine.
45. Barth, op. cit., p. 242. Italics mine.
46. A version of this paper was read at the University of London. I am indebted to the faculty of that university, especially Stewart Sutherland and Keith Ward, and also to John Hick, Gordon Kaufman and Scott Shalkowski, for helpful discussions on ideas in this paper. I also wish to thank the National Endowment for the Humanities for a Summer Stipend Award which supported my work on this paper.

It's Time to Talk About Trust

JUNE O'CONNOR

Joseph Runzo assists our debate by highlighting it precisely *as debate*. Runzo the realist admirably lingers over the genuine validity and plausibility of the questions and objections to realism raised by non-realists, *given their differing assumptions*. These radically differing assumptions, earlier explicated by Hick, urge us, I believe, to face the fundamental role that *trust* plays in philosophy and theology. I shall return to this point.

Realist Runzo's six arguments on behalf of non-realism immediately raise for me a set of questions: Do they touch what religious realists regard as the heart of the matter (namely that God exists independently of the mind and of human thought)? Or are they not examples of what Hick terms 'associated issues' which are often confused with the realist/non-realist debate and which need to be stripped away if our discussion is to be clearly focussed and fruitful? In short, we are not talking about different things when we speak of realism?

Certainly realism can be described in a one-liner: realism claims that God exists independently of belief. But there are notable variations on this claim, as the conference papers make clear. Don Cupitt regards realism, rather, as a stance that holds that a metaphysical good news underpins our lives and that the God in whom ethical standards are invested assures us that ultimately all will be well. (Cupitt's own view is other than this. For him Christianity starts when Christ realises prior to his passion that he is not going to be bailed out.) Realism and non-realism have as much to do with the sense of assurance or non-assurance in one's fundamental reading of the universe as it does with metaphysical claims or denials.

D.Z. Phillips demonstrates the ambiguity of terms by noting that he has been accepted as a realist and non-realist both. He calls himself neither realist or non-realist, finding these terms to be merely 'battle cries'. Phillips is less interested in making claims about the nature of God as dependent or independent of human thought than he is in analysing the God-language that is used by both sides.

Disagreement about the central topic thus characterises our discussion. Joseph Runzo identifies the fundamental point to be 'the

question of sufficient reason' which can be reduced to a consideration of whether or not God functions as a necessary or non-necessary
feature in a given world-view. John Hick had earlier named the
fundamental ('real') issue of the debate to be that of our assumptions
about the nature or structure of the universe as good, bad or indifferent. For Hick, the realist sees at the heart of the structure of the
universe a transcendent and ultimate Reality which is our final
good, so that living in relation to that Reality is to live in accordance
with reality and not illusion. The widely acknowledged fact that
human beings are in radical need of transformation explains in part
the human quest for assistance from and receptivity to transcendent
Reality. Since non-realism accepts and asserts a naturalistic view of
life and allows no non-natural facts, it differs from a (critical) realist
religious perspective in this very fundamental way: non-realism
offers a profound pessimism in so far as we alone and this life alone
constitute the resources for our own fulfilment and transformation.
Not a happy thought to Hick who is impressed by (which is to say
depressed by?) the multitudes of human beings whose potential has
been forever denied because of untimely death from disease, torture,
slavery, starvation, slaughter by enemies and other forms of oppression. Thus in differing ways, both Runzo and Hick seek to cut
through the multiplicity of claims and counter-claims and isolate the
heart of the matter.

Runzo's threefold defence of theological realism as more coherent
and comprehensive and offering a better explanation and motivation for the religious life offers insight into Runzo's theology, but, I
think, will not and cannot cut ice with non-realists. (a) Finding
meaning in the Kantian categories of noumenal and phenomenal,
Runzo sees these as radically and integrally related aspects of reality. The phenomenon of religious experience is thus to be understood as a genuine and trustworthy expression (which is not to say
the only or unique expression) of the noumenal God in Godself. Yet
the non-realists reject the noumenal God of Kant as they reject the
transcendent Reality of Hick. (b) Runzo's affirmation of reason and
cognition as foundational to the religious life does not function to
further his argument, but only to repudiate non-cognitivism. Non-
realists, like realists, value reason in the analysis of religion. Reason
is a tool for assessing claims, is neither a claim nor a denial in itself.
(c) Runzo's critique that non-realism runs the risk and danger of
reducing the religious life to a morally good life is an assertion, not
an argument. While Runzo the realist finds this to be an inadequate

rendering of the religious life, someone like Cupitt the non-realist not only affirms this position but adds the further claim that envisioning the Christian religious life essentially as a moral and spiritual enterprise is an improved, indeed superior and more realistic (!) view that perpetuating a metaphysically based view. Runzo's defence, then, illuminates us about his standpoint, but is unable to alter the assumptions of the non-realist.

Runzo's proposal for a 'modified theological realism', not dissimilar to the critical religious realism proposed by Hick, is further supported by three additional bases: (a) since there is no proof that things do not exist in themselves (for only the crassest verificationism would say so), things might exist in themselves; (b) the religious experiences of humankind described across the world and throughout the centuries suggest that these experiences are a response to a divine noumenal reality; and (c) our faith in God means that we can trust our conceptions and experiences, that is trust that the phenomenal is a real expression of the noumenal. Runzo's modified theological realism, in sum, recommends to us (a) a possible truth, (b) cross-cultural testimony, and (c) faith that our concepts and beliefs are trustworthy.

Yet surely I am not alone in anticipating the following non-realist response: (a) that it is true also that things might not exist in themselves; (b) to the extent that the religions of the world share in the illusion of a transcendent ontological referent that exists independently of human thought, the project of unmasking these illusions in Christianity is applicable to these other religions as well; and (c) that non-realists, too, trust their conceptions and experiences and that it is precisely these conceptions and experiences that move them to demythologise and remythologise religion in the name of accuracy and autonomy. Runzo's thesis does aid the debate, not by being compelling, which it is not, but by telling us how Runzo thinks about these important matters and where he stands on the issues.

And so I return to my opening remarks about trust, wanting to linger on the central role that trust plays in philosophical and theological enquiry. Runzo gives glimpses into those views and values which win and nourish his trust. The non-realist does the same. Such reflection can be seen as a matter of where those reflecting place their trust and why. On what grounds does it rest? In what ways does it function? What ends does it serve? I think we would do well to give sustained attention to the place of trust in philosophical and theological reflection. In this 'debate', none of the principals has voiced the foundational character and role of trust in philosophical and theological discourse, nor have they described the trajectories of their lives, those contexts in which trust is aroused, tested and altered.

I suggest that we would gain insight further and faster in a discussion such as this by laying out in narrative form our own personal trajectories, giving emphasis to the intellectual and other prominent influences that mark our life stories. Could we not understand one another more accurately and more quickly by being specific about the settings of our lives in which selected events, persons, experiences, symbols and arguments have compelled our attention, grasped our affection, and evoked our trust?

Such an approach has worked elsewhere. I think that a dialogue such as this one could benefit, for example, from the experience and experiment described by Sidney and Daniel Callahan who are major voices in the abortion debate. Sidney is pro-life on abortion, Daniel pro-choice. The question that fascinated them most is best described in their own words:

> Ever since the topic of abortion became of professional interest to us, in the 1960s, we have disagreed. At one time, while Daniel was writing a book on the subject, *Abortion: Law, Choice and Morality* (1970), we talked about the subject every day for the four years of the book's gestation . . . Over the years, every argument, every statistic, every historical example cited in the literature has been discussed by the two of us. As Eliza Doolittle says about 'words' in *My Fair Lady*, 'There's not a one I haven't heard.'
>
> And yet we still disagree. How can it be, we ask ourselves, that intelligent people of goodwill who know all the same facts and all the same arguments still come down on different sides of the controversy?

Driven by that question, the Callahans invited a group of thinkers known for differing views on abortion to meet with one another and talk. Convinced by their studies in psychology and philosophy that one's position on important matters reflects deep and pervasive premises about the self and the world, they asked the book's participants to back up a bit and give sustained attention to the prior assumptions and deeper values that inform their judgments. They were 'looking for a shift in focus from the tip of the iceberg – the public debate on abortion morality and policy – to the submerged underlying mass.' Participants were thus asked to provide autobio-graphical statements describing the development of their ideas and addressing the question of how and why they weigh and order their values as they do. The result: a rich set of essays entitled *Abortion: Understanding Differences* (ed. Sidney Callahan and Daniel Callahan, New York: Plenum, 1984). This kind of exchange, I believe, would deepen, hasten and enrich understanding of our differences in the realist/non-realist debate in religion as well.

An example: Runzo alerts us to the centrality of autonomy in Don Cupitt's non-realism. I for one would like to hear Cupitt talk about this central value more personally. Given his observation/interpre-tation that 'modern people increasingly demand autonomy' and that heteronomous religion is no longer a viable option but is at most a kind of affectation, I would like us to pursue these perceptions and judgments against the backgrounds of our lives. What is for him a given and a good, is for me a problem and a danger. When I analyse the experience of freedom, which Cupitt calls autonomy, I see and feel and remember images that appear quite different from those implied by Cupitt. I am not inclined to accept autonomy as a good, over against heteronomy or theonomy which are seen as restricting and constricting evils. I find all three of these terms inadequate and thus I cast about for another option, yet lack a term to name it. I grasp at words not yet formulated – 'ouronomy', 'communonomy', wanting to capture one word that means freedom-in-through-and-due-to-community.

Freedom, I think, is less a goal treasured by the single self than an expansion of the self made possible by others. Freedom occurs through invitation, through the calling forth of one's attention, con-cerns, ability to wonder, capacity to notice, to give, to create, to act, to do. Freedom does involve *my* actualisation, *my* expression, *my* decision and is not merely a dependence on others. But most often my growth into freedom is initiated from without, is stimulated in a way that I would not, perhaps could not, give to or do to myself. I tap my freedom, I find, precisely in so far as I am encouraged and called forth by others.

When I reflect on the meaning and place of freedom in my life, I am much more drawn to a view of freedom reminiscent of St Augus-tine, wherein one's greatest freedom consists in wanting and desir-ing and willing and choosing that which one is: gifted creature in relation. As *creature*, I am free to the extent that I recognise that standing, to the extent that I am in touch with and in tune with that reality and with the origin and destiny of my reality, whom I call God. As *gifted*, I am free to the extent that I recognise and utilise those gifts of critical intelligence, imagination, empathy, creativity, intentionality, choice, capacity to act, ability to relate, and the like. The enlightenment, rationalist, empiricist world-view urges me to place the spotlight on my giftedness and to recognise that talk about God is superfluous, a distraction from the rich resources present in the self.

Yet that rendering of experience is for me incomplete. I experience self as one gifted first of all and pre-eminently with life from without. My contingency shouts loudly. Not consulted about whether to exist or not, I simply find myself existing. And the longer I exist the more gifts I find, not because I have 'achieved autonomy' (though I have indeed become actualised in ways not true in younger years) but because I have had my gifts called out of me by the enabling and empowering presence of friends and adversaries, family and stranger, and, I think/believe, a God I've met in prayer and in people, in nature and in thought.

And so although I do not identify with nor value as much as he the sense of autonomy Cupitt writes about, I wish better to understand why he is drawn to it not only as a given but also as a good. And I wish to have him consider what I see when I say 'autonomy' and 'freedom'. I cite this as one minute example of what might be involved if we were to examine and voice that submerged underlying mass of convictions, dispositions and inclinations that shape our assumptions and give direction to our arguments. This fuller form of exchange would, I trust (there it is, once again), enrich the quality and enhance the clarity of debates such as this.

9

The Religious Necessity of Realism

PAUL BADHAM

Don Cupitt is undoubtedly right that ever since the enlightenment there has been a steady ebbing of the Sea of Faith,[1] and that Christian thinkers who are sensitive to the thought of their own day find themselves increasingly forced to abandon or reinterpret the claims of historic Christianity. Compared with their ancestors in the faith, almost all contemporary Christians are to a greater or lesser extent non-realist in their understanding of at least some elements in Christian doctrine. For example, a Christian speaking of the divine inspiration of the Bible will not usually claim that God literally dictated the text to the human scribes. Nor are Christians usually happy to spell out any clear or coherent presentation of how God can be thought of as acting in history, or providentially determining what happens to each one of us. Liberal Christians have felt uneasy at the notion of Christ's death literally bringing at-one-ment with God by changing God's attitude to the human race, and few can be found to defend a full-blooded account of hell or judgment. More controversially, it has been common for radical Christian thinkers to remove any biological content to the concept of the virgin birth, or any objective content to belief in the resurrection of Jesus, his second coming, or a life after death. In proposing that Christians should take leave of the notion of an objective God, Cupitt is taking the final step on a road along which many Christians have been walking.

Cupitt believes that modern European thought has decisively undermined the historic claims of Christianity. Yet he thinks that some religious values have been an inspiration for good, and that it would be a tragedy if these values were to be lost to humanity simply because the thought-forms which nourished them in the past seem on the verge of perishing forever. Ostensibly therefore Don

Cupitt claims that non-realism enables religious values to be preserved, while untenable propositional claims are abandoned.[2]

In one sense therefore Cupitt might be thought to be doing what liberal Protestants claimed to be doing, that is to liberate the kernel of true faith from the husk of outmoded thought. But there is a difference between pruning over-luxuriant growth, and pulling up all the flowers by the roots. Liberals characteristically affirmed all the old beliefs but suggested they be re-interpreted in the light of modern knowledge. Thus, for example, liberals abandoned belief in a six-day creation in favour of belief in God creating through evolution; a degree-Christology replaced an ontological Christology; and exemplarist theories of the atonement replaced objective ones. But in all cases the heart of the belief system remained in place. This is not the case with non-realism which proposes that the heart be removed. And though it is essential to Cupitt's case that 'religious values' can be preserved, there are major difficulties in giving content to this notion for the values to which theistic religions have given most importance depend on a realist view of God.

At the heart of all theistic faith is the belief that through prayer, worship, religious or mystical experience or vision it is possible to enter into a relationship with God. This belief in a divine encounter is utterly undermined by the claim that such experiences do not have any transcendent source, but arise solely from the subjectivity of the believer. Hence the unknown author of the Epistle to the Hebrews was expressing an important psychological truth about belief when he said that whoever would draw to God must believe both that he exists and that he rewards those who seek him.[3] Throughout the centuries countless deeply religious men and women have been haunted by the fear that their faith might be based on a delusion. This was indeed Muhammad's first response to his sense of a divine call, that it might be nothing more than the product of his own deranged imagination.[4] Four centuries later, shortly after the completion of his elegant Platonic argument for God's existence, St Anselm found himself tortured by the thought that perhaps the all-perfect God of his beautifully constructed thought-system was precisely that, and no more. For Anselm this undercut the whole of his religious life. He found himself unable to sleep, eat, pray or fulfil his duties as prior, such was 'the agony and conflict of his thoughts'.[5] For if God exists in the mind alone, and not in reality also, he could not be that perfect being who alone could be worthy of human devotion. As we know Anselm ultimately underwent an overwhelming religious experience which he described thus:

I have found a fulness of joy that is more than full. It is a joy that fills the whole heart, mind, and soul. Indeed it fills the whole of a man, and yet joy beyond measure remains.[6]

On the basis of this experience St Anselm was led to what might be, for the believer personally, a legitimate conclusion: 'This *is* so truly that it is not possible to think of it as not existing.'[7] And this fact about what is necessary for the personal faith of the devout believer is not affected by the falsity of St Anselm's subsequent application of this as an argument for others concerning God's necessary existence. The most that can be legitimately claimed is that belief in God's reality is a necessary condition for believing that one has entered into a living relationship with him.

What is significant is that both Muhammad and Anselm took for granted that if their religious experience *had been* auto-induced, and not inspired by a transcendent source, it would thereby have been falsified. Hitherto this has been the all but unanimous view of all Jews, Christians and Muslims, as well as of scholars opposed to these traditions. This is why over the past two centuries, psychological or sociological theories, such as those of Feuerbach, Marx or Freud, which have offered alternative explanations for religious feelings have been felt to provide the most damaging critiques of religion. I suggest that they remain so, for if one starts from within the Judaeo-Christian tradition it is clear that the supreme religious value, as summarised by the Torah, and as endorsed by Jesus, is that God be loved with the whole heart, soul (mind) and strength.[8] And God cannot be truly loved if we believe him to be only a non-real concept of our own choosing. Moreover, if we explore what loving God means by reference to the Psalms of the Old Testament or the Epistles of the New, it is clear that the love of God has two components: personal emotional commitment and devotion, and the thought that such devotion will naturally lead to a wish to keep God's commandments.[9] Comparable claims can be made for Islam and Sikhism, where what is of supreme religious value is the attitude of adoring submission to God and of obedience to his holy will. In all these theistic traditions, as well as in Bhakti Hinduism, loving devotion to, or humble adoration of, God as a transcendent reality is seen as the supreme religious value. And hence any account of 'religious values' which ignores these dimensions ignores aspects which seem to be at the heart of the religious quest of most of the human race.

From the perspective of the one who prays, religious experience cannot be classified as non-real. When prayer is experienced in terms of encounter, or personal relationship, or of communion, it cannot, without contradiction, be thought by the believer to be subjective. Only a realist understanding of theism can allow for the genuine possibility of this type of religious experiencing, and if this is thought to be of value then a non-realist understanding of theology cannot be religiously satisfying.

Don Cupitt recognises this. Consequently although he wishes 'formal' modes of worship to continue, he denies that the ecstatic, personal or mystical forms of worship have any authentic place in Christianity. He believes that mystical experience is 'pagan rather than Christian', and derives from 'thwarted eroticism'. In fact this kind of religion 'just is sublimated and purified eroticism'.[10] Cupitt believes that 'modern anthropomorphic theism with its demand for a *felt* relation to a personal God has become a different religion from the more austere faith of the ancient and medieval periods'.[11] He thinks that modern piety with its idea of 'an intimate one-to-one rapport with a vividly experienced guiding and loving fatherly presence' is very different from ancient and medieval prayer which 'was relatively formal, distant and highly ritualised.'[12] Hence Cupitt thinks that the idea of a felt relationship to God, so far from being the essence of faith, is simply a heterodox and modern[13] distortion of it, which has gained power in contemporary Christianity for reasons which Freudian psychology can help us to understand.[14] 'Faith in a personal God' is for Cupitt a 'state of erotic fixation or enslavement' from which we need deliverance.[15]

At this point the issue hinges on what one believes is important in the Christian religion. If one accepts a basically Freudian explanation of theistic religious experience, and if one also accepts Cupitt's historical judgment that belief in a relationship with a personal God represents a modern deviation from authentic Christian spirituality, then the fact that this kind of piety would not be available to a person who accepted non-realism is of no significance. On the other hand, if one thinks that not all mystical experience can be categorised as 'sublimated eroticism', and that many mature and happily married Christians have a strong sense of communion with God, and if one thinks that from the psalmists onwards a personal relationship with God has been part and parcel of the Judaeo-Christian tradition then one would come to a very different conclusion. My own reading of the historical data is that the prophets and psalmists in ancient Israel had a very profound sense of closeness to God, and that this understanding was greatly developed in New

Testament Christianity. Within the historic tradition I would see the Confessions of St Augustine, the writings of the Cappadocian Fathers, the prayers of St Anselm, the hymns of St Bernard and the poems of the Medieval Mystics of England as testifying through the ages to the experience of intimate, immediate and close relationship with God as the living heart and fount of Christian spirituality.[16] Hence I would argue that theological realism is a religious necessity.

Turning from personal and mystical prayer to the liturgical worship of which Don Cupitt approves, I fail to see why he feels that participation in such worship is sensible for a person with a non-realist faith. He makes a reasoned case for believing that worship could be justified for both an atheist and non-realist Christian for the effect it could have on the inwardness of the worshipper, and he believes that since 'the aim of worship is to declare one's complete and *disinterested* commitment to religious values,'[17] there is no need to postulate the existence of a divine being to validate such worship. His discussion is in many ways reminiscent of Kant's justification for worship in his *Religion within the limits of reason alone*. Kant believed that godliness should 'merely serve as a means of strengthening that which in itself goes to make a better man, to wit, the virtuous disposition' and consequently the only authentic purpose of prayer or worship is to establish goodness *in ourselves*, and to spread abroad such goodness within the ethical community.[18] However Kant recognised that this was all completely theoretical since that worship actually on offer in the Christian Churches was not appropriate for the purposes he had in mind, and indeed unhelpful to it. Hence he never actually attended public worship, and even made a point of leaving university processions at the church door.[19]

The point is that worship in all the Christian Churches is thoroughly realist, and increasingly under the influence of the ecumenical and liturgical movements is becoming more and more uniform focusing on the Eucharist, and therein rehearsing a constant succession of propositional claims about God and his saving activity in the life and work of Christ. Liberal Christians often find their worshipping marred by the pre-critical way these claims are presented, but by a process of internal reinterpretation they are enabled to continue in their participation. For liberals characteristically believe themselves not to be abandoning, but to be reappropriating, essential truths contained in outmoded forms. It is much harder to see why a non-realist should worship, because for the non-realist there is no inner core of truth to be discovered.

Don Cupitt has sought to meet this objection by pointing out that much of Christian worship consists of Old Testament material which reflects a religion, society and culture utterly removed from the thought-world of the contemporary Christian.[20] If for two thousand years Christians have used in their worship the hymn book of the second Jewish Temple without endorsing the belief system assumed by it, why cannot the contemporary non-realist celebrate a Christian Eucharist with just as much ease? But this analogy will not do. Christians have not used the Old Testament in its own right. In pre-critical days a tradition of reinterpretation led the Old Testament to be read through Christian spectacles, and reinterpreted to illustrate Christian themes. Since the rise of criticism the Old Testament has been less and less used and, at least in the main Sunday worship, only such carefully selected extracts as accord with Christian ideals continue to be read. In particular the Psalms have been used, not as alien literature, but because they articulate what Christians wish to say. Hence I reject the analogy and suggest that only for a realist faith does Christian worship remain a sensible activity.

It should be noted that the arguments I have hitherto used in associating worship with realism apply even more strongly in other religious contexts. Since celibacy is regarded as sinful in Zoroastrianism, and is not valued in Islam, Freudian interpretations of their worship are much less plausible. In the case of Islamic worship the prayer is wholly centred on the adoration and praise of God and would become a nonsensical activity if God were thought to be unreal. The same also applies to Sikhism and to Hindu worship in the Bhakti tradition.

It might be thought that I have laid too much weight on religious 'feeling'. But I have done so because the possibility of a personal relationship with God is of crucial importance to a realist account of faith today. The strength of the non-realist case is that many professed theists have an entirely secular world-view in that their expectations of life are not affected by their belief in God. For most Christians, belief in particular providence perished with the rise of actuarial statistics, the indiscriminate slaughter of the First World War, and the holocaust of European Jewry in the Second. And though some may continue to believe in special divine intervention or answered prayer, the problems of fitting such alleged instances into any coherent theodicy seem insuperable. So what difference does belief in God make? Unless some answer can be given to this question the non-realist case is established.

Only two answers seem possible: first that through the existence of a personal relationship with God human situations can be transformed from within; second that in the light of the quality of the personal relationship with God it may seem for the believer plausible to hope that God will wish to sustain the relationship through death. Are these answers intelligible? First, at least some believers do claim that their consciousness of God's presence has utterly transformed otherwise intolerable situations. Bishop Leonard Wilson of Birmingham, who ordained me, affirmed that he had never been so conscious of God's sustaining and redeeming love than when he was being tortured in Changi prisoner-of-war camp. In external terms God did precisely nothing. No particular providence rescued him from his torturers, and yet his sense of the presence of God suffering with him in his distress, not merely transformed the situation for him then, but subsequently sustained him in his faith for the rest of his life. This is no isolated case, but is typical of the record of countless Christian martyrs and sufferers through the ages. Now of course there are problems with such claims. No doubt a psychological theory of compensatory projection can be constructed, and cases can be raised, as in the instance of Jesus's cry of dereliction from the cross, when God seems wholly to abandon the sufferer at precisely the time when he was most needed. Nevertheless it is significant that belief in divine grace can make a difference to the human experience of events in the world, both in some cases of suffering, and also through conversion experiences. It may be impossible to demonstrate to others that such experiences arise from anything other than the human subconscious. But it is essential for the believer to suppose that they come from a transcendent source. The experience has its transforming power because it is believed to come from a real God.

Belief in a life after death is another case where a difference between realist and non-realist interpretations of faith becomes apparent. For Christians who interpret life after death as a factual claim, their belief stems from their trust in the constancy of God, his power and his love. I believe it can be shown that throughout the history of Christian thought belief in a future life was of supreme importance, that it was understood in a thoroughly realist sense, and that it significantly affected the way Christians looked at life.

Don Cupitt however, believes that 'it is spiritually important that one should not believe in life after death but should instead strive to attain the goal of the spiritual life in history.'[21] He believes that faith in a future life should be rejected on religious grounds because it conflicts with his understanding of *disinterestedness* as the supreme spiritual value. To love God for the sake of benefits whether in this life or the next would be spiritually corrupting. Hence in prayer we should learn to expect no benefits whether earthly or heavenly, but follow St John of the Cross in the purgative way up the Ascent of Mount Carmel.[22] In this context Cupitt (but not St John of the Cross!) believes that 'it is a great help to be a religious person who does not believe in life after death.' For realising the finality of our death helps to liberate us from self-concern. Hence on religious grounds we should reject realist claims about a future life, quite apart from the fact that the is 'no chance' of them being realised since we are 'quite certain to die and be annihilated'.[23]

On one point I fully agree with Don Cupitt: virtue is its own reward and ought to be done for its own sake irrespective of any notion of subsequent reward or punishment in a future life. However, on the substantive issue, I think that a Christian realist must call into question Cupitt's interpretation of *disinterestedness* as an absolute value. The doctrine is not Biblical, but entered Christian thought from Cicero's work, *On Friendship*. Peter Abélard was the first Christian writer to argue that our love for God should be wholly disinterested, and Etienne Gilson has shown that Abélard came to this view, not simply from reading Cicero, but because he felt that the selfless and enduring love of Héloïse for him throughout the calamities of his life represented the highest form of human love.[24] Though I would agree that Héloïse's fidelity was indeed commendable, it would seem better for all concerned when love is able to be mutually fulfilling. And though God should be loved simply because he is love, I do not think Abélard was being necessarily inconsistent when he also looked forward to the joys of heaven in his great hymn 'O Quanta Qualia'. To love God for the sake of heaven would indeed be akin to using friendship as a means of place-seeking. But to find joy in religious experience, and to look forward to the beatific vision is not a distortion, but a fulfilment of what a relationship with God can be. As Austin Farrer put it: 'Heaven is not a payment for walking with God; its where the road goes.'[25]

It is not surprising that Don Cupitt should highlight those elements in earlier Christian tradition which have spoken of the unknowability of God, of the importance of a disinterested approach to him, and of the Dark Night of the Soul in which prayer seems to go dead. He sees a non-realist account of theology as the natural successor to such teachings. And it is indeed true that many of the greatest thinkers of the Christian past would have been dismayed by the confident anthromorphism of much contemporary preaching, and the auto-induced religious euphoria of some charismatic developments. Christian apologetic can be *too* realist, and may present a too easily conceptualised idol in place of the one who transcends all that we can imagine or describe.

Nevertheless the fact remains that though the greatest fathers of the Church were conscious of the ambiguity of human language, and the limitations of human thought, nevertheless, they were in the end theological realists. They believed that in the darkness they had indeed encountered the holy and living God in whom they lived and moved and had their being.[26] Of none was this more true than St John of the Cross. Cupitt encourages his readers and his students to suppose that this great Doctor of the Church arrived at the same concept of the *nihil* as himself.[27] He is able to do this only by consciously deciding to disregard all the Saint's poems. For the poems speak at length of 'the sense of God living constantly in the soul, of the warmth of reciprocal love, and of God's goodness in all things' and they clearly emerge from the Saint's 'direct and joyful experience of God'.[28] Any similarity between the *via negativa* of the mystical tradition and the non-realism of contemporary Christian philosophy is very much a matter of the surface only and does not extend to the depths of historic faith.

What is valued most in the Christian tradition is a sense of the presence of God. This supreme value is contingently dependent on the believer remaining convinced that God exists in reality as well as in our minds. It may be that our whole culture is passing through a Dark Night of the Soul, and that a genuine recovery of faith may be a future possibility. This possibility will be realised if, and only if, Christians can defend the objective reality of the being of God.

Notes

1. Don Cupitt, *The Sea of Faith* (London: BBC, 1984).
2. Don Cupitt, *Taking Leave of God* (London: SCM Press, 1980), p. 82.
3. Hebrews 11:6.
4. W. Montgomery Watt, *Muhammad* (Oxford University Press, 1961), pp. 21–2.
5. R.W. Church, *St Anselm* (London: Macmillan, 1899), p. 85.

6. St Anselm, *Prayers and Meditations* (Harmondsworth: Penguin Classics, 1973), p. 265.
7. Ibid., p. 245.
8. Deuteronomy 6:4; Mark 12:30.
9. Psalm 119, 41–48, 1 John 5:3.
10. Don Cupitt, *Life Lines* (London: SCM Press, 1986), p. 49.
11. Ibid., p. 55.
12. Ibid., p. 56.
13. Ibid.
14. Ibid., p. 110.
15. Ibid., p. 109.
16. John Burnaby, *Amor Dei* (London: Hodder, 1938).
17. Cupitt, *Taking Leave of God*, op. cit., p. 69.
18. Immanuel Kant, *Religion Within the Limits of Reason Alone* (New York: Harper & Row, Harper Torchbooks, 1960), pp. 171 and 181.
19. Ibid., p. xxix.
20. Cupitt, *Taking Leave of God*, op. cit., pp. 134–5.
21. Ibid., p. 10.
22. Ibid., p. 138.
23. Ibid., p. 161.
24. Burnaby, op. cit., p. 257.
25. Austin Farrer, *Saving Belief* (London: Hodder, 1964), p. 140.
26. Cf. Vladimir Lossky, *The Mystical Theology of the Eastern Church* (London: James Clarke, 1957), Chapter 2.
27. Cupitt, *Taking Leave of God*, op. cit., p. 139.
28. Rowan Williams, *The Wound of Knowledge* (London: Darton, Longman & Todd, 1979), p. 175.

How Real Is Realism? A Response to Paul Badham

D.Z. PHILLIPS

I have some difficulty in responding to Paul Badham's paper, since it is not always clear to me when he is speaking philosophically, theologically or religiously. Sharp boundaries cannot always be drawn between these modes of address, but they are different, and one's response varies accordingly. Conscious, therefore, that I am being selective in what I shall discuss, I am going to restrict myself to comments on what I take to be Badham's realism, and ask: How real is realism?

First I want to note the way in which he, along with others in the conference, have tried to show the necessity of realism, simply by appealing to ordinary uses of the word 'real', as though quoting the latter, *of itself*, establishes the former. Here are two examples from Badham. First:

> From the perspective of the one who prays, religious experience cannot be classified as non-real. . . . Only a realist understanding of theism can allow for the genuine possibility of this type of religious experiencing . . .
>
> (pp. 185–6)

Second:

> the greatest fathers of the Church . . . were in the end theological realists. They believed that in the darkness they had indeed encountered the holy and living God in whom they lived and moved and had their being.
>
> (p. 191)

The suggestion seems to be that since the believers say their experiences are real, and the Church fathers say that they have encountered the living God, that realism is established. But that begs the philosophical issue entirely. My claim is that realism (a philosophical or theological view) distorts these religious uses of 'real' and 'encounter'. I cannot be refuted simply by quoting the ordinary use, since it is the grammar of such ordinary use which is under discussion.

But what of Badham's realism? Can *it* be refuted? It certainly can. In fact, there is a tension in his paper which brings out well what is philosophically at stake. Let us begin by noticing his reference (p. 185) to Anselm's religious experience:

> I have found a fulness of joy that is more than full. It is a joy that fills the whole heart, mind, and soul. Indeed, it fills the whole of a man, and yet joy beyond measure remains.

If we ask what we mean by saying that someone's heart, mind and soul are filled with the joy of God, the answer will not refer to passive mental phenomena, but to the activities, joyous activities, of the person in question. As Badham says later, for believers, 'God's presence has utterly transformed otherwise intolerable situations' (p. 189), for example torture in prisoner-of-war camps. To emphasise the internal connections involved between God's presence and such transformations, Simone Weil said that if she wanted to know whether the Spirit of God was in a man, she listened, not to what he said about God, but to what he said about the world. As Badham says, Anselm said of his experience, 'This *is* so truly that it is not possible to think of it as not existing' (p. 185). Again, that reminds me of Simone Weil's remark that she knew that God existed in that she could not believe that the love she knew could be a delusion. So far, Badham seems to be saying that it is in contexts such as these that issues concerning the reality of God have their *sense*. As he says, rightly:

> This is why over the past two centuries . . . theories, such as those of Feuerbach, Marx or Freud, which have offered alternative explanations for religious feelings have been felt to provide the most damaging critique of religion.
>
> (p. 185)

The tension in Badham's paper is between promising emphases we have noted so far, and his slide into problematic realism. The slide is explicit in the following passage:

> Within the historic tradition I would see the Confessions of Augustine, the writings of the Cappadocian Fathers, the prayers of St

Anselm, the hymns of St Bernard and the poems of the Medieval Mystics of England as testifying through the ages of the experience of intimate, immediate and close relationship with God as the living heart and fount of Christian spirituality.

(p. 187)

In the light of the previous remarks I have quoted, I do not think Badham would object to saying, not simply that these religious activities testify to a relationship with God, but that they provide the contexts in which talk of such a relationship has its sense. But, then, on the heels of this, Badham concludes, 'Hence I would argue that theological realism is a religious necessity' (p. 187). As we shall see, Badham's realism, like that of Penelhum and Trigg, will place belief outside those very contexts in which, he would say, important religious experiences have their sense.

In my paper, 'On Really Believing', I said of Penelhum and Trigg:

According to Penelhum, anyone committed to realism 'would hold that the supernatural facts which he thinks faith requires must indeed *be* facts for faith to be true, so that if they are not facts, but fantasies (or, even worse, not coherently explainable) then faith is unjustified.

(p. 85)

The realist admits that faith, believing, has consequences which constitute the commitments which make up living religiously, but he insists, to use Roger Trigg's words, that 'The belief is distinct from the commitments which may follow it, and is the justification for it' (p. 75). Badham's dilemma is this: his examples of belief have their *sense* in terms of the religious life, but he wants to make the religious life depend on beliefs which are supposed to have *their sense* outside any religious context. My question is: *What would it mean to say that a person held these latter beliefs? Realism makes it impossible to give a coherent reply.* Let me illustrate this.

Badham holds that prayer, worship, religious or mystical experience, all depend on a belief which he says is at the heart of all theistic belief, namely, that through these activities 'it is possible to enter into a relationship with God' (p. 184). But now let us ask what it means to ascribe this belief to a person. How do we know that someone has the belief that it is possible to encounter God in prayer, worship, etc.? Normally, by looking to the role this belief plays on the person's religious life. But Badham has made the religious life depend on the belief. What, then, is the *sense* of the belief? But more is to follow. Badham makes the sense of this abstracted belief dependent on a further belief. You have to believe that your belief that God can be encountered in prayer has a transcendent source (see p. 185). So let us ask: How would we find out that a man believed that his belief that he could encounter God in prayer has a transcendent source? Badham has cut the belief off from any context dependent on a prior belief. Thus, I am now able to include Badham in my earlier comments on Penelhum and Trigg:

> 'I believe' is not a report or description of a mental state. It is doing something, making an assertion. But according to [Trigg, Penelhum and Badham], the essence of 'believing' cannot be found in action, in doing anything, since, according to them, action is itself based on something called 'belief'.
>
> (p. 88)

But what, then, is 'believing'? It has been rendered entirely vacuous, as vacuous as the realism which leads to its unnecessary postulation.

Let me turn now to one major, unhappy consequence of his realism, to which Badham confesses: that in terms of realism, we cannot meet what Badham admits is the most serious challenge to faith in the last two centuries, namely the attempts of Feuerbach, Freud and Marx to explain it away. Badham says that all religious practices depend on a supposition, namely that they came from a transcendent source. But, as I have shown, that 'supposition' is cut off, by Badham's realism, from any context of application in which its sense could be mediated. As a result, it is defenceless against the contrary suppositions of Feuerbach, Freud and Marx. We saw in my paper that Penelhum allows the possibility that religious serenity could be the product of brainwashing, drugs, music or the sources attributed to it by Freud and Marx (see p. 98). In the same way, Badham says, 'It may be impossible to demonstrate to others that such experiences arise from anything other than the human subconscious' (p. 189). These concessions are necessary only if the realism of these philosophers is embraced.

If we look at the language of religious experience in the context of religious belief and practice in which it occurs, it is possible to show, as I tried to argue in *Relation Without Explanation*, that there are conceptual confusions involved *in terms of their own procedures*, in sociological and psychoanalytic attempts to explain religion away. It is foolish to cast aside, as lightly as Badham does, the possibility of this conceptual critique. So much for criticism of these alleged explanations of religion. As far as religious tests of the spirits, to see whether they are of God or no, are concerned, Badham, like Penelhum, when not in the grip of realism, would look in practice to the dispositions of the person involved. They would look to the role belief played in his life, that is to religious life. But by making 'belief' a justification of the religious life, realism cuts it off from the very context in which it can be shown whether the belief is of God, or a product of one of the modes of projection of which it can be accused. Badham's 'suppositions', like Trigg's propositions, are left bereft of any context for them to be anything. Yet it is these suppositions which, according to Badham, are fundamental to theism.

Realism tries to say something important, but confuses it. What it wishes to say is that whether something is the case is independent of what we say or think. Notice that this is a thesis about *truth*, and it wishes to emphasise an important point, namely that we cannot make truth-claims at will. For example, I *cannot* say there is a chair in the next room, yet have nothing to do with the familiar ways in which we would check this fact. What do I mean when I say I *cannot* say . . . I mean that if I said 'There is a chair in the next room,' while ignoring the familiar ways of checking, *I would not be making an assertion at all. I would not be saying anything.* But what these procedures lay down *is the sense, not the truth* of the proposition, 'There is a chair in the next room.' The procedures do not make the proposition, 'There is a chair in the next room' true. What *that* depends on is there being a chair in the next room.

Similarly, religious language does not determine the truth of the proposition 'God exists'. What *that* depends on is there being a God. What religious language determines is *the sense* of the proposition. But by placing religious belief outside all religious practices, realists like Penelhum, Trigg and Badham can give no indication of that sense. What they do, of course, is to assume that the sense is already given. They *assume* that they know what the belief and its 'correspondence to the facts' amounts to, namely what it would amount to in observation statements.[1] As I said in my paper:

> . . . theological realism takes itself to be the expression of a truism: we cannot believe in God unless there is a God to believe in. If that were denied, it seems belief would be robbed of its object. Aren't

we all realists? What we need to realise is that, as yet, *no* grammatical work has been done to elucidate the relations between belief and its object.

(p. 87)

If the grammatical work is done, what is the result? Before ending, I want to comment very briefly on the two answers Hick attributes to me in this context. I am not going to say that Hick attributes *false* theses to me. That is because the theses are unintelligible. Here is the first thesis I am supposed to hold: 'God is not so much an idea in our minds as an element in our language' (see p. 8) What do we normally mean by an element in our language? I suppose nouns, verbs, the copula, etc. Do I identify God with one of these? Do I think people worship a verb or pray to a copula? Of course, we can ask whether the word 'God' is a substantive or a proper name. But, here, we are asking questions to clarify the grammar of the word 'God'. Realism, as we have seen, thinks, wrongly, that this 'grammar' can be taken for granted.

The second unintelligible thesis Hick attributes to me is, 'God exists' *means* that the concept operates effectively in the language. False propositions are an effective use of language. Here is one of them: 'John Hick does not exist'. But if 'exists' means 'effective use', then 'John Hick does not exist' means the same as 'John Hick exists'. Of course, what I have said is that we have to look to 'effective use' to clarify the concepts which puzzle us, the concept of God included. This is what realists will not do. Instead, like Penelhum, Trigg and Badham, they sever belief, religious belief included, from those very realms of discourse and activity where really believing has its sense.

Note

1. In this and the previous paragraph I have drawn on observations made by Peter Winch in a number of papers in his collection, *Trying to Make Sense* (Oxford: Blackwell, 1987). The ways in which he shows how Wittgenstein cuts through the realist/anti-realist controversies in philosophy are highly relevant to the concerns of this volume.

The Religious Adequacy of Non-Realism

DON CUPITT

Those who take a realistic view of God tend to see the non-realist as being close to atheism, and therefore are perhaps too ready to suppose that his position must be religiously inadequate. Yet there are many counter-examples. The early Schleiermacher was a non-realist, whose view of religion as being something like a cosmic attitude seemed to his contemporaries to be not less but more religiously liberating than the rather petrified orthodoxy of the day. Jung always insisted that the subjective God who is the Unconscious or the Shadow is a far more potent and fearsome figure than the objective God of the Church. Many or most people will agree that the purely abstract late paintings of Mark Rothko are more profoundly religious than other more conventionally representational religious art. The distinguished novelist Iris Murdoch in her most recent statements seems to be ready to acknowledge that her position is now that of a non-realistic and fully demythologised Christianity.

We could add many more examples. So far as there is a common doctrine, it runs somewhat as follows: God should not be thought of as having objective, individual existence, but as having many names. God is Death, Christ, Nothingness, the Good, the Void, the Shadow. The names signify a transcendent Otherness that is dreadful to us. When we encounter it and experience it inwardly it shows us that we are a mere aggregate of parts held together by nothing, utterly contingent and mortal. This cuts the nerve of our egoism, freeing us to become kinder to other mortals and to ourselves.

To save us God must make us nothing, and to make us nothing God must himself (or itself) be Nothingness. Thus the non-realist Christian is close to Buddhism. By contrast, a good deal of popular realistic Christianity seems to view God as an immensely powerful Ego, self-existent and omnipotent, the Great I Am. He is infinite substance, characterised by aseity and necessity of being. But I maintain that this view of God is radically incompatible with the general teachings of the religions, that we need to become less egoistic and more selfless. The way to salvation, for Christians in particular, is by the death of the self in union with Christ. The aim is to learn to accept contingency, not to become armoured against it, and so to become less egoistic and not more so.

Thus I conclude that the non-realistic account of God is alone religiously adequate.

Part Five
A Final Overview

10

Great Expectations: Philosophy, Ontology and Religion

D.Z. PHILLIPS

Contributors to this volume were invited to reflect on issues raised in the course of it. In responding to the invitation, I hope to show that some of these issues are central, not simply in the philosophy of religion, but in philosophy generally.

Many realists came to this dialogue with great expectations, expectations that they would be defending and non-realists would be attacking the following thesis: The truth of the proposition, 'God exists' is independent of anything we say or think. But realists' expectations were dashed, since no one wanted to dispute this thesis. Their false expectations were the result of their misunderstanding of what they had taken to be Wittgenstein's anti-realism. What Wittgenstein's critique of realism insists on is that *the sense, not the truth* of the proposition 'God exists' depends on what we say in religious discourse.

It emerged that some realist contributors were open to Wittgenstein's objections. They did put *the sense**of 'I believe in God' beyond all possible contexts, thus robbing the belief of any intelligibility. This is evident, for example, in Paul Badham's paper 'The Religious Necessity of Realism', and I tried to highlight this in my reply. Badham says that religious practices depend on the belief that God is active in them. But if we ask what that belief amounts to, no intelligible answer is forthcoming. The belief cannot get its sense from the practices, since it has been made the logically prior foundation of them. The same difficulty faces the realists who want to make religious practices depend on the existential supposition of God's existence. 'Suppositions', like 'beliefs', need some context to make

203

them intelligible. The supposition that God exists cannot get its sense from religious practices, since it is supposed to be the logically prior foundation, or rationale, of these practices. The realist's metaphysical notions of 'belief' and 'supposition' are, thus, fatally isolated. It must be said that a minority of realists represented in this volume, those who wished to defend the thesis that *the truth* of propositions is independent of what we say or think, have distanced themselves from their fellow realists' conceptions of 'belief' and 'existential supposition'. They, too, agreed that such conceptions are incoherent.

Once we recognise the necessity of looking to religious discourse to find the sense of what is said of God, we recognise, too, that only in religious discourse can we find what is meant by referring to God's independent reality. In his paper, 'Realism, Non-Realism and Atheism: Why Believe in an Objectively Real God?', Joseph Runzo argues that 'to say that religious "pictures" *do* refer to some object, or *do* describe matters of fact is not to deny that their significance is found in the role they have in people's lives' (p. 158). This is true, but the significance of referring to God must be *shown to be* a matter of referring to an object or matter of fact. In my own work, I have argued that the surroundings of religious belief show these to be misleading comparisons. Instead of waiting on the surroundings, we allow positivism to affect our expectations. If God is not a 'something', we think, surely, he must be a 'nothing'. As with John Hick, in 'Religious Realism and Non-Realism: Defining the Issue', the desire for facts is insatiable: if God's existence, or our continued existence after death, are not empirical facts, then they must be non-natural facts. Facts, facts, nothing but facts!

In his paper, 'Ludwig Feuerbach's Philosophy of God', Jack Verheyden quotes the following interesting remark by Feuerbach:

> Thus what theology and philosophy have held to be God; the Absolute, the Infinite, is not God; but that which they have held not to be God is God; namely, the attribute, the quality, whatever has reality. Hence he alone is the true atheist to whom the predicates of the divine being, – for example, love, wisdom, justice, – are nothing; not he to whom merely the subject of these predicates is nothing. And in no wise is the negation of the subject necessarily also a negation of the predicates considered in themselves.
>
> (*The Essence of Faith According to Luther*, p. 21, quoted by Verheyden on p. 32)

In 'God is love', the 'is' is taken to be one of predication, whereas 'God is love' is a rule for one use of the word 'God'. Thinking that 'God' is used as a name, and that it is meant to refer to an object, Feuerbach, Santayana and Dewey saw no alternative but 'to deny the subject'. Their denial of the subject, however, is a direct result of metaphysical and, no doubt, their own, assumptions concerning the sense in which the word 'God' refers. They could not see (to adapt a remark of Wittgenstein's from another context) that if 'God' is not a 'something', it is not a 'nothing' either.

The non-realist assumes, along with the realist, that traditional religion depends on traditional metaphysics. The same assumptions are at work in Don Cupitt's paper, 'Anti-Realist Faith', when he says: 'Now consider how completely we have reversed the traditional outlook of Christian Platonism. The world above and all the absolutes have gone' (p. 49). This conclusion would only follow if the ordinary religious 'absolutes' depend on some form of Platonism. But why assume this? Much of the Wittgensteinian critique in the philosophy of religion consists of showing the independence of religious beliefs from the efforts of metaphysical systems to give them a rational foundation.

Realists in this volume often assume that religious belief depends, implicitly or explicitly, on philosophical conceptions of ontology. Thus, in his paper, 'A Critique of Don Cupitt's Christian Buddhism', Brian Hebblethwaite says,

It is the same ultimate reality to which reason appeals as that to which religious experience appeals. There is no need to drive a wedge between the God of the Bible and the God of the philosophers. The philosophers are only exploring the rational side of the case for accepting that to which the religious sense gives prima facie plausibility.

(p. 140)

This suggestion that 'probably' should be put before everything the Bible asserts, hardly does justice to the nature of religious belief. This has been pointed out, not only by philosophers of religion influenced by Wittgenstein, but also by reformed epistemologists such as Alvin Plantinga. On the other hand, reformed epistemologists would probably side with Hebblethwaite in wanting to resist what the latter called the Wittgensteinian reduction of ontology to language (see p. 137). But this resistance must be philosophically justified.

There are dangers, sometimes, apparent in the conference, of making realism a philosophical orthodoxy. There may or may not be a place for orthodoxy in religion, but there is no place for it in philosophy. No conclusions about a person's religious beliefs can be drawn from his adherence or otherwise to philosophical realism. Thus, the alleged dependence of religious belief on some kind of 'ontology' is itself a philosophical issue.

Consider the following remarks. First, Hick: 'It is time now to specify the non-realist religious point of view . . . centrally it interprets religious language, not as referring to a transcendent reality or realities' (p. 7). Second, Francis Cook in his paper, 'Zen and the Problem of Language', refers to 'the Buddhist conviction that concepts and their verbal expression are totally inadequate for grasping the true nature of things' (p. 63). Third, Runzo suggests that one form of anti-realism depends on 'the idea that language itself must fail to successfully denote or even refer to [a transcendent] being' (p. 155). All three speak as though it *makes sense* to speak of language referring to reality. *But language as such does not refer to anything, either successfully or unsuccessfully.* We make various kinds of reference, some successful, some unsuccessful, *in* language. We can then explore the logic of these references, including references to God. By talking of language itself as a referent, this much-needed work is hampered. For example, is Cook turning religious notions of inadequacy into epistemological inadequacies? When we say 'God is beyond mortal telling', we are no more failing to worship, than someone who says, 'Words can't tell you how grateful I am' is failing to express thanks. Similarly, Runzo turns active faith in God into an epistemological faith that *that* faith is about God.

Such philosophical endeavours end in the same incoherence which characterised the efforts to place religious belief and existential suppositions concerning God beyond religious practices. If we say that language, as such, refers to reality, the concept of reference employed and the reality supposed to be referred to are *entirely* unmediated. They have no context in which to have any sense. 'Ontology', like the metaphysical notions of 'belief' and 'supposition', has been placed beyond any context in which it could have sense. Thus, how could Hick's critical realist ever know, in *this* context, that any revision is nearer to reality than what it revised? Non-metaphorically, of course, what we mean by 'more correct' gets its sense from the grammar of the diverse activities in which corrections are made.

Wittgenstein emphasises that the distinction between 'the real' and 'the unreal', what it comes to, varies with different realms of discourse. The non-metaphysical task of philosophy is the modest one of exploring the grammars of these different contexts. Within certain religious traditions, there is talk of God as 'the creator of all things'. A philosopher may think this talk refers to a super-explanation of all things. If he falls into this assumption, the philosopher turns talk of God's reality into a metaphysical system, thereby doing a disservice to both philosophy and religion.

There are pressing problems to be discussed which this volume has hardly touched on. If we say that there are different concepts of reality, what happens when they clash, and when they compete for our allegiance? Runzo raises these important issues in his paper, but obscures what is at stake by treating the competing and clashing conceptions of reality as though *they* were competing hypotheses about 'ultimate reality'. Thus, Runzo would inherit all the logical difficulties we have already outlined. This is not the place to develop what I take to be an alternative account of the way conceptions of reality compete for our allegiance. It is an issue which was explored illuminatingly by Newman and Wittgenstein. I discuss their conclusions in the first part of *Faith After Foundationalism* (Routledge, 1988) called: 'Can There Be A Religious Epistemology?'

This question brings us back to underlying differences in our conceptions of philosophy which were at work in the conference, although they were not made explicit. According to the conception of philosophy as descriptive metaphysics, philosophy attempts to determine whether 'ultimate reality' is 'one' or 'many', 'personal' or 'impersonal', 'good' or 'evil', etc., etc. But if this conception of 'ultimate reality' is isolated, logically cut off from any context which could give it sense, these speculations are idle. According to the conception of philosophy shown in Wittgenstein's work, our task is to rescue the wonderfulness of the ordinary from the grip of the metaphysical tendencies to which we are all prone. These metaphysical and non-metaphysical conceptions of philosophy were clearly at work in the conference. To note this fact, of course, does not resolve the conflict between them, or show, philosophically, what is at stake. A fruitful topic for future discussion might be: 'What do we expect from the philosophy of religion?', a question which would engage the attention of foundationalists, evidentialists, reformed epistemologists and those influenced by Wittgenstein in the philosophy of religion.

11

Reflections on Realism vs. Non-Realism

BRIAN HEBBLETHWAITE

Dewi Phillips's Wittgensteinian animadversions failed to persuade us that there is not an issue of substance between the realists and the non-realists in talk of God. The starkness of Don Cupitt's anti-realism, his insistence that the history of thought has made belief in an objective God impossible and that Christian God-talk must consequently be wholly reinterpreted in merely human terms, made it absolutely clear that, whatever the difficulties in articulating the 'grammar' of traditional Christian God-talk, Cupitt's version was something very different from what the vast majority of Christian believers and Christian worshippers have thought they were holding and doing.

It became apparent early on that the realists had a double task on their hands – to show against Phillips that the very meaning of Christian God-talk entailed reference to an objective *ground* of the world's being and destiny, and to show against Cupitt that belief in such a ground is not only possible in the modern world, but actually required by the evidence. But what evidence? The realists were divided on this question. Could appeal to religious experience by itself sustain the case for objective theism, or must there be supporting arguments as well, establishing a rational as well as an experiential case for theism?

Phillips's manifest suspicion of the idea that Christian belief could ever be *dependent* on such metaphysical argument tended to obscure the point at issue here. For no one wanted to insist that we have to *rely* on such tentative arguments for belief in God to be a life-determining possibility. On the contrary it is the philosopher and the theologian, trying to spell out the *meaning* of Christian God-talk, who have to abstract, for rational scrutiny, the cognitive *implications* of religious talk of the One who is Creator, Redeemer and Reconciler of all. But the *relevance* of concern with the rationality of Christian belief in God to the faith of the ordinary believer is shown when the latter is subjected to Cupitt's radical reinterpretation. Phillips's insistence on internal criteria entirely lacked the intellectual means to resist that subjectivist deconstruction.

Hick's repeated claim that critical rather than naive realism was the issue of the conference betrayed a number of ambiguities. It was fair enough to suggest that many of the anti-metaphysical arguments appear to be directed more at naive than at critical realism. Certainly the case for critical realism is simply not being considered by those who dismiss belief in the transcendent as infantile or as being rendered impossible by advances in science or critical history. But Hick's defence of critical realism tended to be undermined by his own refusal to consider the theistic arguments and by his decision to rely entirely on religious experience in all its world-wide diversity. There is indeed an argument from religious experience for the reality of God, but, unless supported by the rational arguments, it is extremely vulnerable to alternative psychological and sociological explanations, as Cupitt was quick to point out. Hick's pluralism, seeking to accommodate all forms of human experience of the transcendent, theistic and monistic, personal and impersonal, into a single global interpretation of religion, tended to erode the cognitive significance of religious experience. So much had to be conceded to the constructivists. So great was the consequent agnosticism about the ultimate or the 'Real'. In particular, the theistic arguments, which posit an ultimate mind or intention – and thus a personal spiritual source – behind the whole cosmic process got no more serious attention from Hick than they did from Phillips or Cupitt.

A more robust resort to metaphysical arguments – together with critical reflection on alleged divine revelation – will show, against Hick, that rational choices can be made between the various worldviews in the history of religions. It will show, against Phillips, that Christianity is committed to objective theism in the metaphysical as well as the religious sense. And it will show, against Cupitt, that the 'last thirty years', indeed the last two hundred years, do not by any means present us with a single cultural trend, leading inexorably to an extreme anti-realism. On the contrary, the manifest incoherencies of Cupitt's position, its problems over reflexivity, its inability to account for anything, let alone the claims of beauty, goodness and truth, and its implausible denial of countless believers' experience of the reality and love of God, will surely send us back to theological realism as the only possible way of making sense of revelation, religion, value and rationality, and of a world containing all these things.

Index